THE SECRET OF TSL

The Revolutionary Discovery That Raises School Performance

William G. Ouchi

SIMON & SCHUSTER

New York • London • Toronto • Sydney

Simon & Schuster
1230 Avenue of the Americas
New York, NY 10020

First Simon & Schuster hardcover edition September 2009

SIMON & SCHUSTER and colophon are registered trademarks
of Simon & Schuster, Inc.

For information about special discounts for bulk purchases,
please contact Simon & Schuster Special Sales at
1-866-506-1949 or business@simonandschuster.com.

The Simon & Schuster Speakers Bureau can bring authors to your live event.
For more information or to book an event contact the Simon & Schuster Speakers
Bureau at 1-866-248-3049 or visit our website at www.simonspeakers.com.

Designed by Dana Sloan

Manufactured in the United States of America

10   9   8   7   6   5   4   3   2   1

Library of Congress Cataloging-in-Publication Data

Ouchi, William G.
    The secret of TSL / William G. Ouchi.
        p.   cm.
    Includes bibliographical references and index.
1. Class size—United States—Case studies.   2. Schools—
Decentralization—United States—Case studies.   3. School
districts—United States—Case studies.   I. Title.

LB3013.2.O93   2009
371.2'51—dc22   2008055250

ISBN 978-1-4391-2158-0
ISBN 978-1-4391-4127-4 (ebook)

To Ethan, Will, Ryan, Hana, and Dylan.
May you always love books!

CONTENTS

THE SECRET OF TSL

1

WHY GOOD SCHOOLS ARE THE RESULT OF GOOD MANAGEMENT

A Revolution Is Under Way

Virtually everyone who teaches in our K–12 schools is aware that most school districts today are run the way businesses were forty or fifty years ago: top-down, autocratic, and bureaucratic. Teachers and principals have to use books that are selected by someone in the central office who does not know their school; they must follow a daily schedule set by that central office; and all schools are assigned the same complement of teachers, attendance clerks, and so on—according to the central office formula. Students have to attend the "zone" schools to which they are assigned by that same central office. That educational straitjacket is widely disliked by families and by teachers, but until recently, there has been no alternative.

Now, however, a quiet revolution is under way. That revolution allows each school in some districts the power to make more and more of its own budgetary, personnel, and instructional decisions and permits families to decide which public school their children will attend. Power is being shifted from central office staffs to families, principals, and teachers, and the results so far show that students are doing better, parents and teachers are more satisfied, and school districts may never be the same. It may be too early in this dramatic period of change to declare that top-down management is dead. Most of our nation's schools still report to strongly centralized staffs. The eight districts that have been pioneering this move to decentralization are inventing and learning as they go. Some of them have made costly missteps. Their story is not one of easy change— it's a nuanced story of victories and of defeats. This book describes that quiet revolution, what it means, and how every school district can learn from the successes and the failures of the pioneers.

Excellent Schools, Excellent School Districts

Most people know of at least one excellent public school, perhaps a school that they attended or one they worked in or that a child they know attends now. High-quality public schools offer living proof that public education can rise to the level of excellence, yet they also stand out as exceptions to the rule and thereby raise questions of incalculable consequence for American public education: Is it possible for a school district with dozens or hundreds or even a thousand schools to achieve high quality in virtually every school? Is there something about large school districts that inevitably kills the spirit of the teachers and principals, or is there a way to general excellence through fundamental changes in how we organize public education in this country?

The answers, as I will demonstrate in this book, are in the positive. Ask yourself what you believe is the single most important factor in the success of a school district. Ask anyone you know the same question. Ninety percent of the time, the answer will be "teachers." Then ask how, as a practical matter, a school district's student performance can be raised. Now the answer won't be so clear. This book will demonstrate that the most important element to the success of a school district is management. Good managers will organize schools effectively and will attract and retain good teachers. Without good management, even talented teachers will fail.

Why Big School Districts Need to Decentralize

I am a professor at the UCLA Anderson School of Management, a graduate school of business. I have spent more than thirty years studying very large companies, such as General Motors, Toyota, Intel, and Macy's. In the corporate world, it is considered reasonable to expect high quality throughout a company, even a very large company. After all, Toyota built its reputation by making every one of its plants a high-quality operation, not by having some good plants among several poor ones. McDonald's built its reputation by making every one of its stores deliver quality service to every customer, every time—not by delivering high-quality service sometimes to some customers. If Toyota and McDonald's can do this, why can't large public-school systems? As I have suggested, the answer has to do, more than anything else, with the way public education is organized and managed in this country today.

More than a quarter of a century ago, corporations and scholars recognized that large size brings major negative consequences and that the chief antidote to these pathologies is to decentralize decision making down to the operating subunits. A fundamental flaw in public education in the United States is that this lesson has not yet been applied to school districts.

Over time, school districts have become very large. Since 1932, the number of students enrolled in public schools in the United States has more than doubled, from 24 million to about 50 million. Meanwhile, the number of school districts has declined from about 127,000 to about 16,000.[1] This means that school districts today on average have fifteen times as many students as their predecessors did seventy-five years ago. Business organizations, functioning in a competitive world, long ago understood that they could not survive that much growth without decentralizing. In a competitive setting, the rule is decentralize or fail. But school districts, not living in a competitive world, have not changed their form. They remain about as centralized today as when they were one-fifteenth their present size. In fact, as a result of growth in the size of school districts, they are actually far more centralized today, in the sense that in each district, one central office staff now makes the decisions that affect fifteen times as many students as before.

Many districts think they've already tried decentralization and found that it did not work. For example, the nation's three largest cities—New York, Los Angeles, and Chicago—have at one time or another grouped their schools into "communities" of several dozen schools or have created subregions of schools and have delegated limited decision powers to the assistant superintendents who run each subregion. Invariably, these districts were disappointed with the results and soon abandoned the experiment. These ineffective approaches to decentralization were bound to fail, because they did not place decision making where it makes a difference—with the principals. If principals are under the thumb of bureaucrats, it does not matter whether the bureaucrats are in a regional office or in the central office. What matters is whether or not the principal has the executive power required to exercise the leadership fundamental to the success of educating children.

About twenty years ago, I became interested in helping public schools to improve. For many years, I volunteered in a local organization that gave advice to our local school district, and I couldn't help but notice that more often than not the best schools were outliers and renegades, that they followed a set of principles that were in conflict with the desires and dictates of the school board, the superintendent, and the central office staff. That did not make sense to me. Why would any school district not celebrate its successful schools? Why would it not try to have all of its schools emulate them? I wanted to get to the bottom of these questions, so I've spent the past eight years organizing research teams and visiting a total of 665 schools across the United States.

My Research Team Visits 665 Schools and Brings You Their Stories

In my first study (of 223 schools in nine districts), I wanted to find out if decentralized decision making—that is, giving power over the school budget to principals—would result in higher student achievement.[2] The answer was a clear "yes." In that study I compared the three largest centralized districts in the country to the three largest decentralized districts and to the three largest Catholic school districts. That study demonstrated that a school district can empower its principals with real, meaningful autonomy. But I did not know at that time what principals did with that freedom to make them successful.

By the time we launched the second round of research, eight

large U.S. districts had begun serious decentralization—Boston, Chicago, Houston, New York, Oakland, San Francisco, Seattle, and St. Paul—and we were able to study them all, drawing a total sample of 442 schools from these eight districts. To my knowledge, ours is the only large-scale study of school district decentralization. In all likelihood this reflects the fact that only in the past few years have any U.S. districts implemented true decentralization by giving principals substantial control of their budgets—as much as 87.2 percent of the budget in St. Paul, Minnesota, 85.0 percent in New York City, and 73.7 percent in Houston. Far more typical of the country as a whole are the cases of Los Angeles,[3] in which principals control 6.7 percent of their school budgets, and Hawaii, where principals control about 4 percent, according to the Hawaii state auditor. Indeed, as recently as 2001, New York City principals controlled only 6.1 percent of their budgets, before the far-reaching reforms introduced by Chancellor Joel Klein during the administration of Mayor Michael Bloomberg.

None of this is to suggest that success requires only that districts grant a large measure of autonomy to their principals: that step, while necessary, has to be accompanied by four other policies—(1) school choice, (2) development of effective principals, (3) accountability, and (4) weighted student formula budgeting. Together, as we will explore in coming chapters, these Five Pillars of School Empowerment can produce dramatic improvements in achievement for all students, from those in affluent neighborhoods to those in inner-city ghettos. (I will provide information about student achievement in the chapters that follow.)

Let me hasten to add that this book deals primarily with the improvements that can be made in the performance of students if the school district is organized and managed in a decentralized fashion. While organization and management are crucially important and may qualify as the least appreciated aspects of education, there are several other major factors that matter, which are not covered in this book, although they too are of crucial importance. The performance of students is greatly influenced, for example, by the training and skill of their teachers. A great teacher can overcome many bureaucratic obstacles, but even the most dedicated teacher will eventually lose heart in a badly managed school. Also of great importance are a curriculum that is well designed and properly implemented and an approach to standardized testing that makes sense. Also important are the development of very young children even before they begin school and children's physical and emotional health. These important topics are beyond the scope of this book, which focuses on the management of the school district within which teachers and students interact each day. Based on my research, I can assert with confidence that when a school district grows beyond about three thousand students, the one thing that will most improve the academic performance of students is better management.

The New Educational Debate: Management Matters—A Lot!

When Enron, Countrywide, or General Motors get into trouble, we automatically point the finger of blame at the top corporate management. We assume that the branch managers and the front-line employees are operating within a set of policies that were set at the top and that those policies must be in some way defective. We don't blame secretaries, customer-service representatives, and auto workers. Nor do we blame the customers, because we know that any large organization has all kinds of customers, some of whom are hard to please, and that it's the responsibility of the company to learn how to deal with all kinds of people.

For some reason, though, when a school district is in a state of chronic failure, otherwise levelheaded people blame the teachers or the teachers unions or, even more strangely, the students and their parents! Perhaps this is because the public does not typically think of a school district as an organization but rather as a collection of schools, which in turn are viewed as a random collection of students and teachers. As a result, there is a general tendency to explain poor performance as the result of shortcomings of teachers or students, which is really no different from blaming the assembly-line workers or customers at General Motors for that company's performance problems. A good teacher who is overwhelmed by too many students, confusing schedules, and frustrated parents cannot be successful. An inexperienced new teacher who is assigned to a chaotic school will not develop into a strong classroom performer. Strong teachers are developed, coached, and protected by strong principals.

For their part, strong principals have to be decision makers who can make a myriad of choices each day on the spot—for example, to modify curricula and schedules as needed or to add new reading specialists in place of less important staff positions in order to meet the needs of students and teachers. Principals who are capable of these kinds of decisions aren't born; they have to be selected and trained and then furnished with a set of districtwide policies that give them autonomy and hold them accountable for student performance as well as for teacher and parent satisfaction. At the same time, the central office staff must be organized to serve the unique needs of each school rather than to enforce a one-size-fits-all policy.

Organizing School Districts for Success

How can school districts be organized for success?

First, by achieving the right balance between staff positions and classroom positions. The tendency in school districts today is to have far too many staff jobs, so that, according to one study, only 43 percent of school district employees nationwide are "regularly engaged in classroom teaching."[4]

This isn't the same as having an insufficient number of credentialed teachers on district payrolls, because as many as one-third of a district's credentialed teachers may be in staff jobs, not in the classroom. This maldistribution of human resources comes about because state school funds are sent to the district headquarters, which then decides how much of the money to keep for district staff and how much to allocate to schools. Research has shown that, over time and economic cycles, school districts tend to lay off teachers disproportionately (instead of staff) when budgets are tight and then to hire both teachers and staff when times are good.[5] As a result, with each economic cycle the staff become a larger and larger fraction of a district's total employees.

One goal of decentralization is to reverse this trend by sending the money directly to the principals. That way, the central office cannot lay off teachers in a down cycle, and principals are unlikely to do this unless those cuts are unavoidable. The result, we have found, is vastly fewer staff and many more teachers in decentralized districts.

This vicious cycle of centralized districts begets a second organizational pathology. When a district has too few classroom teachers, student loads per teacher rise to the point where teachers can no longer know their students well enough to establish a bond of trust with them. Without this trust, a teacher can neither establish an orderly classroom nor push a student to do his or her best, and the teacher's job often becomes frustrating and constantly stressful. Under these conditions, many veteran teachers understandably want to escape the classroom and get into staff jobs, and the result is that they create pressures within the district to create yet more staff jobs to which they can migrate. We've found that when a district is run in a decentralized way, staff positions decline, teaching loads decline dramatically, and most teachers no longer have the desire to escape the classroom, because now they know their students and enjoy their teaching.

Perhaps most important, successful school districts tend to have low TSLs—low Total Student Loads per teacher. Total Student Load is little known to most people, yet it is crucial to classroom success.

The Most Important Fact About a School May Be Total Student Load

Total Student Load may be the single most important fact to know about a school, particularly a middle school or high school. But by and large, TSL is still largely a secret, and few people know why it is important.

Total student load is not the same as class size, although the two are related. To put it simply, TSL is the number of students that a teacher has to get to know each term and the number of papers that a teacher has to grade each time. For example, in most New York City middle or high schools, the union contract specifies a maximum of 170 students in five classes of 34 students per class. That means that if a teacher assigns a paper, he or she must read, grade, and write constructive comments on 170 papers. Ask any teacher if he or she can do this for two or three ten- to fifteen-page papers each semester, and they'll tell you that it's impossible. Such a student load also means that each semester teachers must get to know 170 new adolescents and form a sufficient bond with each one to be able to reach those students, support them, and push them to do their best. Teachers will tell you that's impossible, too.

Our research shows that Total Student Load has a very powerful effect on student performance, and that the decentralized schools of New York City have achieved particular success by reducing TSL to levels previously unheard of in public education.[6] A principal who has control over staffing, curriculum, and schedule can strategically manage these variables to greatly reduce Total Student Loads. In most districts, though, principals have little or no control over these variables, and we have found that most every school in those districts has a high TSL as a result.

It would be useful to be able to compare these Total Student Loads to national data on all public schools, but, since TSL is still largely a secret, no such data exist. We do know that the TSL of 87.7 in New York City's first Empowerment Schools is low compared to what prevails in most schools across the country. In most school districts, the contract between the teachers union and the district specifies the maximum class size and number of classes per teacher that is permitted. From these figures, we can calculate the maximum TSL. In Los Angeles, for example, the maximum high school TSL permitted by the teachers union contract is 225 (five classes of forty-five students), although many teachers are above that figure. In Clark County, Nevada, where school construction has not kept up with the explosive population growth in Las Vegas, TSL at some high schools reaches 260, as teachers are encouraged to "sell back" their free or prep period and teach an extra class for additional pay. In doing so, teachers are giving up their allocated time each day for grading papers and for preparing for the next day's classes, which must negatively impact the quality of instruction in their classes.

As we've indicated earlier, Total Student Load is a different concept from class size. Consider a teacher who teaches five classes of thirty-five students for a TSL of 175. We can reduce her TSL to a much more manageable 105 either by reducing the number of her classes to three or by reducing her class size to twenty-one. Both solutions would be far too expensive, however, to be implemented on a large scale in our public schools.

The challenge for management (that is, principals and superintendents) is how to get TSL down to the neighborhood of 80 students per teacher in a way that is affordable for a public-school district. What decentralized districts have done—New York City most consistently—is to empower principals to find creative ways to drive down TSL without increasing costs. This cannot be done by top-down, central office mandates, but, as we will see in the following chapters, it can be done by empowering principals to make their own budget decisions. With budget autonomy, principals can work with teachers and staff to find ways unique to their school to reduce TSL dramatically.

One school, for example, may not need or want security guards or professional development staff, while another may not need attendance clerks or registrars. Allowing principals to make these staffing decisions and to use the money saved for more classroom teachers is part of the solution to reducing TSL.

Principals have also used their freedom to shape curricula and schedules to reduce TSL. In several schools we found that principals had combined the English class and the social studies class into a single humanities course or had combined math and science into a Math-Science Integrated (MSI) course. At least one principal invented a way to schedule classes so that all students could have a one-on-one "office hour" visit with any teacher they desired. We will describe these initiatives in greater detail in the chapters to come. The result of these kinds of adjustments is often a dramatically lower level of TSL, but without any increase in school budgets.

TSL Has a Huge Impact on Student Performance

As part of our research we analyzed three years of data on student performance at each of the eight decentralizing urban districts. In analyzing student performance, we tested the other variables that might affect student performance, including class size, teachers' years experience, percent of teachers who have full or partial credentials, use of professional development coaches, minutes devoted per week to math and to literacy instruction, and a few dozen additional factors. Among these, only TSL had a noticeable effect on student performance in every district, and that effect was large.[7]

In New York City, for example, we found a virtuous relationship among three factors—the principal's control over budget, Total Student Load, and student performance. An increase of ten percentage points in the principal's control of budget was associated, all else being equal, with a reduction in TSL of twenty-five students per teacher and an increase of eleven percentage points in the percentage of students who reach the federal government standard of "proficient or above" in standardized math tests. Further studies will be required to tell us whether, as seems likely, there is a ceiling on this effect as a principal's autonomy rises to even higher levels. Even so, the magnitude of this improvement in performance is far larger than that of any reform strategy tested in other research. Studies of school reform typically reveal gains that are a fraction of what we found.

I've already noted that we analyzed several different kinds of innovations that schools often use, and we found that the only change that has a noticeable effect on student performance is reduction in Total Student Load. While those other variables are surely of great importance, I am now drawn to the conclusion that focusing on these individual factors is like pouring new wine into old wineskins. It's the container—in this case the school district—that must be radically redesigned, if changes in curriculum and professional development are to be truly effective.

Total Student Load is a cold statistic that represents a set of human relationships between teachers and their students. A low middle or high school TSL, in the range of 80, means that teachers can know their students and that students are aware that teachers understand them and care about them to the point that, if they slack off or miss school, the teacher will call home. A low TSL may also mean that teachers have enough time out of the classroom to make themselves available to their students and to encourage students to come to see them during office hours. One-on-one encouragement that a student is too embarrassed to seek in front of a class can make the difference between a student's giving up and continuing to work hard in school.

School districts do not measure and report to parents or the public the degree of trust between students and their teachers (except in New York City, as we shall see later). Nor, they feel, is there a practical way for districts to measure or report on student motivation, which is a direct consequence of the student-teacher bond (New York City now measures this, too). Every teacher will tell you, though, that until students trust a teacher, they will not open up to the teacher's efforts. I can affirm this myself as a classroom business school teacher of thirty-eight years.

How can a teacher establish a personal bond of trust with 140 or 225 or more new students each term? Experience shows that it cannot be done. When TSL approaches 80 students per teacher, however, this bond does develop and student motivation and performance rise, sometimes dramatically, on a district-wide basis.

Principals as Managers or as Instructional Leaders: Is There a Difference?

School officials often complain to me that decentralization or school empowerment means trying to turn principals into CEOs of schools; principals, they will say, are not meant to be business managers but instructional leaders. Many principals, to my dismay, echo this sentiment.

I confess that I'm always chagrined at this complaint, even though I understand what motivates it. Most school districts, after all, have largely taken their principals out of decision making and so have often selected as principals people who don't want responsibility, authority, or accountability. Almost all school districts have standard staffing formulas—the number of teachers of each kind, of assistant principals, attendance clerks, assistant registrars, counselors, and so on, depending on school enrollment. Principals are generally not involved in deciding either how many or which teachers, assistant registrars, or attendance clerks to hire; it is as if these individuals are widgets. As we shall see, though, a math teacher who would also like to teach a gym class is not a substitute for a math teacher who only wants to teach math, and the decision of which one to hire should be left to the principal. Empowered principals in the decentralized districts of our study overwhelmingly involve teachers in these decisions, sometimes to the point of having the entire teaching staff vote on the decision, which is then binding.

Unsurprisingly, principals in traditional, centralized districts have become accustomed to having little power or authority. As a tradeoff, they also have little accountability, which explains why weak principals can manage to hang on to their jobs for what seems forever. In this arrangement the central staff are happy because they enjoy virtually unquestioned power; principals are happy because they have total job security and are not accountable for anything; but teachers, students, and parents suffer the consequences.

To principals who object that they should be instructional leaders instead of executives, I have some pertinent questions: What does it mean to be the instructional leader of your school? Do you control the staffing? How about the use of teacher's aides? How about the choice of the teachers you hire? Do you get to set the curriculum that would make the most sense in your school? What about choosing the books and materials? How about selecting the bell schedule (number of periods a day)? How about the professional development budget?

If the answer to all those questions is no, as it almost invariably is, then what does it mean to be called the instructional leader? If the school district decides on how to staff each school, which personnel to send to each school, and what books the schools must use; if principals do not decide what professional development courses need to be provided to teachers but instead have to send teachers to courses selected or designed by the central staff; if principals do not control the curriculum, schedule, or budget, then in what way is the principal the instructional leader of the school? What else is there to control that is instructionally important?

If there is any vital job for a principal, it is precisely to control the major instructional variables of budget, staffing, curriculum, schedule, and professional development. Those are the levers through which the instructional leader of a school, the principal, can build a great school by attracting, developing, and retaining strong teachers.

Large school districts that follow the traditional centralized approach to management have a chronic shortage of qualified principals. That should come as no surprise. No one wants a job that has great responsibility and no power and in which he will be publicly criticized for all failures. New York City's school district used to be like that. New York City had a chronic shortage of credentialed principals back when it was a centralized, top-down, enrollment-formula district. Today, with its new decentralized approach that empowers principals, New York City makes sure that new principals are trained and ready. Some of the new principals are being trained in a fifteen-month program run by the Leadership Academy, and all new principals receive at least one year of coaching support through the academy. Instead of a shortage of principals, New York City now has approximately six hundred qualified applicants each year for the sixty-five openings in each new class at the Leadership Academy, about which we will learn more in a later chapter.

Why Small Schools Make a Difference— It's Not What You Think!

The decentralizing districts that we have studied are moving to replace their large schools with small schools of about 350 to 600 students each. A few large schools remain and are successful, and there is no reason not to keep these schools as they are. The trend, though, is to replace large, 3,000-student schools with small schools. Small schools are advantageous in large part because they are easier to manage. A small school will have about twenty to twenty-five teachers and only three to five non-teaching staff. Inexperienced but bright neophyte principals who have proven themselves as excellent teachers can handle that assignment. The experience in our eight cities shows that there are large numbers of capable teachers who are eager to become principals in these small schools in districts that give principals autonomy. All of a sudden, the job of principal can become more attractive, just as reducing Total Student Load can make being a teacher attractive.

Many district officials will agree that this seems to be an appealing idea but will then plead that switching to small schools is just not possible, because the capital funds are lacking to build all of the new small schools. To these people I would say, visit New York City. I have visited school after school in that city that has made the conversion from one large school to several small schools with a capital budget of fifty dollars.

How is that possible? In one case, I visited an old building of four floors that housed a school of 3,200 students in the South Bronx. The district went to this school with a bucket of yellow paint and a large paint brush (thus the fifty dollars). On each of the four floors, they painted a bright yellow stripe down the middle of the floor and declared that henceforth the right side of the hallway would be one school, and the left side of the hallway would be home to another school. In this way, they turned the four floors into eight schools of 400 students each. On average, though, the conversion of an old large school into several small schools in New York City does necessitate some reconfiguration, and the average cost for converting each small school is about $100,000, according to the district.

It's true that the new principals did not have nicely designed offices and that all of the schools have to share a library, lunchroom, gymnasium, and other facilities. The principals have a council that meets regularly to coordinate use of the shared resources. There is no question, however, that small schools are more manageable, that the number of candidates who can effectively manage small schools is vastly larger than the pool of qualified principals for very large schools, and that inadequate capital funds is a weak excuse for failure to take this step.

Here a cautionary note is in order. In some school districts, small schools have been created en masse through large outside grants. In some cases, the districts that accepted this money did not understand the concept of empowering schools. As a result, they created lots of small schools but did not empower their principals. What they demonstrated is that if you convert a large, failing urban school in a centralized district into several small schools that are also run in a centralized, top-down fashion, you will now have several small, failing urban schools! Unfortunately, these districts may think that they have tried decentralization, when in fact they have not.

Haven't We Already Tried Decentralization and Found That It Did Not Work?

Many school districts think that they've already tried decentralization and have found that it did not work. As I indicated earlier, they most likely tried superficial approaches that were bound to fail, because they did not place decision making where it makes a difference—in the hands of principals.

Many districts have implemented site-based management, commonly known as SBM, and have found it wanting, too. That may seem pretty strong evidence that decentralization does not work, because SBM involves the creation of a school site council at each school. Yet the mere fact that a school council has been created does not mean that either the school or the principal has decision-making power. Moreover, even if school councils did have real power, that fact would vitiate the accountability system, thus creating another serious problem.

The new approach to school empowerment typically grants control over the budget to the principals, not to school committees. Some districts, such as San Francisco and St. Paul, do require that every school have a site council made up of teachers, parents, and community members and that the council have the power to approve the school plan and budget, but other empowered districts, such as Houston and Oakland, have councils that are advisory and do not have final decision powers. New York City vests the decision power in its principals but requires that each principal consult with a school site council.

It is prudent to grant budget autonomy to a principal? Not only is it prudent, it is absolutely necessary if there is to be any accountability. In 1988, Chicago implemented a state law that provided that every school in the city had to have an elected council of parents, teachers, and community members. Councils had the power to hire and fire principals and to approve a large part of each school's budget. What followed was infighting and accusations of graft, patronage, and sometimes of outright stealing by members of the school councils. In the end, a new mayor, Richard Daley, persuaded the state to pass another law that gave the mayor the power to appoint the city's school board and through it to control school budgets.

A related example comes from New York City. In 1966, the state legislature passed a law that created elected school boards for each of the thirty-two community subdistricts in New York City. Only about 5 percent of eligible voters turned out for local school board elections, though, and in some cases a board member was elected with as few as 238 votes.[8] The result, as in Chicago, was chaos. After more than two decades of grand jury investigations and exposés by watchdog groups and newspapers, the citizens of New York were fed up with the widespread impression that these local school boards had used their vast budgets to become centers of patronage and political power. A new state law, passed in 1996, stripped the local boards of their budget control, giving all financial control to the chancellor of the New York City Department of Education, where it remains today.

Accountability has to mean that an identifiable person or persons bear direct responsibility for the use of budgets and that, if they use the money badly, they will either lose their jobs or suffer some other major consequence. Where school site committees with decision powers are used, accountability is compromised, because parents and community volunteers cannot be fired or sued for poor school performance, and no teacher can be held accountable for anything that is not included in the union contract. This is not to say that a principal should exercise totalitarian control over the school budget. To the contrary, every district that has empowered principals with budget control has also created an elaborate accountability system to see that teachers, parents, and others are part of the decision process, as we shall see in the section on accountability.

What About Vouchers and Charter Schools?

Some people argue that school district decentralization is nothing but a weak form of what they consider to be "true" choice— vouchers and charter schools. They may be right, in the sense that decentralization, as we shall see, has strong features of choice, because all of our eight districts permit families to pick any public school within the district (with preference given to neighborhood children) without seeking a waiver from their local or "zone" school. Why not go all the way, these people argue, and permit families to receive a voucher that they can spend at any public or private school?

My answer is based on practical experience. California has had two initiatives over the past fifteen years that would have created statewide vouchers. The first initiative was backed with a campaign of some $50 million, the second with a campaign said to have cost $70 million. Both initiatives lost by very large margins of about 70 percent to 30 percent. Anyone who has been involved in politics will tell you that when you spend that much money on a campaign and still lose that big, it's time to move on to the next issue.

Nonetheless, there are successful voucher systems in some states, and the United States Supreme Court has ruled that vouchers may even be used to attend Catholic schools under certain conditions. Perhaps a time will come when a system of vouchers that will provide equality of access will be invented. Until then, vouchers will remain a very small part of our educational system.

Charter schools, in contrast, have grown briskly since 1991, when they were first permitted in the state of Minnesota, and they now enroll about 3 percent of all U.S. students in the forty states that have passed charter school laws. Charter schools enroll between 25 percent and 55 percent of the students in Dayton, Detroit, New Orleans, and Washington, D.C., and about 7 percent of all students in Los Angeles.

Charter schools bear a strong resemblance to strongly decentralized school districts. For one thing, they are public schools: they charge no tuition, and they must accept all comers, though in some cases they may require an admissions test (as some district public schools do, for that matter). Charter school principals typically enjoy full autonomy in much the same manner as principals of empowered or autonomous schools in St. Paul, Boston, or New York City. In fact, one could argue that a fully decentralized school district operates as though it had converted all of its schools into charter schools.

It is also notable that every one of the eight decentralizing urban districts in our study except Seattle is competing against charter schools (the state of Washington does not yet permit charter schools). In many cases, our research team concluded that it is the success of charter schools in raising student achievement that has encouraged superintendents to decentralize, since charter schools have proved that public schools can be run with a high degree of autonomy and be successful. The popularity of charter schools with teachers and parents has also made the case that small schools are desirable, and the freedom of choice that has drawn many families to charter schools has also had an impact on school district managers.

Charter schools may well have an even more profound benefit for public education. Charter schools are always schools of choice. No student is assigned to a charter school. Charter schools can survive only if they can continue to attract enough students to make their budgets. In other words, they compete against other charter schools and the school district for students, even though they sometimes partner with that same district by participating in joint planning and other activities.

We do not know whether the decentralization of our eight large school districts will survive the test of time. Even if decentralization produces superior student achievement, the world of political decisions is such that a new president of the United States, a new mayor of Boston, Chicago, or New York, or a new governor of California, Minnesota, Texas, or Washington could sweep away even the most successful school district reforms. One force that will push back against any potential backtracking in decentralized districts is the continued success of charter schools. A large and successful population of charter schools in any city serves as a constant, visible reminder of the efficacy of local school autonomy and of school choice. In the face of that daily reminder of the strength of decentralized decision making, it will be far more difficult than it would be otherwise to reverse the progress that is taking place in these eight districts.

That being the case, why don't we simply convert all school districts to charter schools, rather than attempt the arduous task of reforming those districts? My answer is that these decentralizing districts are, in effect, doing just that. If Boston or Chicago spreads its pilot-school model to all of its schools as Houston, New York City, Oakland, Seattle, St. Paul, and San Francisco have done, then these districts will be indistinguishable from very large charter school systems, with the one difference that they will have traditional union contracts, while charter schools tend to be non-union. The Boston Pilot Schools have an abbreviated union contract, but all of the other seven districts have found ways to bring about decentralization while maintaining more traditional union contracts (other than Houston, because Texas does not permit collective bargaining, but the state does have associations of teachers). As long as collective bargaining is not incompatible with successful school empowerment (and apparently it is not), there is no reason to doubt that decentralized districts can be as successful, or even more successful, than charter schools.

There is another element in the argument about replacing existing school districts with charter schools. New York City has 1,467 schools and Los Angeles 878. Many of these are large schools. To replace these schools with small charter schools (most charter schools to date are small) would mean having perhaps 3,000 charter schools in New York City and 1,700 or more in Los Angeles. As a practical matter, who is going to open and run that many schools? Will it be thousands of mom-and-pop operators, each with one or two charter schools? Who, then, will oversee the quality of education and the proper use of public funds at these schools? No county or state is equipped to do so, and if those education agencies were to build new bureaucracies to take on the task, the result twenty years from now might well be an even larger and more cumbersome set of educational bureaucracies.

Clearly, any practical plan for large-scale charter school growth would require that a small number of very large charter school operators rise up. Each of these would operate perhaps five hundred or a thousand charter schools. Each would then be a large school district and prone to the familiar pathologies of large size. Perhaps with time and good management, these new charter school behemoths could be created. I would argue, though, that it is far more practical, given the success of the eight districts described in this book, to work the problem from the other side, by decentralizing the districts that we have now.

Decentralization on a Large Scale

The decentralization of entire school districts is new to the United States, where it dates only to the mid-1990s, but it has been practiced for nearly three decades in Canada, Great Britain, New Zealand, and Tokyo (though not elsewhere in Japan). All of these districts roughly follow the pattern first invented in the approximately eighty-thousand-student Edmonton Public Schools more than thirty years ago.[9]

Edmonton is a blue-collar city and has the largest percentage of low-income students in the province of Alberta. Edmonton Public Schools operates 197 schools for its approximately eighty thousand students, more than Boston, Oakland, San Francisco, St. Paul, or Seattle. The district must compete directly against local Catholic schools, which are funded on an equal basis by the government and enroll about 30 percent of the city's students.

In 1973, former principal and hog farmer Mike Strembitsky became superintendent. Applying his common sense and his dislike of central bureaucracy, he invented the system of decentralization that is now being implemented in all eight of our study districts. Strembitsky served for twenty-two years as superintendent, long enough to cement this approach in place. Today, several superintendents later, Edmonton still adheres to this system. The district website includes this statement: "Our Philosophy: . . . Choice is the foundation of our district's approach to education . . . We believe that the 'one size fits all' model of education is no longer appropriate."

More than thirty years after it began decentralization, Edmonton now has a four-year high school graduation rate that is 68 percent and rising, above the 55.8 percent of New York City. Edmonton students take the provincial Diploma Examination, roughly comparable to New York State's Regents Examinations, or can elect to receive a "school awarded" diploma, as in New York City. Students must pass two of the diploma examinations to receive the provincial diploma. In 2007, 86.5 percent of students passed the English exam (compared to the provincial passing rate of 87.7 percent), and 82.2 percent passed in math (compared to 81.1 percent for the province). These results are impressive, given that Edmonton has a higher proportion of low-income students than any other district in the province. Data on the racial breakdown of scores are not available; Canadian school districts are not allowed to collect data on the race of their students.

Edmonton also pioneered annual satisfaction surveys of students, parents, school employees, and principals. In 2007, 1,057 Edmonton residents who have no children in the public schools were surveyed, and more than 80 percent responded that they were satisfied with the overall quality of education provided by the public schools. Nearly 60 percent of that sample said that they felt the education provided by the district was equal to or better than that provided by private schools, and nearly 95 percent said that they felt Edmonton Public Schools provided a quality of education that is better than elsewhere in Canada. Among parents of Edmonton students, about 97 percent were satisfied with the overall quality of education, and more than 90 percent were satisfied with their child's school principal. More than 85 percent expressed satisfaction with the district's Board of Trustees. Among high school students, 80 percent reported that their schoolwork is "interesting," and 90 percent said that they get help from their teachers when needed. Among elementary students, nearly 90 percent found their schoolwork interesting, and more than 95 percent said that they get help when they need it. In addition, every school administers these surveys to parents, students, principals, and school employees every year and posts the results publicly.

Edmonton Public Schools provides a benchmark by which we can evaluate the progress of the eight U.S. districts of this book. The basic elements of decentralization that were developed and refined over thirty years of experience there have stood the test of time. They make up the framework that has guided the reforms in all eight of our study districts. Of equal importance is that Edmonton has maintained its decentralized organization through several decades, through the normal turnover of elected school board members, and through several superintendents.

Decentralizing Is More Like Building a Marriage Than Building a House

As we will see in the chapters to follow, decentralization is more an ongoing process than a fix-it-once-and-leave-it-alone construction project. Once a district has successfully decentralized, its task has just begun. Someday, school districts all over the country might be decentralized. If and when that day arrives, it will be much easier to maintain a decentralized form, because every new superintendent, school board member, principal, and teacher will accept the idea as natural. Now, however, a decentralized district is pretty much alone, surrounded by traditional, centralized, top-down districts and their people. Under those circumstances, it's a constant struggle to keep decentralization going.

No superintendent stays in office forever, and neither does a school board member or a mayor. Turnover in the governance system is inevitable, and whenever new people arrive at the top of the decentralized district, the autonomy of the schools will face a new peril. Until decentralization someday becomes the national norm, new superintendents and school board members will come in with the traditional, top-down, centralized idea of how a district should be managed. In the stories of the school districts that follow, we'll see the struggle that sometimes ensues after a major succession in the apparatus of governance. As a result of this constant process of change, many decentralizing districts find themselves living in a nuanced world rather than one that is all one way or another. There is reason for optimism even in the face of these challenges, though, because the heart of a decentralizing district lies in the entrepreneurial, independent spirit of the principals and teachers. Once they have tasted the freedom that goes with decentralization, they never entirely lose their desire to keep it.

Now that we've laid out some basics, we're ready to dive into the subtleties and the practicalities of empowering schools in a decentralized district. Let's start our coast-to-coast tour of school district decentralization.

2

THE FIVE PILLARS OF SCHOOL EMPOWERMENT

Beginning in the year 2000, I set out to learn more about good schools in big school districts. I wanted to find out what it would take for a district to enable all of its schools to be good schools. As I explained in the previous chapter, my study of corporate organizations had led me to believe that any school district can be composed of consistently good, high-performing schools.

My Visits to Schools: Study One

Study One was completed a few years ago, as I described earlier. I will briefly summarize it here because it provides some useful background for Study Two, which forms the basis of this book.

During Study One, I assembled a team of about ten research assistants to help me, some of whom were former teachers and one of whom had also been a principal. They were my teachers, since I have never worked in a K–12 school. Together, over a period of three years, we visited 223 schools across the United States. We visited the three largest school districts: New York City, Los Angeles, and Chicago. We visited the three largest Catholic school systems: Chicago, Los Angeles, and New York. In addition, we had heard of three districts that had developed a new, bold approach of granting full empowerment, or autonomy, to every school. These included Edmonton, Canada; Seattle, which had borrowed the Edmonton model in the mid-1990s; and Houston, which had learned from Edmonton at about the same time as Seattle. We visited these three as well. At each of the 223 schools that we sampled in these nine districts we interviewed the principal, observed several classes, and inspected the organization and activities of the central office staff. We also analyzed data on the standardized test results of the students. What we learned was that when we compared student performance in the three old-line U.S. districts, all of which were run in a top-down, centralized fashion, to the three decentralized districts of Edmonton, Seattle, and Houston, the decentralized districts produced better student performance on standardized tests. I described those results in a book and some articles.[1]

This study demonstrated that when a district grants autonomy to its principals, they run their schools in a way that creates superior student performance—not in just a few of the schools, in most of the schools.

Here's one example of what we learned in Seattle during that first study. We visited the John Hay Elementary School, K–5, in the Queen Anne Hill neighborhood, a middle-and upper-middle-income part of the city. Thirty percent were students of color, and 24 percent were from low-income families. The principal at the time was Joanne Testa-Cross, who has since retired from the school district. Under previous management, Seattle had been a traditional, centralized district, and Testa-Cross was given only $25,000 a year to spend as she and her staff saw fit. The school district's central office staff hired the mixture of teachers, registrars, attendance clerks, and other personnel that it thought was best for all elementary schools. After the new decentralized system was introduced, Testa-Cross suddenly controlled all $2 million per year of the school's budget. She used her new autonomy to cancel some existing programs and instead brought in full-time specialists, new curricula chosen by the teachers, and twelve part-time retired teachers to serve as tutors. The result? Fourth grade math scores on the state WASL test went from 36 percent satisfactory in 1998 to 61 percent in 2001!

I found many schools in all three decentralized districts that had used their new empowerment to improve the performance of their students. While some schools had embraced their new autonomy with more enthusiasm than others, enough schools in all of the decentralized districts had done so that we reported that principals in Houston now controlled nearly 59 percent of their budgets, in Seattle about 79 percent, and in Edmonton, about 92 percent. By comparison, principals in Chicago controlled slightly more than 19 percent of their budgets, in Los Angeles about 7 percent, and in New York City only about 6 percent.

Centralized versus Decentralized School Districts: Principals' Control over Budget in 2000*

Traditional, Centralized Districts	Decentralized Districts
Chicago 19.3%	Edmonton 91.7%
Los Angeles 6.7%	Houston 58.6%
New York City 6.1%	Seattle 79.3%

* All of the tables presented in this book can also be found in the appendixes for easy reference.

The central office in each city dictated how the rest of the money was spent.

This analysis confirmed that the basic principles of organization that hold for large businesses also hold for large school districts: large size tends to produce bureaucratization, rigidity, and top-heavy administration, which drag down the performance of any organization. The cure both in businesses and in school districts is decentralization. Decentralization in school districts works. Now, however, we faced a new and more intricate challenge: to find out what it is that principals do with their autonomy that enables their schools to succeed, and to find out how a superintendent can have enough surveillance over empowered principals to keep an eye on any principals who don't know what to do, while at the same time giving enough freedom to the strong principals to enable them to create truly great schools. This required a second study.

Finding Out What Empowered Principals Do with Their Autonomy: Study Two

Theodore Sizer, one of the great scholars of school management, visited eighty successful schools across the country and then wrote three wonderful books about them.[2] I've studied those books and had the opportunity to interview Ted and his wife and research partner Nancy Sizer for this book, and much of my research for this book has been influenced by their ideas. Sizer's ideas included the now-popular notion that small schools are inherently superior due to their greater intimacy and sense of community, that a curriculum should follow the dictum that "less is more" by reducing the number of courses to the minimum, and that no teacher should have responsibility for more than a total of 80 students. Beyond that number, he argued, teachers lose track of their students. Sizer and his colleagues at Brown University, along with a group of principals, founded the Coalition of Essential Schools in 1984. This group, which has grown today to a few thousand schools, maintains regular contact and several of the Coalition principals were instrumental in shaping the reforms in our eight study districts (see Sizer, *Horace's School*, 1992, pp. 207–21, for a full list of the nine principles of the Coalition and a list of the early schools).

After the publication of my book *Making Schools Work*, a few superintendents had contacted me and said they wanted to implement the ideas that I had found in Edmonton, Houston, and Seattle. A few other school districts learned about the Edmonton transformation on their own. As a result, by 2005 there were eight U.S. districts that were implementing Edmonton-style decentralization, giving decision authority to principals. I felt that in order to be thorough, I was going to have to visit all eight of them.

I assembled a new research team, and we drew a sample this time that was even larger than before, 442 schools in eight districts: Boston, Chicago, Houston, New York City, Oakland, San Francisco, Seattle, and St. Paul. I bought a new suitcase, asked my wife for her forbearance yet again, and off we went. Our districts spanned the nation, from coast to coast and from north to south. I looked forward to revisiting Houston and Seattle after a hiatus of five years and wondered whether I would find that they had maintained their commitment to school empowerment. I knew that the superintendents in St. Paul and San Francisco had worked with Mike Strembitsky and were well informed about the Edmonton approach to decentralization. The superintendents in both Chicago and New York City had read my earlier book and had contacted me. Both of them seemed to be serious about implementing decentralization in their districts, which were the third largest (Chicago) and the largest (New

York City) in the nation. The Oakland superintendent had been a student in a class for aspiring superintendents that I had taught, and I anticipated that he'd be serious about his reform. Boston had a set of twenty Pilot Schools, said to be autonomous from the central office, but I knew little about them. All in all, it was an exciting prospect.

As I made my visits, I was reminded that schools are about children and young adults. They're about the development of human beings and about the adults who devote their careers to this mission. It's rejuvenating to see second graders give their teacher spontaneous hugs. While I have great admiration for IBM, too, no one there gives hugs, at least not that I have ever seen.

Along the way I learned how Phalen Lake Elementary School in St. Paul, Minnesota, used its freedom from central office mandates to craft a model program that meets the needs of 150 new, non-English-speaking Hmong students from Thailand. I found out why Vanguard High School in Manhattan draws dozens of educators to study its methods every week, and I saw how elite Lowell High School in San Francisco makes it possible for every one of its 2,600 students to visit each of their teachers for a one-on-one session when they need to. I discovered Total Student Load, which has the power to improve every school. Most of the schools in this book are successes, and each of them is unique. In one sense, this book is very much about uniqueness, about the fact that when schools are given freedom they each find a way to create a school that is like no other. In another sense this book is about how, at a deeper level, these schools are all the same in that they rely upon a common set of freedoms, which I call the Five Pillars of School Empowerment.

The Five Pillars of School Empowerment

A school district that is decentralized is one that has empowered its principals to make the operating decisions about how best to implement the policies established by the state and the local school board. In order to empower all schools, a school district must have all of the essential Five Pillars of School Empowerment, which fit together into an integrated whole. They are as follows:

1. Real choices for families
2. Empowering schools with the Four Freedoms (control over budget, staffing, curriculum, and scheduling)
3. Effective principals
4. A system of accountability
5. Weighted student formula budgeting

Let's briefly review these, and then we'll be ready for a deeper look to see what we can learn from the eight school districts and 442 schools that have acquired the Five Pillars and achieved some degree of empowerment.

THE FIRST PILLAR: FAMILIES HAVE REAL CHOICES

In most school districts, students are assigned by the central office to the local school nearest to their home. At the elementary level, that's not a bad idea, because most families prefer to have their children attend a school near home. Because most elementary schools in a single district offer the same curriculum, it would seem that one school ought to be as good as another, although parents will typically seek out the school that is reputed to have the best teachers.

This may be the usual way of doing things, but is it really the best way? Not in decentralized districts. In all eight of the empowered districts, parents have a choice of where their child will go to school, and they don't have to receive special dispensation from anyone to do it. In New York City, for example, every family lists up to twelve schools that they'd like for each child. Schools that are oversubscribed select their students with the help of a district-run computerized algorithm that matches students with schools, with preference given to neighborhood families. Almost everyone gets one of the schools on his or her list.

Empowered schools choose their own teachers to fill every opening, too. The district personnel office still must check applicants to make sure that their credentials are in order, but it's up to each principal to choose the teachers that will meet specific needs. In that way, each school can develop an instructional program that is tailored to its specific group of students, rather than having a generic, Brand X set of teachers who may be talented individually but may not fit well together as a team. A baseball team, after all, doesn't need nine catchers!

Consider TechBoston Academy high school, in Dorchester, Massachusetts, a Boston Pilot School. TechBoston was formerly called Dorchester High, but it was known as "Dumpchester" or "Dumbchester," because everybody who had failed everywhere else was sent there. Now it's a school of choice. Boston has implemented school empowerment on a pilot basis and now has 20 such schools (out of 144 total schools), the Pilot Schools. TechBoston Academy is in its fifth year as an empowered school and has about 300 students. Compared to traditional high schools of 1,500 or more students, it's a small school. Fifty-four percent of the students are black, 30 percent are Hispanic, 6 percent are Asian, and 10 percent are white; 13 percent are eligible for special education, and 85 percent are from low-income families. Average daily attendance is 92 percent, and the dropout rate is 9 percent per year, which is high but not unusual for a low-income population. Of those who graduate, the school says that 96 percent go to college, and 80 percent go to a four-year college. It's a "school of choice" because in Boston, all schools, whether they are Pilot Schools or not, are schools of choice. Each K–5, 6–8, and K–8 school is placed in one of three geographical zones, and families can apply to any elementary or middle school within their zone. If a family lives near a zone border, it may also apply to schools that are in a neighboring zone within one mile. For high school, every family may apply to any of the thirty regular high schools and the three "test" or selective-admissions high schools in Boston. The school counselor at TechBoston observes that "we don't pick our kids . . . some of them want to be here because of the technology. Some of them, their parents want them to be here because it's . . . a small school and we're really tight and we really focus on the students." Half of the TechBoston students come from the neighborhood, and the other half come in through the lottery that randomly selects them from the applicant pool, which is larger than TechBoston can accommodate.

The rigorous discipline and focus at TechBoston Academy means that it is not for everyone, but it does not have to be. It only has to be able to attract enough students to make its budget, and it does that easily every year. In a real sense, it's the parents that are being empowered when the schools are schools of choice. The parents are voting with their feet for the schools they like. Some people believe that low-income, inner-city families don't care as much as middle-class families about the education of their children. TechBoston, and hundreds of other inner-city schools of choice around the nation, demonstrate how untrue that is.

School choice has a second, very important effect: it produces competition among the schools. When the district central office assigns students to schools, principals know that whether their school performs well or badly, it will have the same number of students and the same budget. If the students and their parents are unhappy, the school doesn't have to respond because the students don't have a choice—they'll be back next year, like it or not. Their only alternative is to drop out of school entirely. Imagine how life would be if we were each assigned an automobile, an apartment, and a restaurant by the government and had no choice. What would happen to the quality of cars, apartments, and restaurants?

Without school choice, there is no reason for a school district to grant managerial autonomy to principals. Principals have little incentive to want to improve their student performance or their communication with parents, because a high-performing school will have the same enrollment as a failing school. Under a choice system, though, everything will change. Failing schools will quickly see a decline in enrollment, the school budget will be cut, the number of teachers will have to drop, and so forth. School buildings are very expensive to build, especially in urban areas, and the district wants every seat to be full in every school. In a choice district, strong schools will be full beyond their capacity with students who are staying away from the weak schools. It may be possible for a principal in a non-choice district to make excuses for poor performance, but under a choice system, a principal who has a half-empty school doesn't have a leg to stand on.

THE SECOND PILLAR: SCHOOLS ARE EMPOWERED WITH THE FOUR FREEDOMS

One of the most important discoveries of this second study is that empowered principals have not one but four freedoms that are equally essential to success. These are:

1. Control over the school budget
2. Control over the staffing pattern
3. Control over the curriculum
4. Control over the schedule

1. Control over the School Budget

Let's summarize a few of the basics about budgetary control. In most of the approximately 16,850 school districts of the United States, a principal controls only about $10,000 to $25,000 of discretionary money each year. That money can be used for school field trips, instructional consultants, and so on. In centralized districts, moreover, not all of the school district's funds make it as far as the schools. When the central office controls the money, it usually finds ways to keep a "pinch" or more for itself. That pinch is often as much as 30 percent or more of the entire district budget, which is spent on central office staff. Not only that, but central office staffers usually create lots of non-teaching jobs to be filled at each school, and then they send veteran, credentialed teachers to those jobs. Let's remember that only 43 percent of school district employees are regularly engaged in classroom teaching.

In an empowered school, by comparison, the principal has the authority to decide how to spend the school's money, and the district sees to it that most of the money gets to the schools. That happens in large part because the policy of sending dollars rather than positions to each school makes it easy for teachers and parents to understand where the money is going. Once they understand, they create pressure for the central office to send more of the total district budget to the schools, so that it can be spent in the classroom rather than on central office staff. The largest expense in every school is staff, which usually accounts for more than 90 percent of the budget. Principals may also use their discretion in other ways. For example, the Young Achievers Science and Mathematics Pilot School in Boston (K–8) believes in experiential education, so it uses a good deal of its money on student projects around the city of Boston. Another example is the Mission Hill School in Boston (K–8), a Pilot School where the principal allocates one thousand dollars to each teacher, every year, to spend on classroom materials so that teachers can tailor their materials to their curriculum.

The Boston Pilot Schools receive administrative support from the Center for Collaborative Education, a nonprofit organization headed by Dan French. French explains how the Pilot Schools got control of that central office money: "We helped the budget office itemize every single central office cost there was . . . and said Pilot Schools can either choose the service, or if they don't want the service . . . add it to our lump-sum budget." At Young Achievers, the principal sums it up this way: "One of our autonomies as a Pilot School is to decide how you spend your money."

Our research was conducted during 2005–6, with additional investigations continuing through 2008. Most of the statistical data, though, come from the 2005 calendar year. In a few cases the data have changed substantially since that time, and in those cases the more recent numbers are also cited. We found that there were large differences among our eight decentralizing districts in the principals' control of the school budget, as the table that follows illustrates.

There are several things worth noting in this table. First is that the districts have implemented local school empowerment in very different ways. Chicago, which has the lowest budget control for principals at 13.9 percent, was very new in its implementation and was in the process of increasing that figure. San Francisco, which was also low, at 22.8 percent, had intentionally

Principals' Control over Budget in
Decentralizing Districts as of 2005

Boston*	75.0%
Chicago*	13.9%
Houston	73.7%
New York City*	85.0%
Oakland	60.5%
San Francisco	22.8%
Seattle	47.7%
St. Paul	87.2%

* In Boston, Chicago, and New York City, these data apply only to the schools that are part of the empowerment program. In the other districts, all schools are part of the empowerment program. Percentages are the average of principals who were interviewed in each city.

held back most of the budget control from principals—partly in response to a consent decree. Seattle, at 47.7 percent, had slipped considerably from its 2000 local budget control figure of 79.3 percent. A new superintendent explained that he felt that budget decentralization had gone too far in Seattle and needed to be reined in. The opposite trend was evident in Houston, which increased local budget control from 58.6 percent in 2000 to 73.7 percent in 2005, while making two changes in superintendent during that time. Oakland, under a brand-new state appointed administrator (the district had been declared insolvent and the state of California had taken over), had gone all the way from traditional centralized control to 60.5 percent local budget control in just two years. Finally, Boston (75.0 percent), New York City (85.0 percent), and St. Paul (87.2 percent) exhibited the greatest delegation of budget control to principals, approaching the 91.7 percent in Edmonton that I measured in 2000. (As an aside, Edmonton appears to be increasing this percentage as well.)

In two of the cities, Boston and Chicago, we were able to compare budget control among the schools that had been empowered versus control in the traditional schools. In one other, New York City, only some of the schools had been empowered by 2005, but we were not granted permission to gather data in any of the traditional schools. We do know from Study One, however, that in 2000, when all of New York City's schools were run in the traditional manner, principals controlled 6.1 percent of the money spent in their schools. In each of the remaining five districts, all of the schools had been empowered, so there were no traditionally managed schools available for a comparison with empowered schools. Among the two districts that permitted this comparison, we found that the Pilot Schools in Boston control on average 75.0 percent of their money, while traditionally managed schools control 27.8 percent. In Chicago, the empowered schools controlled 13.9 percent of their money, compared to 10.8 percent in traditional schools. Keep in mind that Chicago was at the time only in its first year of implementing decentralization.

I'd like to add an explanation on how we measured each school's budget control. In both 2000 and 2005 we followed the same procedure. We sat down with the principals in our sample and reviewed with them specific budget categories, including staff salaries, professional development consultants and courses, books and materials, substitute teacher expenditures, parent programs, and so on. We asked them to estimate what percentage of each of these budgets they controlled and how much was controlled by the central office. If they were not sure, we asked them to look up the numbers while we waited. The percentages that resulted often differ, sometimes substantially, from the official district reports of local budget control. That difference is sometimes due to the fact that the principal's supervisor will typically interpret district policy according to his or her taste, and some of those middle managers are quite authoritarian, while others are not. As a result, the district policy might call for decentralization of, say, 50 percent of the money to the schools, but if the assistant superintendents who oversee principals are top-down managers, the principals may be under orders to use their "discretion" as they are told. In reality, those principals may control only 25 percent or less of the money, despite the district's policy to the contrary. A truly decentralized district will have trained and will monitor its assistant superintendents so that they do in fact grant to principals all of the empowerment that is intended by the district—or it may have eliminated that middle layer of management entirely, as in New York City and in Chicago's empowered Autonomous Management and Performance Schools.

In other cases, school districts may adopt low estimates of budget decentralization so as not to surprise or worry the public (people may think that the principals are running amok with public funds!) or may publish high estimates in order to create the impression of progress and reform. Our method was intended to measure how much budget control principals felt they actually had, not how much the district officials said they were supposed to have, and we have high confidence that our measures are valid.

There are some people who doubt that any superintendent has the power to bring about change in a large school district. Our data make it clear that belief is incorrect. The changes in principals' control over school budgets were large and took place within one year after the new policy was announced. I know of no large business organization that responds more quickly to this kind of change. The changes that took place between 2000 and 2005 in Houston (from 58.6 to 73.7 percent), from 2002 to

2006 in New York City (from 6.1 to 85.0 percent) and from 2005 to 2007 in Seattle (a decline from 79.3 percent to 47.7 percent) make it clear that school decentralization or centralization policies set by the school board and superintendent register very quickly throughout the schools.

2. Control over the Staffing Pattern

This concept might be unfamiliar, but it is both simple and important. Control over the school staffing pattern does not mean that the principal can set the salaries of teachers, and it does not mean that the principal can override the provisions that have resulted from collective bargaining with teachers unions. It means that the decision about how many employees of which types to hire has been removed from central office staffers and delegated to principals. In the traditional approach (used in almost all school districts today), central office analysts decide how many teachers an elementary, middle, or high school should have for every so many students, typically based on a district formula computed according to the number of students enrolled in each school. In a similar manner, districts determine how many registrars, assistant registrars, attendance clerks, counselors, assistant principals, and so on each school should have. Then, another central office department hires the personnel and assigns them to the schools. The principal has nothing to say about the resulting staffing pattern in her school. Most districts claim that any principal may depart from the standard staffing formula by requesting a variance from the central office. All principals will tell you that these variances are so bureaucratically difficult to get that it's not worth it to apply.

The most important instructional decision that a principal can make is how many administrative staff positions to trade for more classroom teachers. Some high schools in tough neighborhoods, for example, may want to have a dozen security guards, while other schools may want none. The district, however, will send the same formulaic number of security guards to every school, based on enrollment.

Consider Phalen Lake Elementary School, K–6, in St. Paul, Minnesota. In 2003, Phalen Lake received the Minnesota Title I Award for outstanding academic achievement, the only St. Paul elementary school to be so recognized. You might be surprised to learn that many recent Southeast Asian immigrants have settled in St. Paul and that their children are a major presence in the schools. Of the 669 students at Phalen Lake, 57 percent are Asian, 18 percent African American, 14 percent are Caucasian, and 10 percent are Hispanic. Fifty-nine percent are English Language Learners, largely recent Hmong arrivals from Thailand, and 92 percent are from low-income families.

Although Phalen Lake has as many challenges as a school can have, it is succeeding. From 2001 to 2005 in grade 5, for example, student reading performance on the Minnesota test shows that the number of students at level 4 in reading, the second highest, has increased from 20 percent to 37 percent, and level 5, the highest, has improved from 0 to 12 percent. Improvement in math has mirrored these results. Using the federal No Child Left Behind (NCLB) standard, among Phalen Lake fifth graders, 62 percent are proficient or above in English, while 74 percent meet that standard in math.

Patricia Harvey was the superintendent who brought school choice and empowerment to St. Paul. Dr. Harvey had worked with Edmonton superintendent Mike Strembitsky after his retirement, and under her leadership, several St. Paul teams visited Edmonton, bringing back new ideas.

At Phalen Lake, Principal Jan Hopke-Almer is explaining that she uses part of her budget to bring all of the new kindergarten students in before school begins, for testing in English. The children who need additional English language development are evenly divided among the five kindergarten classes when school begins. With its large population of English Language Learners (ELL), the school has developed several programs that aim to get everyone reading and writing as quickly as possible, and this requires a uniquely designed instructional approach, the STAR system.

It's now 8:30 a.m. on the second day of our visit to Phalen Lake Elementary, time for the STAR [Student Teachers As Readers] program to begin in the school library. There are five tables, each with two or three children who are working on their reading with a teacher. One of the tables is staffed by the teacher who has charge of this first grade class. An English Language Learner specialist is at another table, and the other three tables each have a teacher's assistant who is trained to work with ELLs. During the day, all of the students in grades 1–6 will rotate through the library for their STAR time. At one of the tables, a student is reading a book titled *Copy Cat,* and the teacher is helping the student to sound out the title. The first page of *Copy Cat* reads: "I go up the path. You go up the path." At another table, the students are playing Alphabet Bingo. At a third table, the ELL teacher, a Caucasian woman, is talking with three students in Hmong.

It is September 22, the third week of school, and the students have just completed the testing that provides each child with a detailed profile of his or her reading level. They will take this diagnostic test three times each year so that teachers can tailor their instruction to the specific needs of each student. During today's session of twenty to twenty-five minutes, each student will have two "cold" practice readings of a new passage and one "hot" reading that the teacher will score for the number of words the student can read correctly in sixty seconds. Each student will chart his or her score on a bar graph that will enable the student to see his or her progress during the year. Often, the STAR workshops have one or two volunteers from local companies who help out regularly. In addition, two or three teachers and local college and high school students provide one-on-one tutoring during the day to students who need the additional help. This approach to reading requires that the teachers and paraprofessionals be highly trained in working with ELLs and that they have a strong desire to serve ELL students. The principal could not have assembled an award-winning staff or have so many skilled ELL instructors without control over her staffing pattern.

In a second grade classroom, twenty-three children are seated on the carpeted floor while the teacher holds up a book and an audiotape that they will hear. Also in the room is a Reading Recovery specialist who spends half of her time assisting teachers and the other half working intensively with selected students, one-on-one. During her classroom time, the Reading Recovery teacher takes students in groups of four to her own room, where she works with each group on guided reading. The classroom teacher does the same, taking four students at a time at her desk for guided reading instruction, while the remaining students work independently as they await their turns. The second grade classes have staggered their language arts time so that the Reading Recovery specialist can get to each one. This way, the two adults will each have half of the twenty-three students during reading instruction each day. The teacher explains that every day, these second grade students spend 90 to 120 minutes on reading skills and 45 to 60 additional minutes on writing.

In another second grade class, the classroom teacher is sitting at a kidney-shaped table doing guided reading with three students, while the ELL teacher works in another corner with two students, and a master's degree student teacher has a group of six students who are listening to a taped recording through headphones. The other nine students in this twenty-student class are working independently for now, but they will rotate through these stations, too.

This is a successful reading program. The concentration of the staffing pattern on reading teachers is obvious. But how can Phalen Lake Elementary School afford to have, in addition to 29 fully credentialed classroom teachers, another 10 credentialed ELL teachers, 3 credentialed reading specialists, 7 ELL education assistants, 10 classroom aides who supervise small-group reading, and 3.4 additional licensed specialists (one of them is part-time)? The answer: principals who want to change the staff allocations that are in the 50 percent controlled by the central office bring in their site council chair or the clerk who works on their budget, and they sit down and talk about it. First, the district provides, out of its 50 percent of the district budget, additional funds for special education and ELL students, and second, Phalen Lake gave up its assistant principal for two years and thus has only two administrators. It has no media specialists, no deans, no full-time counselor, no math specialists, no professional development coaches, only two custodians, and two office clerical staff. Third, the principal has made her limited funds go as far as possible by blending fully credentialed teachers with less-expensive paraprofessional education assistants and classroom aides who are trained in the specific skills that they need. Other schools have these paraprofessionals, too, but often they are mismatched to the school and end up running the copy machine or serving on playground or lunchroom duty. Phalen Lake has made choices both about what kinds of staff to hire and about which applicants will match the specific needs of the students. That is what control over the staffing pattern is for. It's also worth pointing out that the principal at Phalen Lake is exactly the kind of motivated, take-charge educational leader who can take full advantage of an empowered school in a decentralized district. A passive principal surely would not have attacked Phalen Lake's literacy issues with the same energy or creativity, but then in St. Paul's accountability system, a passive principal would not last long.

Central office has had to make substantial changes in its way of doing things to support empowered schools. For example, the finance department in the St. Paul central office has developed a computerized staffing planner that enables principals to enter the positions that they'd like to have, and the program will then show them the total cost of those positions for a year. Principals know their budgets, of course, and must stay within them. Because the unforeseen often happens, the St. Paul district allows an elementary principal to go over budget by up to $5,000, a middle school principal by $10,000, and a high school principal by $15,000. That deficit must be made up in the next year. If a new principal takes over at a school that has a deficit, he or she must make up that inherited deficit. If the deficit is large, the new principal is allowed to repay it over two years rather than one, but according to the finance staff at central, in most cases the principal wants to take care of it as soon as possible. As a result, principals in St. Paul reported to us that, on the average, they control 87.2 percent of their budgets, although the district says that principals officially control only 50 percent.

3. Control over the Curriculum

The first topic in discussing curriculum always has to be the distinction between standards, which are always set at the state level, and curriculum, which can be set by the state, the school district, or the individual school—depending on the policies of the state and the local school district. The state standards define what students at each grade level should learn. For example, the California standards for eighth grade English include the following:

Eighth Grade Reading Standards

1.0 Word Analysis, Fluency, and Systematic Vocabulary Development
    1.1 Analyze idioms, analogies, metaphors, and similes to infer the literal and figurative meanings of phrases . . .
    1.3 Use word meanings within the appropriate context and show ability to verify those meanings by definition, restatement, example, comparison, or contrast.

The standards attempt to set out clearly the skills and areas of knowledge that students must learn at each grade level. They do not, however, prescribe whether that learning should be accomplished by reading Shakespeare or Maya Angelou, and they also do not tell the schools whether the reading goals should be accomplished through an integrated study of the Middle East in both social studies and English, or whether those subjects should cover completely independent topics. Those and many other decisions about how to deliver the state standards make up the curriculum of a school.

Some school districts have made the centralized decision that all elementary students will study from the materials of one publisher, such as Success for All, Open Court, or Reading Mastery, or that all mathematics instruction will be from one publisher's series. Other districts have delegated those decisions to the schools. In a few cases, states have chosen to limit all schools to one or two choices of reading or mathematics books, as in California's elementary schools. Proponents of the centralized approach argue that in today's world, students move from one district to another with such frequency that all schools should be required to use the same books and materials to provide consistency for the students. Advocates of school empowerment argue that because the needs of each school are unique, each school should be free to choose its own materials. Our eight decentralizing districts vary on this issue, but let's see what one school has done with its choices.

The Lilla G. Frederick Pilot Middle School is on the Roxbury-Dorchester border, not far from TechBoston Academy. The school has about 660 students in grades 6, 7, and 8. Lilla Frederick is a brand-new school built on a site that previously was a gang hangout, a drug zone, and worse. The neighborhood petitioned Boston superintendent Tom Payzant to build a new school on the site, and that new school is now the pride of the community. The building is entirely free of graffiti, neighbors turn out for community cookouts hosted by the school, and they occasionally call Principal Debra Socia to tell her that they can see that her car is still in the lot, it's late, and she should go home!

Lilla Frederick is divided into four small schools, each of which is "cored" and "looped," which is a unique approach to both curriculum and scheduling. In each of the four schools, there are two sixth grade teachers. One of them offers a "cored" humanities course that combines the curricula of English and social studies in teaching two classes of about twenty-five students each. The other sixth grade teacher covers both math and science in a Math-Science Integrated (MSI) class. One result of this integrated curriculum is that each sixth grade teacher has a total of about forty-five to fifty children, all of whom they get to know intimately. In other words, the humanities teacher teaches two subjects, English and social studies, to one class of twenty-five and then repeats that instruction for a second class of twenty-five. She has thus taught four normal periods, but instead of having four classes of twenty-five, she has two classes of twenty-five.

Grades 7 and 8 are "looped" but not cored. This means that a seventh grade math teacher teaches only math and has four classes of about twenty students each. That teacher "loops," or stays with the same group of eighty students when they move to eighth grade. In this way, the teacher can get to know all of her students very well, although she has nearly twice as many students as each sixth grade teacher, because she stays with them for two years and thus can work with each student in a sustained way on their math development. The same applies to the other subjects of science, English, and social studies: all are looped for grades 7 and 8, but the subjects are separated, rather than integrated across disciplines as in grade 6. The tradeoff that the principal and teachers have made is that every teacher in grades 6, 7, and 8 must become expert on twice as much material as in a traditional curriculum (either a second subject or a second grade level), but each has closer contact with a small group of students. As Principal Deb Socia says, "One of our highest priorities is around this whole idea that children do better when they know adults well" (Interview of November 3, 2006), and because the school controls its curriculum, it has been able to achieve that goal.

4. Control over the Schedule

Few non-educators appreciate the importance of local school control over the schedule of classes. In most districts, the central office dictates that the school day shall consist of seven periods of forty-five minutes each plus a lunch break, and that's it. No one may depart from that official schedule. In some cases, the state even dictates the class schedule to all school districts!

Not in San Francisco's empowered schools, though. Consider Lowell High School, a National Blue Ribbon School of Excellence. Lowell has 2,600 students, of whom more than 50 percent are Chinese American, about 18 percent are other Asian-Pacifics, 14 percent are Caucasian, 6 percent are Filipino, about 7 percent are Latino, and about 3 percent are African American. Each year the school will administer about 2,600 Advanced Placement exams, and the typical student will graduate with three to six AP course credits. Lowell offers instruction in nine foreign languages, including Mandarin, Japanese, Korean, and Hebrew, and eleven sections of AP economics. The typical teacher has four classes of 30 to 35 students each, for a total of 120 to 140 students. Each of the school's approximately ninety student clubs has an adult advisor, and the advanced drama class performed twenty-four different plays last year. Lowell not only has a lot going on, it's packed with students and has a severe shortage of classrooms.

These are selected students, because Lowell is what is known as a selective-admissions school. It enrolls about 723 of the 2,200 who apply for ninth grade each year. Lowell counts among its alumni three Nobel laureates, Supreme Court justice Stephen Breyer, and Yale University president Richard Levin. Selective-admissions schools seem to be gaining in popularity around the United States, with several having opened in Chicago and other cities over the past few years. While some people feel that these schools legitimate an attitude of elitism that does not belong in public education, others celebrate selective-admissions schools for their ability to attract to public schools the children of doctors, lawyers, and scientists. Public schools, they feel, must offer something for everyone, lest they become purely the last resort for the immigrants and the poor and slip out of the mainstream of American life.

One impression that a visitor to Lowell has is that these bright, motivated, and well-prepared students have tremendous mental energy, and they want to do more, experience more, and take more classes. Apparently no one minds the relatively large classes of thirty to thirty-five students, perhaps because the schedule is designed to encourage both greater choice in courses and greater individual attention, and because these students do not want or need the kind of intimate attention that we've seen at schools that serve predominantly low-income students.

We are now visiting an AP physics course, and the subject for today is astrophysics, the science of stars and planets. This class, like all classes at Lowell, is designed around modules of twenty minutes. On Monday, all classes meet for two modules, or forty minutes. On Tuesday, Wednesday, and Thursday, some classes meet for sixty minutes (Tuesday), then forty minutes (Wednesday), then sixty (Thursday), while other classes have the opposite schedule. On Fridays, a class might be either forty or sixty minutes. Every class will have three forties and two sixties in one week and three sixties and two forties the next week. This schedule was necessary to get in all of the elective courses that the students at Lowell High want to take. The academically intense atmosphere attracts a certain kind of teacher, as former principal Paul Cheng notes. "Many teachers like to work in a large setting. They would have worked in a smaller school, but then they come to work at Lowell. I have had teachers who tell me that they rejected assignments to smaller schools because they felt a certain sense of energy, a certain sense of enthusiasm, a certain sense of high school life that was real to them." Cheng also observes that his teachers work under more stress than others; they know they have to work twice as hard, because students will challenge them, and parents will challenge them. "Sometimes it's not just the grades but what they know, because we have parents who are professionals and are really specialists in their field. Say in the science area, for example, we have parents who are professors at UC San Francisco or who are medical doctors."

One important result of the modular schedule is that in addition to the universal one teacher preparation period each day, teachers have additional "holes" in their schedule when they are not teaching and not in a preparation period. During those times, teachers are in their offices, available to students. Former principal Cheng continues, "So you can see where those holes are when they can see students, and that is what is unique about Lowell, what the kids remember, and what I think has a large impact on the forming of relationships with teachers that is very hard to find in the more structured high school schedule. That is why, I think, a lot of problems are prevented, you know, by teachers knowing somebody is in trouble, and they found out not during class or during prep, but they ran into them or they came to them in the office or in the hallways. So the conversations go on all the time in our building, you will see that." Students at Lowell all take at least the state-required number of instructional minutes every day, and teachers are in class for the required number of minutes, but the unique schedule allows for one-on-one interaction. As former principal Cheng asserts, "I have not heard of any other high school in the U.S. that has this module schedule. If you find one, let me know!"

Paul Cheng and his teachers used their control over their schedule to make the most of their school, but they had to make some tradeoffs. Teachers of English, history, and other writing-intensive courses have 120 to 140 students, too many for them to assign long papers that require detailed comments from the teacher. As a result, writing skills are the major area of weakness among Lowell students, and many have difficulty with their college application essays. Traditionally managed schools have to cope with the same large numbers of students per teacher, but without the freedom to arrange the kind of unique schedule that Lowell has. Lowell's bright, motivated students will make up their writing deficiency as college freshmen, and although Lowell doesn't have the financial resources to do everything as well as it would like, it accomplishes a great deal with what it has, because it has control over its schedule. Still, it seems that the quality of student writing has suffered, which perhaps is no surprise, given Lowell's relatively high Total Student Load.

THE THIRD PILLAR: EFFECTIVE PRINCIPALS

Effective principals are not born, they're developed. The early training requires the development of skill as a teacher, for the most part. Occasionally, a former military or businessperson can become a very successful principal, but that's rare. In order to understand what a principal must be to be successful, it's necessary to understand what a principal must do. What a good principal does is to teach her teachers how to be more effective. In other words, to be successful, a principal must be a strong teacher of other adults.

Several years ago, I spent a week with one of New York City's most effective local district superintendents. What I remember best about that week was the day that I spent with her as she conducted her monthly meeting with her thirty or so principals. Most area superintendents use their monthly meeting to go over the latest new regulations from the central office, to review the upcoming student testing schedules, and to tell the principals other administrative trivia in which they have little or no interest. Not in this case.

The topic for the day was math instruction. All of us were given several sheets of math problems to solve, and we furrowed our brows and licked our pencils as we worked them out. After we were done, the superintendent, acting like our math teacher for the day, asked each of us to describe out loud how we had solved one problem or another. To my surprise, we discovered that each problem had been solved through very different methods by different people, yet all of them were correct. On one problem, one person had solved the problem through algebra, another through estimation procedures, and others had used different methods. The principals already knew people used different methods to solve math problems, but they weren't as ready for the next step, which was for us to answer the question, How would you move a new teacher or veteran teacher to broaden her repertoire of teaching methods so that she can recognize and encourage every student to follow the path that is most comfortable for him or her? We spent the next hours in small groups discussing this challenge, followed by a general discussion of what we'd learned.

If a superintendent should be a teacher of principals, then every principal should be a teacher of teachers, and all of them should be students of education. That is the fundamental role of a principal—to be a teacher of teachers—and thus in one sense it's only a small step for an effective teacher to learn to become an effective principal. Former principal and now senior school district official Eric Nadelstern of New York City put it this way. Question: "What do you look for in a principal?" Nadelstern: "Great teacher, I'm looking for our best teachers. I'm trying to convince those teachers that it's the same job. It's just the students change. So instead of working with fifteen-year-olds, they work with teachers—with adults." (Interview of March 31, 2006)

There is another essential activity that all principals must be able to execute, and that is to learn how to interpret test data from students and to use those data to design and custom-fit an instructional program to each student. Teachers must be able to do that as well, but they need to learn it from their principal. In addition, a principal must be able to interpret the data from all of the students in her school and then decide what staffing her school should have and what professional development activities her teachers most need. Most teachers won't learn that on the job, so aspiring principals have to learn it outside of the classroom, which they can do through a combination of apprenticeship as an assistant principal and formal training programs provided by the district.

Principals also must develop the leadership skills to create a team of teachers and other staff who can work in an integrated effort to make a successful school. Many people already have those skills, while others can learn them. The district must learn to recognize both, so that they can become principals.

In a decentralized district whose principals are empowered, the principals must also be willing to make decisions every day and to accept the consequences of those decisions, be they good or bad. A successful principal, like any other manager, must be able to shrug off the defeats and move on to new challenges with optimism. Not everyone has that ability, and the district must have a selection process that can recognize those people. That selection process must also be able to pick out the teachers who have the inner strength to buck the system when necessary, to stand up to an outdated district rule or an autocratic supervisor and advocate for their teachers and their students.

Few school districts have adequate methods for recruiting, selecting, training, and coaching their principals. The decentralizing districts that we studied all realized that having such a system is an essential requirement. In a decentralized district, the principals are the system. Decentralized districts do not rely on large rule books and extensive central office orders to make things happen in the schools, because those methods are far too rigid and bureaucratic to meet the needs of a diverse student population. Instead, these districts rely on their principals to make wise decisions about how to operate a school so that it is custom-fitted to the needs of the students it is trying to serve.

Empowered schools must have effective principals. There is no substitute. Weak principals must be coached, retrained, or replaced. Good teachers should not be abandoned to weak principals—not in any school, and definitely not in a decentralized school district. Good principalship cannot be inspected in, just as good quality in automobiles cannot be inspected in. Evaluation, monitoring, and accountability are essential, but they serve primarily to identify weak principals and to reward the effective ones. Accountability systems cannot create good principals. Only thoughtful recruitment, selection, training, and coaching can do that.

THE FOURTH PILLAR: A SYSTEM OF ACCOUNTABILITY

When educators hear the term "accountability," they often fear that it means teacher-bashing, but not here. The focus of this book is on empowered schools, and the point person in each of those schools is the principal. When principals are empowered, they must at the same time be embedded in a web of accountability. That web must be simultaneously loose enough to give each principal lots of elbow room but tight enough to keep them focused on student performance, budget performance, and communication with teachers, parents, and the community.

The basic system of accountability for empowered schools was developed beginning in the 1970s by Edmonton superintendent Mike Strembitsky, and it's as good today as it was then. It has three basic elements. First is accountability for student performance. Ever since the signing of No Child Left Behind into law in 2002, every public school in America has been required to have a target for its Adequate Yearly Progress, or AYP. If a school fails to make its AYP target for several years in a row, it suffers a series of increasingly severe consequences, which can culminate in the closing of the school or a conversion of a district school into a charter school. The districts in our study have gone far beyond that basic federal requirement to create much more demanding and specific performance improvement goals of several kinds. We'll review those in detail later on.

The second aspect of principal accountability is responsibility to stay within the approved school budget. As we have already seen in the case of St. Paul, empowered principals have to pay back deficits from the next year's budget. If principals are to be held accountable for financial performance, they must be told far enough in advance what their budget for next year will be, so that they can make their spending plans accordingly. During the school year, they must have access to a frequent, preferably real-time computerized financial system that lets them see every day whether their spending is above, below, or right on their budgetary target. For example, when a school is 22 percent of the way through the school year, the principal needs to know whether she has spent more or less than 22 percent of her budget. That way, principals can make midcourse spending corrections and stay on budget. No principal wants to underspend her budget, because that means she has cut or delayed valuable educational programs that would help to boost student performance. No principal wants to be over budget, either, because that will get her in trouble with headquarters and because she will have to cut valuable programs from the following school year, again undermining student performance.

For its part, the district central office must update each school's budget in the fall, after classes have begun and every school knows how many students it actually has. The budget is created several months before school begins, and usually a school will actually have more or fewer students than planned. Once the true number of students is known, each school's budget can be adjusted up or down. This small bit of uncertainty about the budget means that principals will have to maintain a bit of flexibility in their spending plans so that they can easily accommodate this budget "true-up."

The third aspect of accountability has to do with the perceptions of students, teachers, and parents. Do these key stakeholders feel that the school is safe? Do they feel that the school is setting high expectations for its students? Do parents feel welcome to visit the school, and do they feel that their ideas are heard? Above all, how do teachers and parents feel about the leadership that the principal is providing to the school—do teachers trust the principal, and do parents feel that the principal cares about their views of the school? Also important is the question of how principals feel about the quality of service that they receive from the central office staffs, whether in purchasing, finance, personnel, or building maintenance. All of these accountabilities can be brought to the surface through simple annual questionnaires, with the results made public. If you feel that your school district is one where no one is accountable for anything, you will find lots to digest in the discussions of accountability to follow. Accountability questionnaires are beginning to appear in several decentralized school districts, following the practice that was first established in Edmonton.

THE FIFTH PILLAR: WEIGHTED STUDENT FORMULA BUDGETING

Once a school district has decided that it will send money rather than positions to each school, it has to decide how much money to send. It would make no sense to send the same amount of money to each school regardless of enrollment. Nor would it make sense to send every school the same amount of money per student, whether the student body is 2 percent special education students or 25 percent special education students. In fact, there is no logical way to allocate money to schools. Instead, the solution that has evolved is to allocate the money to the students, let the students choose their schools, and then have the money follow the students to the schools. This innovation is known as Weighted Student Formula budgeting, or WSF.

Weighted Student Formula budgeting determines how much money will be allocated to each student, based on preexisting state funding definitions and known student characteristics. For example, all states allocate additional funds for students who have been classified as eligible for special education. Each such student has, by state law, an Individualized Education Plan (IEP), which may specify, for example, that one student must receive an hour of occupational therapy each day, while another student requires the assistance of a speech pathologist. Students who are blind or deaf require more extensive assistance. The cost of each of these additional special education services can be calculated, and then each student can be assigned an overall weight, ranging from 1.0 for a student who requires no special services up to 9.2 (in Seattle's system as of 2001). The student's weight is then multiplied by the basic allocation ($2,616 in Seattle for 2001) to arrive at the total funds assigned to each student. In this example, a student who has no characteristics that warrant additional funding would take $2,616 with her to the school of her choice, while the student with a maximum weight of 9.2 would take $24,067 to her school. The student chooses the public school she prefers, and the money follows her to the school. The school combines the money from all of its students to calculate its total budget for the year (each school also receives a flat foundational grant to cover the necessary costs of a principal, one office assistant, and other basics).

Several studies of WSF budgeting have demonstrated that this system greatly reduces the inequities in most school districts.[3] In most districts, the practice of allocating teaching and other positions to schools from central office funds has proven to be susceptible to pressure from well-connected schools, with the result that the greatest funding goes to the schools with the greatest clout, rather than to the schools with the children who need the services for which the states originally provided the funds. In addition, teachers unions in almost all districts have won the right for tenured teachers to change schools when an opening occurs, based not on their qualifications but on their seniority. In many though not all cases, this right has resulted in the most experienced teachers migrating to the schools serving the highest-income populations. These schools, whose students have the fewest special needs, end up with the most experienced teachers and the highest teacher payroll, sometimes twice as much per student as in poor neighborhoods. In this manner, the policy of the state, which is to provide extra funds for the students who need it most, is turned on its head. Under Weighted Student Formula budgeting, a school district sends money rather than positions to schools. It can then choose to bill each school for its actual teacher salaries, creating an NBA-like salary cap. The result will be that principals of schools in wealthy neighborhoods will not be able to afford to take only experienced teachers, while schools in poorer neighborhoods should for the first time be able to have some of those experienced teachers.

Many educators feel that adding new teachers to a mature faculty tends to improve the enthusiasm and creativity of the entire school, with the result that the salary cap system actually benefits the schools in wealthy neighborhoods. There is widespread agreement that in poor neighborhoods, schools that have few experienced teachers will benefit from the salary cap system, as they end up with more money than before and can either add more new teachers (who receive the lowest salaries) than they had before and thus reduce TSL, or they can choose to add veteran teachers, who can serve as mentors to those with less experience. So far, it appears that schools in low-income neighborhoods will choose to do some of each.

WSF budgeting serves a second, equally important function. The traditional system of allocating positions to schools based on enrollment is so complex as to be completely impenetrable to most principals, teachers, and parents. WSF budgeting, by comparison, is easy for everyone to understand. The district can publish an annual budget for each school that displays the average student weight and the total budget. Parents and teachers understand how much money is available to the school, and they typically then take an interest in how that money is spent for the benefit of students. As is usual in our democratic system of government, full disclosure is often all that is needed for effective oversight by parents and teachers to take place.

Weighted Student Formula budgeting, in combination with the other four Pillars of School Empowerment, results in a better-informed school community that cares about a school and a school that is empowered to take the actions necessary for improvement. Add in the influence of families who have a choice among public schools and strong accountability measures in the hands of school district managers, and the result is that schools will have both the incentive and the ability to use their control over budgets, staffing, curriculum, and schedule to reduce Total Student Load and, finally, improve student performance.

How the Four Freedoms Can Be Used to
Drive Down Total Student Load

We've argued that Total Student Load is the single most important fact to know about a middle or high school because it, more than any other factor that a district can influence, will raise student academic performance. A few scholars have emphasized TSL, including Ted Sizer,[4] Debbie Meier,[5] and Arthur Powell.[6] TSL has been of central importance to the Coalition of Essential Schools (CES), a national association founded by Ted Sizer. CES holds that no teacher should have a Total Student Load greater than 80 students. Beyond that number, students cease to be individual personalities who are known by their teacher, and they become a faceless crowd instead. But by and large, TSL is still a secret, and almost no one knows what it is or why it is important. Do your own test. Ask a teacher, a principal, or any school official that you know what the average TSL is for their school or district. I'll bet that you will receive a puzzled look in reply.

We've noted earlier that TSL is the number of papers that a teacher has to grade and the number of students that a teacher has to get to know each term, but let's consider an example. In New York City's famous Bronx High School of Science, an elite school that takes only the top test takers, each teacher in the English Department has the union contract maximum of 170 students. That means that teachers who assign a major paper must read, grade, and write constructive comments on 170 papers. That isn't possible for long papers, and the result is that the brilliant students at Bronx Science (and at many other U.S. high schools) are typically assigned to write papers of no more than five pages! They may graduate as accomplished students of math, but many will flounder in their college courses that require the writing of long, analytical papers. At the recommended level of eighty students or fewer, though, every teacher can get to know every student, can assign complex work and respond effectively to it, and students can prosper in their studies.

Our research reveals that TSL can be reduced by empowering principals to make their own decisions about how to spend the school's budget, but this reduction cannot be achieved through top-down central office mandates. The reason, as we shall soon see, is that a top-down, one-size-fits-all approach to reducing TSL is too expensive, but every principal who has appropriate discretion over budgets can work with her teachers and together find methods unique to their school that will drive down TSL while staying within the budget.

These unique solutions can be categorized into two types. One type recognizes that some schools don't need certain administrative staff positions, and other schools can do without other positions. Allowing principals to make these staffing decisions and to use the money saved for more classroom teachers is part of the solution to reducing TSL. Why can't the central office staff simply dictate that schools shall all now have fewer administrative staff and more classroom teachers? The reason is that any standardized rule must meet the needs of every school. Thus, because some schools will need at least one security guard for every 250 students, all schools will have to have security guards allocated to them at that ratio. In fact, though, the needs of each school are unique, and thus the only way to drive down staff ratios is to leave the staffing decisions to the principal and to require that the principal consult with teachers and others.

The second type of individual solution involves creative use of the freedom over curriculum and schedule. We've already described how we found that several principals had combined classes such as English and social studies into a humanities course or had combined math and science into a Math-Science Integrated (MSI) course. Other principals had invented new ways to schedule classes that were unique, in order to guarantee that every student can have a one-on-one "office hour" visit with every teacher if they so desire.

TSL has a slightly different look in elementary schools, where typically one teacher has a class of twenty to thirty-five students for the full school day. We found that when elementary principals enjoy budget autonomy, they often come up with very creative curriculum, scheduling, and staffing arrangements that drive down TSL for English and math, the two most crucial subjects in most urban elementary schools. Schools that have predominantly children from middle-class and professional families can use the same approach but focus it on strengthening coursework for high-achieving students. For example, Phalen Lake Elementary School in St. Paul and John Hay in Seattle arrived at similar, creative solutions. In each case, these schools traditionally had taught the English language arts (reading and writing) in grades K–3 at about 8:00 a.m. every day, right when school begins, when the students are fresh and at their maximum attentiveness. That's typical all across the United States. However, in these two schools the teachers and the principals working together hit upon the idea of staggering the times when they teach ELA and using their budget flexibility to add one full-time reading specialist. They were then able to ask the paraprofessionals (classroom aides), student teaching interns, and volunteers to descend in numbers upon each K–3 classroom during ELA time. They also sent one or two classes to the computer lab when the others were having ELA, thus freeing those teachers to help out on ELA instruction while the computer lab teachers had their students. The result was that they are now teaching the crucial reading and writing skills in groups of three to seven students rather than in entire classes of twenty-five to twenty-eight, and in this new arrangement, each student receives one-on-one instruction within their small group in ELA and math every day. In some schools, both teachers and parents worry that the high-achieving students tend to receive little attention, because teachers focus on those who are farthest behind. With a flexible approach, both the students who are below grade level and those who are above grade level in their reading can receive the attention they need. In order to make these changes, the principals required freedom over their budgets, curriculum, staffing, and schedules, and through district-wide decentralization they had that freedom.

We analyzed data on TSL at each of the eight decentralizing districts. We found that some of the districts have emphasized the reduction of TSL, while others have not. New York City, as we've mentioned, has done this more consistently than the other districts. Boston, like New York, has some empowered schools and some traditional schools. There, TSL for traditional high schools is eighty-five and for empowered schools, or Pilot Schools, TSL is seventy-six, also a substantial gain. Overall, the Boston school district has done a superior job of reducing TSL for all schools, with the result that the difference there between traditional and empowered schools is smaller than in some other decentralizing districts.

We can also compare the Total Student Load of 87.7 in New York City high schools to other districts in which all of the schools have been empowered. The other districts have high school TSLs that range from 123.0 (Oakland) to 160.0 (Houston). We performed similar analyses for elementary and middle schools, and the results are presented in the table that follows.

We were not able to calculate TSL for Chicago's elementary or middle schools, because they are combined in K–8 schools. I would also offer some cautionary notes about interpreting these

Total Student Load in Empowered Schools

	Elementary Schools	Middle Schools	High Schools
Boston	41.8	81.0	76.0
Chicago	——	——	141.9
Houston	33.6	162.0	160.0
New York City	21.5	53.5	87.7
Oakland	23.6	102.7	123.0
San Francisco	25.8	125.9	142.5
Seattle	33.0	111.1	125.7
St. Paul	26.0	150.0	129.0

results, because data always have certain quirks that are not obvious. For example, the TSL for Boston elementary Pilot Schools appears high compared to the other cities. That is because some of the Boston Pilot elementary schools are K–7 or K–8 rather than the traditional K–5 or K–6. Grades 7 and 8 typically have TSLs of 75 to 85 in Boston, which artificially inflates the elementary TSL in our table. The elementary classrooms that we visited in Boston Pilot Schools actually have TSLs of 20 to 23. Keep in mind also that in New York City, at the time we gathered these data (2004–5) only forty-two district schools had received their empowerment, and those are the schools that were included in the study. By September of 2007, New York City chancellor Joel Klein had extended this decentralized approach to all 1,467 schools and all of its approximately 1.1 million students.

It would be valuable to be able to compare these TSLs to national data on all public schools, but since TSL is still largely a secret, no such data exist. In addition, we found that none of the eight districts could provide us with reliable measures of TSL. Instead, we compiled our own data by visiting schools in each district and gathering our own figures. However, we do know that these figures for TSL are low compared to many other cities that have traditional, centralized districts. We've described Los Angeles, where the maximum middle or high school TSL permitted in the teachers union contract is 225 (5 classes of 45 students), and many teachers are at or above that figure. We also mentioned Clark County, Nevada, where TSL at some high schools reaches 260. Imagine the resulting penalty on those students, compared to those who are fortunate enough to be in Boston or New York City empowered high schools with a TSL of 81.0 (in Boston) or 87.7 (in New York City)!

The Seven-Step Logic of Improved Student Performance

There are seven logical steps in decentralization and the improvement of student performance: (1) Large size begets a variety of organizational pathologies, all of which harm performance. In school districts, that means that large district size creates bureaucratic barriers that harm the performance of students. (2) The antidote is always decentralization of key decisions to the operating subunits, such as the schools within a district. (3) The key change is to empower principals by giving them control over how they spend their school budgets and placing principals within a web of accountability. (4) Principals can use that freedom, given proper training and supervision, to make revisions in their staffing, curriculum, and schedule that will have the result of reducing Total Student Load. (5) Reducing TSL enables a bond of trust to develop between teachers and students. (6) Because education works best when it takes place one-on-one, intimately, student performance will rise as TSL drops, as long as the district focuses its principals on student performance.

(7) Much of what we believe is important about curriculum design, scheduling, and staffing should be revised in order to promote reductions in TSL.

The Best Instruction Is One-on-One

It's true that instruction always comes down to the interaction between a teacher and a student. That fundamental truth leads many of us to reach the conclusion that the only things that matter in education are the ability of the teacher and of the student. As we've seen here, though, that image of student and teacher is much less than the whole story. It makes a big difference if that teacher has to get to know 150 students each semester or each year rather than half that number. It matters if elementary school students have the chance to sit at a table with two other students and one experienced reading teacher for ninety minutes each day, and it matters if high school students can have a one-on-one office visit whenever they need help or encouragement from a teacher. In a sense, what we've seen is that teaching and learning work best when it's one-on-one. It doesn't have to be that intimate all of the time, but that kind of personal coaching can be crucial to every student at some point.

Principals emerge in our story as key figures in arranging the possibility for this personalized instruction. Principals in empowered schools have the authority to use their considerable tools of budget, staffing, curriculum, and schedule control to create the opportunities for personalized instruction. Superintendent and school district central offices also play a major role, because principals can enjoy real autonomy only if the central office equips them with the information, the budgetary systems, and the organizational cooperation that make school empowerment a reality. Superintendents, in addition to providing the absolutely essential leadership to bring about district decentralization, must put into place the accountability mechanisms that will provide support and, when necessary, discipline to principals. Principals and superintendents hold the power with which a school district and all of its schools can become great. They can accomplish this through their management approach. Paradoxical as it may seem, this research reveals that when it comes to K–12 education, management matters more than anything else that the school district can control.

At my alma mater, Williams College, we had a saying that the best educational system is Mark Hopkins (the legendary former president of Williams College) on one end of a log and a student on the other. By implication, it's equally true that the worst educational system is Mark Hopkins on one end of a log and 150 students on the other end.

Now that we have our overview, our roadmap, let's pack a bag and set off to learn more about empowered schools. We've identified the essential elements of a great school with examples from several schools. Now, let's see what one school looks like when it has all of these elements.

3

AN EMPOWERED SCHOOL: VANGUARD HIGH SCHOOL

An Empowered School in New York City

It's April in New York City, and Manhattan's First Avenue is clogged with traffic under a light rain, just enough to cause pedestrians to open their umbrellas. There are traffic jams of cars and crowds of people everywhere, and not just because of the rain—New York City is just so massive. The New York City Department of Education is massive, too. It's the largest district in the United States, with more than 1.1 million students. That's about 450,000 students more than the Los Angeles Unified School District, the nation's second biggest.

Yesterday a nor'easter dropped nearly seven inches of rain on the city, a record. People hardly noticed, though, because the city has the infrastructure to deal with large anything, or so it seems. Today, I'm going to visit one of the 1,467 schools of New York

City. I want to find out if the city can deal with big education as well as it deals with big crowds and big rainfall. The last time I visited the schools here, principals controlled only 6.1 percent of their budgets, and one school looked pretty much like another, with a few exceptions. Several principals complained to me that the school district was so top-down and centralized that they felt suffocated by it. However, there were a few isolated schools that managed to be very independent even during those times, and one of those was Vanguard High School, founded in 1993.

New York City mayor Michael Bloomberg and his chancellor of schools Joel Klein began an ambitious reform in 2004 that is converting all of New York City's schools into empowered schools. As a result, one day soon all of the city's schools may be run like Vanguard. It's worth a visit to find out what an empowered school in New York City is like. Not only an empowered school, but one that has sixteen years of experience as an empowered school—a history that is longer than that of even the Boston Pilot Schools, some of which date to the 1990s. Will the central office have eroded Vanguard's initial freedom by now? Will the principal and the teachers have lost some of their initial enthusiasm? After sixteen years, will Vanguard now be like any old school anywhere?

There are other questions that have to do with the immense size of the New York City Department of Education. Is school empowerment an idea that will only work in smaller districts and middle-sized districts? Empowerment might work in Boston, with about 63,000 students, and it might be fine in St. Paul with about 45,000, San Francisco with its approximately 60,000, and Seattle with nearly 50,000, but when it comes to size, New York City is in a class by itself. If New York City can enable schools to have real autonomy, every school district can do it, too.

Vanguard High School and the
Julia Richman Education Complex

Vanguard is on the Upper East Side of Manhattan. The neighborhood is nice yet has a local feeling: on East Sixty-seventh Street there's a Psychic Boutique next to Dominick's Deli and Catering, the Trattoria Cantina Toscana, some apartment buildings, and Vanguard High School, H.S. 449. I'm looking forward to visiting Vanguard because I've heard so much about it. Vanguard is one of the most celebrated high schools in America. It draws a steady stream of visitors who are eager to see how it succeeds with a primarily low-income, minority, inner-city student body. New York City's schools are schools of choice, and Vanguard is open to any student from New York City's five boroughs. Thirty-six percent of Vanguard's students are black, 53 percent are Hispanic, 8 percent are white, and 2 percent are Asian. Sixty-seven percent qualify as low income, and 5 percent are English Language Learners.

Vanguard is one of six schools that share a large old building, and collectively these schools are known as the Julia Richman Education Complex, taking their name from the former high school whose building they occupy. There are four high schools, an elementary school, and a school for autistic children. The founding project manager was Debbie Meier, a strong proponent of Ted Sizer's Coalition of Essential Schools (CES). Vanguard was designed to embody the principles of CES, principles that are similar to our Five Pillars and Four Freedoms, although the CES approach addresses the design of single schools rather than entire school districts, as I am describing in this book.

Debbie Meier was part of a group of young, independent-minded educators who included Seymour Fliegel, who later founded the Center for Educational Innovation; Beth Lief, the founder of New Visions for Public Schools; and Eric Nadelstern, now with the New York City Department of Education. As a group, they wanted to form the Learning Zone, in which all of the schools would have autonomy. Although only Debbie Meier managed to bring her dream into fruition at that time, each of these people was to play an important role in the decentralization of New York City's schools.

For many years, the schools of the Julia Richman Education Complex had to fight to maintain their autonomy against the constant pressures of a monolithic school district that didn't understand or like the idea. They became accustomed to constant criticism and fault finding. Indeed, the Julia Richman leadership council had refused my first request to visit any of their schools in 2005 unless I agreed to permit them to edit whatever I wrote or to publish their rebuttal alongside my comments. That was a request to which I could not agree. This sort of caution toward outsiders was, I suppose, a result of their history of being cast as renegades. Now, however, the school district values and celebrates autonomous schools, including these. Now, Julia Richman and Vanguard do not have to keep their dukes up all of the time.

Today, the principal, Louis Delgado, is stuck at home, dealing with a basement that flooded during yesterday's rains, and he'll be late coming to work. Assistant Principal Ann Purdy has a small office that right now is packed with visitors, including two from Watsonville, California ("the Artichoke Capital of the United States"), a researcher from UCLA, and four more visitors who've just arrived from Oakland, California, and from Stanford University. Julia Richman has become the Yellowstone National Park of schools, with edu-tourists coming through constantly. Ann Purdy sends her guests off to visit classrooms and sets off down the hallway with me in tow.

Miguel (not his real name) is in the twelfth grade at Vanguard. Today, Miguel is in his usual oversized pants, a short-sleeved black shirt over a long-sleeved shirt, and black athletic shoes. Around his neck is a big medallion on a long silver chain, and he's wearing an oversized, chunky watch on one wrist. In other words, he looks like a typical big-city high school student, except that Miguel's attire makes it clear that Vanguard is not a "uniform school" (uniforms are becoming more common among urban schools). Miguel's attire is an apt metaphor for the culture at Vanguard, which does not believe in success through regimentation, but through personal attention.

Miguel is standing at the whiteboard in front of his teacher and six fellow students solving a calculus equation. He's explaining how he is solving the equation as he works his way through it. Miguel is classified as a special education student, which means that he has been tested and found to have one or more learning disabilities. About 22 percent of the 395 students at Vanguard are special ed students. In many cities, students who are designated as special ed are warehoused and forgotten in some dark corner of the school district. It might be that their disability has to do with a speech pathology or a mild diagnosis on the autism spectrum, but most schools don't have or won't take the time to understand each individual student. If special education students are treated as a class rather than as individuals, students like Miguel will be ignored and forgotten. Some say that New York City used to be that way. In any case, it's unusual both that Miguel is studying calculus and that his teacher is not a special ed teacher; instead, she's one of New York City's master teachers, who will earn a bonus of $50,000 over five years for coaching other, mostly young, math teachers. She's one of the school district's best, and she obviously believes that every student can learn calculus, including Miguel.

How Total Student Load Makes a Difference

In the hallway outside of Miguel's classroom are bulletin boards that display student work. One has project reports on the Harlem Renaissance. Another is covered with reports on economics, and a third displays science reports. One of these is a twelve-page paper coauthored by two students about the human papillomavirus, which can cause cervical cancer. There is a fourteen-page report on sliding friction, with exhibits. In all, thirteen science reports are on display, all of them longer than ten pages. This is an unusual display, because in most urban high schools, students write either "short papers" of one to three pages or "long papers" of three to five pages. Few New York City teachers assign ten-page papers these days, because until now, high school teachers in most city high schools had to read and write comments on 170 papers (teachers have five classes of up to thirty-four students) several times a semester.

As we observed earlier, we can think of Total Student Load as the number of papers that a teacher must grade. Think of reading a fourteen-page paper on the human papillomavirus or the Harlem Renaissance and writing thoughtful comments, noting logical development, proper citation of sources, use of analogy, metaphor, and simile, paragraph and sentence structure, homonyms and antonyms, punctuation, grammar, and spelling. Perhaps forty minutes per paper if you're a fast reader and writer. If you have 170 papers, that's 112 hours of work outside of the classroom. If you have 225 papers, it's 148 hours of work. Ergo, the "long paper" in high school is now three to five pages. But not at Vanguard.

How an Innovative Curriculum and Schedule Reduce Total Student Load

Ann leads the way into the fourth floor, which, along with part of the third floor, is Vanguard's territory. The floors shine, and there's not a speck of litter to be seen anywhere. The building, though, is old, with what looks like a dozen coats of paint on the walls. A ninth-grade robotics class is in session. The course is actually a Math-Science Integrated (MSI) course, with robotics to keep it interesting for the students. We've seen this system of integrated courses before, at the Lilla G. Frederick Pilot Middle School in Boston. Here, that system is being implemented at the high school level. The students are seated at tables of two or three, with plastic bins full of Lego parts, including gears, wheels, and an electric motor. Their assignment is to program a set of instructions into the robot so that when they turn it on it will run whatever path they have programmed into it. There are twenty students, slightly more than usual at Vanguard, where each math or science teacher has three "blocks," or double-length classes of combined math and science, of eighteen students each. Classes meet on Monday, Tuesday, Thursday, and Friday for math-science. Wednesday is for tutoring, planning time for teachers, and for teachers to meet to discuss the progress of individual students. So the official academic Total Student Load for a math or science teacher is 54 students (three classes of eighteen students). In addition, every teacher has an advisory of about twelve students that meets for forty minutes every day, so we could also calculate an overall TSL for math and science teachers of 66, though for the purposes of our analysis, the TSL for math and science teachers is 54.

English and social studies teachers have a slightly different schedule. They teach two double-length blocks of humanities, which combines English and social studies, every day, five days a week, plus an elective that has about twelve students and meets twice each week in an eighty-five-minute block. Thus the English and social studies teachers each have an academic TSL of 48 (two classes of eighteen students, plus one elective of twelve students). With advisory, the overall TSL for English and social studies is 60, which is lower than the 66 that math and science teachers have, but math-science meets four days a week, while humanities meets every day. The teachers seem to feel that the workloads are about equal.

How Creative Staffing and Curriculum Reduce Total Student Load

Let's review our Total Student Load calculations. If Vanguard maintained its class size of eighteen but did not have combined MSI and humanities courses, each teacher would have ninety students in academic courses (five times eighteen equals ninety students), plus an advisory of twelve students, for a total TSL of 102. That would be a substantial improvement over the 140 that is typical in most other New York City high schools and the 170 in some New York City high schools. But how can Vanguard afford such small classes? The answer is that Vanguard allocates its scarce staff budget almost entirely to teachers. The teachers have to be willing to do double duty, serving as IT administrators, art or gym teachers, and in other roles to make this system work, but the important thing is that in New York City's empowered schools system, they have the freedom to do so.

Vanguard has a total of thirty-seven employees, of whom thirty are fully credentialed teachers, four are classroom aides, two are administrators—the principal (who also teaches one class) and assistant principal—and one is the office secretary.

There are also eight student teachers assigned to the school at no cost. Vanguard has no other non-teaching personnel. It has no deans, counselors, literacy specialists, math specialists, special education specialists (the regular teachers fill this role), no specialists in art, music, drama, or physical education (as mentioned, regular teachers double in these roles), no separate professional development coaches (one of the math teachers doubles in this role), and no computer staff or IT administrators (three of the teachers double in this role). The Julia Richman Education Complex schools share a library and librarian, a cafeteria and gym, a nurse, security staff, and custodians.

Control over staffing decisions has enabled Vanguard to reduce its Total Student Load to 48 for humanities teachers and 54 for MSI teachers. Vanguard has reduced its TSL by having fewer administrative staff and more classroom teachers, and then it has further reduced TSL by creating block-scheduled integrated courses. Teachers at the most elite private schools typically have TSLs in the range of 60 to 65, so this is a major achievement for Vanguard. My first study included several of these top private schools, and I found that in all of them, teachers serve multiple roles, as they do at Vanguard. In addition, at most private schools the headmaster teaches a course. At elite Harvard-Westlake in Los Angeles, the college counselors and even the chief financial officer all teach. The lesson is that no school has enough money to afford the luxury of having lots of non-teaching administrative staff. Teaching is the core mission, and the rule in most successful schools is that everyone teaches.

In a nutshell, TSL is the difference between private school and public school. The miracle of decentralization is that Vanguard's teachers have the same TSLs as teachers at the most elite private schools in America. However, Vanguard must have control over its staffing to achieve this. If one of the math teachers who doubles as gym teacher should retire, Vanguard needs a re-placement math-credentialed teacher who also wants to and is qualified to teach gym and who also wants to lead an intimate group of students in advisory and who truly believes that every student, including a non-native-English-speaking special educa-tion student, can learn calculus.

There are, of course, no free lunches, and Vanguard has made some tradeoffs. For one thing, Vanguard offers fewer elective courses than many other schools. If each teacher had classes of thirty-four rather than eighteen, there would be a need for only about half as many classes in the basic subjects, and the school could offer more electives. To the teachers at Vanguard, that is not an acceptable strategy because they believe in the philosophy of the Coalition of Essential Schools, that in curriculum design, "less is more." Exposing a student to more different courses, they argue, is not a benefit in developing the skills of thinking, writ-ing, speaking, and developing mathematical and scientific hab-its. They prefer to reduce the number of different courses to the smallest number and to introduce breadth through new topics in each course. Believers in this approach think that the ideal cur-riculum would include only one course that integrates a wealth of topics. If only teachers who have that much breadth were available, someone would surely try it. Others might disagree, and surely the Vanguard approach to curriculum will not appeal equally to all families. However, New York City allows families to choose any public school they want, so it is not necessary for each school to appeal to all families.

A second tradeoff is that each English teacher is teaching both English and social studies, and so is each social studies teacher. The school requires that every humanities teacher have the dem-onstrated skill to do this, but some of the teachers may not have taken the formal step of acquiring a teaching credential from the state of New York in both subjects, and the federal No Child Left Behind law requires that teachers possess a credential in every subject that they teach. The same tradeoff applies to the math teachers and to the science teachers. Some families would prefer that their student learn math from a math specialist and science from a science specialist, and that is not what Vanguard offers.

However, Vanguard does not stint on giving students extra help in their basic academic subjects. Vanguard offers tutoring in humanities for the students who need it, whether after school, during office hours, or on Saturday. There is also a Math Center, open every day from 3:15 (after classes have ended) until 4:30, staffed with two teachers and some college student interns. One of the math teachers keeps track of all of the students who need help. If a student is not studying or is behind on his homework, she sends his faculty advisor a note explaining what assignments and topics the student is behind on. "So their advisors know immediately and will connect," says one teacher. (Interview of April 16, 2007)

A third tradeoff is that Vanguard, with about four hundred students, is a small school. Vanguard cannot possibly match the selection of courses, including the array of Advanced Placement courses, that are available at a school like San Francisco's Lowell High School or in most large schools. Vanguard also does not have a football team, a track or swimming team, or a school band, and some students might miss those activities. But Vanguard does not have to please everyone; it has to attract and please only enough families to meet its budget, and it does that easily.

The Advisory Is the Hub Around Which Everything Else Revolves

Every student at Vanguard is assigned to an advisory, which meets every day before lunch for forty minutes. Advisories consist of twelve to seventeen students with one teacher. Each advisory is a blended group of ninth, tenth, eleventh, and twelfth graders who stay together with the same advisor for all four years of high school. As a result, the advisor does not have many of her advisees in class but instead has a relationship with each advisee that is more akin to a counseling relationship than a teaching one. With permission from the advisor and from the principal, a student may change from one advisory group to another. Advisories are a place to knit the grade levels into a unified student body, a place to discuss social development, and in some schools, to study a curriculum on subjects as diverse as race relations, college preparation, or drug and alcohol abuse. They are also the place where the school becomes a community.

It's day two of our visit to Vanguard, and Principal Louis Delgado is in his office, his flooded basement at home now under control. Principal Delgado has his office door open as always, because he likes to be able to hear and see what is going on in his school at all times. As I approach, he leaps to his feet to greet me. He is a man of about fifty years of age, impeccably dressed in a white shirt, tie, and suit, his salt-and-pepper beard neatly trimmed. He has presence, he radiates energy and purpose, and one surmises that he is a man who is not to be denied. Louis has another group of edu-tourists in his office, this time from Stanford University. They go off to observe classes. Unlike most visitors to Vanguard, we are not mostly interested in visiting classes to observe instructional technique, although we do visit several. Our main interest is in the management, because we want to see how Vanguard is organized and how it makes its most important decisions.

Delgado describes what he looks for in an effective advisory teacher: "I think the key is to be able to listen . . . and not just an empathetic type of listener . . . There's a certain confidentiality attached to it that the students feel like he or she is an advocate but at the same time will put that boot in my butt if I need it" (all quotes from Louis Delgado are from interviews on April 17, 2007). Not all young teachers are emotionally mature or experienced enough to play this role effectively, and as a result, some advisories have co-teacher advisors. The advisor also has primary responsibility to communicate with parents on behalf of the school. For example, Delgado continues, "If a kid is misbehaving in one class, that teacher will communicate with the advisor. That advisor has the option of sitting down with the student and trying to negotiate bridging that gap . . . If it's not going well, the advisor may decide to expand the circle and include the parents. He may decide to expand the circle even further and include me in the equation. We start talking about consequences. But the advisor acts like the dean or the point person. Sometimes the advisor may call a teacher and say, 'His sister just had an accident, and, you know, he's really, really struggling right now.' So it sheds a different light on the situation so that the teacher may be more sympathetic, or more supportive of the kid's reaction."

The system of advisories looks finely tuned today, but at the outset, it was a far different story. Principal Delgado credits Ted Sizer's book *Horace's Compromise*[1] with providing him a conceptual model: "It really gave me a language and at least a framework from which to work. Putting it into practice was a whole different ball game. And it was very, very difficult. And by no stretch of the imagination did we figure this out in the first year. It took me the better part of seven years to get a staff . . . After the seventh year there was some continuity with staff . . . So then we just have one big conversation on how to teach and how to get kids to learn, and what this process is all about—one team. For the last seven years, I've been blessed with pretty much the same team."

Delgado continues, "Well, in the first couple of years, the first year especially, I made a big mistake hiring too many teachers who had never taught before. Maybe ninety percent of our conversations were about classroom management! So for the second year after they all left, I was able to rethink and rehire a new group of teachers. And then I started to think in terms of seasoned teachers with a frame of reference on teaching and learning . . . you know, teachers who can create curriculum, can be creative and also be able to change midstream if they need to make some adjustments. So you need experienced teachers to be able to do that." With a group of seasoned teachers on board, Delgado set out to implement the vision that he had, and that vision depended crucially on the advisory: "The one thing right up front that I made absolutely non-negotiable to the group of teachers was that I wanted to create an advisory system in the school that really connected the school to the parents, the teacher to the kid, and the kid to an adult advisor. I wanted to create an opportunity for the kids to have a relationship with an adult. That was absolutely non-negotiable for me."

What is more important still is the reason that Delgado wanted every student to have a close relationship with a teacher: "I felt that if I could develop getting kids to really establish a relationship with an adult in the school, and everybody was marching to this vision of creating an opportunity for a kid to go to college, that he or she somewhere along the line would relax their shoulders a little bit and leave the street behind . . . and begin to trust a little bit and go on this ride, this four-year, five-year ride that we have for them. In order for an adult teacher in the school to be able to push and pull a kid, you need to have a relationship. Otherwise you get—if they're very defensive—'Who are you? Why do you—why should you care? You're not my mom. You're not my dad.' They'll start questioning. So you need a relationship and based on this advisory, we were able to establish those relationships and really communicate with the families. That's the glue that really holds this school together—that advisory."

Asked whether he felt that his teachers know him, one junior replied, "Unfortunately, yeah. They know us like, really well. It could be a good thing and it can be a bad thing. But most of the time it's a good thing." Another junior added, "Even though I have a hard time, I would rather be in this school and this advisory than in any other school in New York . . . I figure it would be harder for me to just quit and go try somewhere else. It's just like I've been here so long that it's, like, sometimes you get sick with your family and you don't want to be around them, but that's still your family, you always come back to them." Another noted, "Most of my teachers know me pretty well . . . that's part of the reason why I like this school, because the teachers know how hard it is for me, and they understand that I'm set in my ways and I'm kind of complicated. And they know how good I can do, and even though I'm not always doing as good as I can, they always still have faith in me." When asked what happens if he is absent, a senior said, "They call your home, and then the next day, if you missed your homework you still have to—you're still responsible to make it up!" Observed another student, ruefully, "When I left the school, the assistant principal called my mother, like, 'I'm calling to inform you that your child has not come to school.' She's like, 'Nobody informed you that we were leaving for Florida?' And right before that, I had just hung up the phone with the assistant principal! She still called! I'm like, 'Great!' If I was cutting school, I would have still got caught" (all student interviews on April 16, 2007). So we have another discovery: advisories are not simply security blankets for the students. They are a great source of support, but the advisory and the teacher-advisor also prod, push, and keep the pressure on the students to perform. It's a complicated relationship. It's a human relationship.

Teachers appear to favor the advisories, too. Said one, "I did teach in one of the large—I taught in one large school and then I was—I was excessed out into another large school. And when I was excessed from the other large school, I said I had to find a home. I had to find a home 'cause I didn't like teaching. I feel as though it's a factory. The large schools are factories and there's no relationship. And before that I was a counselor, and then I went into teaching. So I went from having relationships with students to not having relationships with students. And I didn't like that. So I went looking and I ended up here. And I've been here ever since, and I don't plan on leaving." This teacher previously had taught the standard five classes of about 30 students each, for a TSL of 150. Now, in addition to her two blocks of humanities, she teaches her advisory and "I teach an all girls' book club (twice each week) and I do the senior activities (twice each week). We do the year book. We do the prom. We do everything!" As for knowing her students, she comments, "If I've taught you, I know you. And I've been here a long time so I know—I realized that I don't know some students when it comes to senior time and then I realize there are some students I never taught and never had them for anything. So, but, as long as I've taught you, I know you, and I know you well." The teacher concludes that "They're my kids . . . I know all their parents." (Interview of April 16, 2007) On the other hand, teaching advisory can be emotionally exhausting, and it takes something out of every teacher. As Principal Delgado puts it, "There's an unbelievable social, emotional investment in the advisory that is critical to getting the intellectual piece in the class." For that reason, Delgado is committed to keeping TSL low: "I said, Look, I'm going to work and I'm going to make sure that I hire as many teachers as possible as long as you have an advisory group and you help connect with students." One result is that classes become even smaller by the spring, when attrition has taken its toll on total enrollment in the school. At the beginning of each school year, each humanities and MSI class has about twenty-five students, and the elective class has about twenty-five as well, for a typical TSL of 75. Says Delgado, "My goal with the teachers is to make sure that they are not responsible, even at our peak time, for eighty students." By spring, classes are down to eighteen or twenty, which is smaller than ideal but a result of the focus on never having TSL at 80 or above. It should be noted as well that Vanguard needs to continue to find ways to reduce that student attrition.

The author Douglas McGregor wrote in *The Human Side of Enterprise*[2] that there are two kinds of managers, Theory X managers, who believe that you cannot trust others to make good decisions, so you should rarely grant autonomy to subordinates, and Theory Y managers, who believe that since most people will sincerely try to do the right thing most of the time, every manager should grant autonomy to others. Vanguard's Delgado is definitely Theory Y, so consistently so that his commitment to participative decision making extends to students. "I wanted to create an opportunity for students to have a voice. And I thought advisory was the way of polishing that voice and then creating a curriculum that empowered students, too. Right up front I felt that there was no way I could reach my students if I didn't empower my students. I could not have a 'top-down' if I was expecting 'bottom-up' in the classroom. So my approach was, how do I empower my teachers so that ultimately I could reach the students? It was my vision fourteen years ago to create this epidemic of hope, and I'm still fired up about it!" Delgado continues, "I was telling the teachers what to do, what to teach. So I wanted to create opportunities for them to deal with concepts, bring in the standards, and then create a curriculum that they felt most comfortable with—different approaches and how to assess it. So once they were empowered to do that, I felt like, you know, we can then empower students so that they have a voice in the discussion."

One senses that a man with Delgado's intensity and impatience does not easily come to accept a drawn-out planning process that engages teachers and students. In another school with a traditional organization, Delgado might well be a driving, top-down principal, rather than the kind of participative leader that he is today. That is the purpose of designing organizational structures in a thoughtful manner. Properly designed, an organization helps and prods ordinary people who have ordinary strengths and weaknesses to behave in extraordinary ways. At Vanguard, the advisory so completely engages and empowers teachers, students, and parents that its principal, no matter his natural inclinations, has become a consultative leader and is unlikely to be authoritarian or dictatorial.

Curriculum Design at Vanguard Involves Everyone

At Vanguard, all of the ninth grade humanities teachers work together to design a curriculum for the year. The same process takes place within the Math-Science Integrated faculty. That's not how it works in most districts, where curriculum specialists in the central office study curricular change and then send new curriculum guidelines to all of the teachers in all of the schools, who are supposed to use a single curriculum no matter how different the needs of their students might be. At Vanguard, in June, the staff reflects on what worked well for them during the past school year and what did not. They evaluate advisory, attendance, cutting of classes by students, student government, and other issues along with curriculum. Teachers work on the major projects in teams, and each team submits a proposal for the additional planning work that they will do over the summer months.

In late August, before school opens, the entire faculty and administration meet for three or four days. They decide together on which of the proposals they are going to fund out of the school budget in the coming school year. All of the teachers work on their own curriculum plans, and most of the teachers are also assigned to work on one of the additional school-wide issues. Because Principal Delgado has control over his school's budget, he is able to pay teachers for this additional time, without seeking special approval from anyone else.

On my day two tour, block two is now over, and the students are in the hallway, headed to advisory. Principal Delgado is in the hallway, talking to students one-on-one. He knows every one of them by name. He's going to make sure that everyone gets into his or her proper classroom, that no one loiters in the hall. Despite his vigilance, he has cultivated a relaxed attitude in the school. Some students are wearing hats or baseball caps, some are wearing the red shirts that are often thought of as gang regalia, and it seems that every student is wearing an oversized coat, the urban fashion of the day. Pretty soon, Delgado will hit the brass gong in his hand that will let the students know that they have two more minutes to get into their classrooms.

The Web of Accountability That Surrounds Vanguard High School

In New York City, a principal enjoys great freedom to decide how to spend his budget, to staff his school with more teachers or more administrators, to design his own curriculum, and to design the school's schedule. In return, the principal is held accountable by the top management of the district for performance, most importantly student performance. Principals sign an agreement to meet an array of student performance goals within five years. If they do not meet these goals, they will be removed from their principalship. In practice, an obviously weak principal is usually removed well before the end of the five-year period.

In 2004, the first twenty-nine schools in New York City were placed into the Autonomy Zone, which later was re-named the Empowerment Schools. Vanguard was in that first cohort. Louis Delgado understood that if he agreed to have Vanguard become an Empowerment School, he would be protecting the freedom to continue to run his school as he saw fit, but in exchange, he would give up job security and would for the first time be held accountable for student improvement. How did he react to that new arrangement? "I was signing stuff without even reading it because I wanted to be held accountable. I wanted the flexibility with the money. I was starving for that. I really wanted that. Raise the stakes? It doesn't matter to me. It's very difficult, high stakes, but it's worse when your hands are strapped and you don't have the funds to do it."

It's doubtful that Louis Delgado fully appreciated just how thorough an accountability system could be. Chancellor Klein had tapped a law professor from Columbia University, James Liebman, to design a different kind of accountability program, one that would not only set clear targets for each principal and make effective use of the city and state tests, but that would also capture the more subtle but often crucially important qualitative sense of each school and make all of this easily understandable to students, teachers, parents, and the public at large. What Liebman created can provide a model for all school districts. Among the accountability elements are four major evaluations of Vanguard, which are also conducted at every school in New York City: (1) the New York State School Report Card, (2) the New York City Learning Environment Survey Report, (3) the New York City Quality Review Report, and (4) the New York City School Progress Report. A fifth element of accountability is perhaps the most important of all, and that is the freedom that every family has to choose the school that they prefer for their child. Finally, there is the direct supervision of the Chief Schools Officer, Eric Nadelstern, backstopped by the personal vigilance of Joel Klein, the schools chancellor.

1. THE NEW YORK STATE SCHOOL REPORT CARD

The four major reports are available to anyone on the New York City Department of Education website. The website is easily accessed and easy to use. The New York State Board of Regents prepares the New York State School Report Card. This report shows enrollment, student demographics, and a variety of evaluative statistics. For example, of the 104 classes offered at Vanguard in the school year 2005–6, 21 percent of the classes were taught by teachers who are not "highly qualified" in their subjects, according to the federal standards. As previously explained, this relatively high percentage results from the fact that some of the teachers have not yet attained state credentials in both math and science or in both English and social studies, but instead are teaching an integrated curriculum and are only credentialed in their primary discipline. Another section says that the school has a top mark in student progress over the past year in English but failed to make adequate progress the year before. The state also reports that of those who graduated in 2006, 63 percent intended to attend a four-year college, and another 14 percent a two-year college. Vanguard will continue to work with students for five years and reports a graduation rate after five years of nearly 100 percent, of whom 95 percent will attend college. The report also shows the percentage of Vanguard students who have passed each of the five state Regents Examinations that are required to receive either a local diploma with a score of 55 or higher, or a Regents Diploma with a score of 65 or higher. In the spring of 2007, 60 percent of the seniors graduated (above the state standard of 55 percent), and of those who graduated, 73 percent received a Regent's Diploma.

2. THE NEW YORK CITY LEARNING ENVIRONMENT SURVEY REPORT

Although Louis Delgado is a principal who listens to his teachers and parents and consults with them on most decisions, not all principals are like him. To guard against a principal who may achieve short-term results by inappropriately pressuring teachers or who may ignore parents or students, Chancellor Joel Klein has instituted the Learning Environment Survey, which publicly reports the results of three annual questionnaires. Twenty-seven percent of Vanguard's parents completed the survey in 2006, below the citywide average of 40 percent. Parents were asked forty-two questions in four broad categories. On the category of "academic expectations" that the school sets for its students, parents gave Vanguard a score in the 96.2 percentile, which means that it was better than 96.2 percent of all the city's schools. On how well the school communicates with parents, Vanguard was better than all other city schools, at the 100th percentile. On "engagement" of parents in visiting the school and feeling welcome to participate in the school, the score was better than 93.1 percent of all city schools, and on "safety and respect" in welcoming children of all races, keeping children safe, and preventing drug use and bullying, Vanguard ranked above 90 percent of all

schools. Principal Delgado might have been particularly grati-
fied on answers to another question, in which only 2 percent of
parents said that they felt the school needed "more effective
school leadership."

Teachers gave Vanguard similarly high marks. Of particular
note is a series of six questions in which teachers were asked to
evaluate the leadership of the school. Sixty-one percent of the
teachers completed the survey. Vanguard teachers gave Principal
Delgado and Assistant Principal Ann Purdy very high marks.
One hundred percent of teachers said that "school's leaders communicate a clear vision for this school," 100 percent agreed that
"school's leaders let staff know what is expected of them," 100
percent felt that "the principal is an effective manager who
makes the school run smoothly," and 100 percent said that "I
trust the principal at his or her word."

Among Vanguard's students, 75 percent completed the survey, and they were positive about their school, if a bit more critical than either parents or teachers. Students gave the school
a 73.3 percentile ranking on "academic expectations," 91.7 on
"communication," 68.2 on "engagement," and 83.3 on "safety
and respect." On some specific questions, 92 percent of the students said that "I feel welcome in my school," while 84 percent
felt that "the adults at my school look out for me." Another 82
percent agreed that "my teachers give me extra help when I need
it," while a lower percentage, 60 percent, agreed that "my school
offers a wide enough variety of classes and activities to keep me
interested in school." It appears that the strategies employed at
Vanguard are producing very much the kinds of reactions from
teachers, parents, and students that were intended.

3. THE NEW YORK CITY QUALITY REVIEW REPORT

The Quality Review Report is written by a team of evaluators from outside the school, in many cases from Great Britain (where all government-supported schools are now run in a decentralized manner), who visit each school each year. They interview the administrators, a sample of teachers, and a sample of students. They review the curriculum, the extracurricular activities, student test scores, the school's atmosphere, and they observe classes. They capture much of what is important but is missed in the statistical reports and standardized test scores. Before they leave the school after their two- or three-day visit, they meet with the principal and give him or her an unvarnished preview of what they've found.

The ten-page Quality Review Report on Vanguard published in 2008 gave the school an overall rating of "well developed," the second-highest possible, just under "outstanding." The comments by the reviewers sound familiar: "The principal provides inspirational leadership to the school. Students and parents value the extensive support and guidance offered by course teachers and advisors. Relationships within the whole school community are very strong, with high levels of mutual respect evident." On the less positive side of the ledger, the Quality Review Report makes clear that in the past the school had not used its extensive database as effectively as possible to set specific learning goals for each individual student, measure the progress of each student toward those goals during the school year, and develop consistent evaluations of student progress from teacher to teacher. However, the 2008 report lauded the school for having addressed those issues, giving it an "outstanding" for its use of student data, saying that "the school has developed an extremely impressive database that brings together the whole range of test and assessment information that it gathers regarding the performance and progress of its student population."

4. THE NEW YORK CITY SCHOOL PROGRESS REPORT

Finally, the Department of Education assessment staff takes all of these inputs, combined with its interviews with senior management of the district, and issues a two-page report card on each school. For the 2006–7 year, Vanguard received an overall grade of B, which is considered deserving of some rewards, while schools that receive marks of D, F, or three Cs in a row face negative consequences. Vanguard's overall score for the year was 66.4 (out of 100), and it received a target score for next year of 69.4. The school had very high scores on its survey of teachers, parents, and students and above-average results on graduation rates, course completion, and Regents Examinations results, but it was weak in the progress made in math by the bottom third of its students, a group that is separately tracked in the performance evaluations of principals. Perhaps that explains why Miguel, who is a special education student, is now studying calculus under a master teacher. No principal can get an A unless every category of students is making good progress.

In my experience, every principal in New York City is acutely aware of his or her overall letter grade. There are, for example, several principals who have student bodies made up primarily of middle-class children and who became accustomed under the old rating system to always being at the top. Under this new accountability system, though, a school is rated according to how well it does with the kinds of students it has, and many of those principals of middle-class and upper-income schools are now bemoaning their grades of B or lower. One such principal complained that although 89 percent of his students had received passing marks on the Regents Examinations in mathematics and 93 percent had done so in English, he still received a mark of B! The reason: given the high-income population of students in his school, he should have 95 percent passing and two-thirds or so scoring at the higher level necessary for the Regents Diploma, rather than the ordinary diploma. It would be a revelation to parents in many middle-class schools across the country if their districts were to adopt New York City's approach to accountability for principals.

There are two ways to react to Vanguard's overall grade. One is surprise that a school with this much dedication to its students and focus on their education could receive a mark as low as B. The other is appreciation for just how serious the district is that every student can learn and that every school can be great. Many school districts would rate Vanguard an A+, and parents would sing its praises. Indeed, as we've seen, educators come from all over the United States to visit Vanguard. In New York City, though, the bar has now been set very high.

Principal Delgado did respond to his school's overall grade of "B" and to the suggestions that he received through the account-ability system. One year later, his school's overall grade had risen to "A," and enrollment was up from 395 students to 425 for 2007–8.

The Accountability System Has Set the Bar High

Now let's step back and take stock of this accountability system. Vanguard is an inner-city high school that is 89 percent black or Hispanic and 67 percent low-income. Yet 61 percent of the students graduate within four years, and according to the principal, nearly 100 percent eventually graduate. Of those who graduate within four years, 77 percent intend to attend college, and according to the principal, eventually 95 percent do so. According to a report by Jay Greene of the University of Arkansas,[3] the national graduation rates are 78 percent for white students, 56 percent for African-American students, and 54 percent for Latino students. In Chicago, Cleveland, Dallas, Detroit, Los Angeles, and Philadelphia, graduation rates are lower than the national averages. Vanguard's graduation rates are somewhat above the national figures and well above the rates for urban schools in big cities.

The accountability reports produced by New York do not compare Vanguard's graduation rate to that of other cities. What is most striking and encouraging is that New York City is not attempting to sugar-coat its results. Instead, Mayor Michael Bloomberg, who has direct responsibility for the schools, and Chancellor Joel Klein, who runs the schools, seem to have adopted the view of some weekend golfers whom I respect: there's no sense in cheating on your score, because you won't be able to tell when you're improving.

Some experts would disagree with the conclusion that New York City has a tough accountability system. They would argue that New York State doesn't have tough enough tests or that New York City is fudging in the way that it calculates graduation rates. To the contrary, my research demonstrates that New York City, along with Boston, has produced the largest gains in student performance of any of the eight decentralizing cities. When it comes to accountability, New York City has set a new national standard for full disclosure to teachers, parents, and the public on the performance of its schools and, notably, of the principals who run those schools. New York City devotes a great deal of its time, energy, and financial resources to its accountability system. Other school districts don't typically pay as much attention to accountability for principals, perhaps because most school districts don't give principals much authority to make decisions.

Now let's expand the view from one school to one large school system.

4

SCALE-UP IN
NEW YORK CITY

New York City serves nearly 1.1 million students in 1,467 schools; 32.3 percent of the students are black, 39.4 percent are Hispanic, 14.3 percent are white, and 13.6 percent are Asian/ Pacific Islander. Seventy-six percent qualify for a free or reduced-price lunch. As already mentioned, this massive school district is implementing a top-to-bottom decentralization that is empowering schools and their principals. While not yet complete, the change is well under way in all important respects. Few if any school districts have ever undertaken an organizational change of this magnitude. If it can be done in New York City, it can be done anywhere. For that reason, examining how New York City developed its program of change should be particularly useful to other school districts.

How I Was Able to Study New York City's Change from the Inside

It is rare for any scholar to have the opportunity to observe first-hand as a large organization works its way through a complete reorganization. Organizational change is always messy, and no top executive wants his missteps to be publicized. Ordinarily, the process of organizational change must be studied after the fact, and the researcher is forced to rely on the recollections of the participants to reconstruct what happened. Those memories, though, are usually filtered through rose-colored lenses, and they are notoriously unreliable. My study of New York City's schools is different because I was there, on-site, and had the chance to watch it as it happened.

During the year 2000, I was studying the schools of New York City for my first book, described earlier. At the time, the district was a very traditional, top-down, centralized organization. While I was completing that study, Mayor Michael Bloomberg was elected, and he appointed Joel Klein as chancellor of the New York City Department of Education. I was invited to lunch with Michael Bloomberg shortly after he had won the election and told him that I thought that New York City should decentralize its school district. Several months later, Chancellor Joel Klein contacted me. Klein was considering the idea of district-wide decentralization, and he sought input from me, as he did from many others. He also agreed to let me continue my research, if I could pass the standard district approval process for outside researchers. As a result, I had the unique good fortune to have visited the schools and gathered data before the decentralization had begun and then to be able to follow them for the next eight years as the changes took place.

One reason for Klein's willingness to allow me access to the entire change process was that he had read the prepublication manuscript of my 2003 book, which he had obtained through his own sources. He was impressed by my description of the decentralizations in Edmonton, Houston, and Seattle, and he wanted to learn more about what my research had yielded. I agreed to serve as a paid consultant, at a modest fee (a total of approximately twelve thousand dollars plus travel expenses), for six months. After that, it was clear that New York was going to make a serious commitment to decentralization. I wanted to study that decentralization and felt that I could no longer take money from the district. For the next several years until early 2008, I served as an unpaid advisor to Klein and to the district. Whether that relationship has clouded my objectivity each reader will have to decide for himself. Joel Klein never asked that I color my results or my writing in any way, nor did he ever ask that I grant him or anyone else the right to review my work in advance of its publication.

Joel Klein—A Nontraditional School District Leader

Joel Klein served as deputy White House counsel to President Bill Clinton, then as chief of the Antitrust Division of the U.S. Department of Justice, then as chairman and CEO of the U.S. operations of Bertelsmann, one of the largest media companies in the world. While he was chief of the Justice Department Antitrust Division, Klein developed a deep suspicion of monopoly in any form. In a great irony and a greater opportunity, Klein is now in charge of one of the largest remaining monopolies in the United States, the New York City Department of Education. He has instinctively gone about the task of demonopolizing the schools with a strong sense of what needs to be done.

Chancellor Klein is a balding, bespectacled, friendly yet intense man of short stature. He greeted me in his shirtsleeves and tie and welcomed me to his cubicle, one of perhaps thirty similar "cubes" in a large room in the Tweed Courthouse, the district's headquarters. Over the next six years, I would learn that he is a man who does not shy away from a difficult problem or a tough adversary, although he always looks for a way to get to his goal with a minimum of conflict. When the educational benefit was clear, though, I saw him consistently make the decision that he felt was best for students, no matter how strong the opposition. In the end, I came to admire him as a leader.

The Seven Steps in Implementing Decentralization in New York City

The story of the transformation of the New York City school system rests on strong leadership implementing a difficult solution. I've identified seven steps in this process.

1. Defining the goal and the strategy
2. The preparation phase
3. The pilot phase
4. Going to scale
5. Preparing the central office staffs for decentralization
6. Selecting and training principals
7. Sustaining the new organization over time

1. DEFINING THE GOAL AND THE STRATEGY

The school is the unit that matters.

JOEL KLEIN
INTERVIEW OF FEBRUARY 9, 2006

New York City's strategy was to improve student performance by allowing each school to elevate itself in its own unique way. The basic theory was that every school, given proper freedom and accountability with skilled leadership from the principal, will improve. Klein and his staff also believed that without an effective principal who has the authority to make decisions, no school can improve. The primary goal was to improve student performance. Every district has that goal, but the goal does not by itself dictate a specific strategy: some might argue that the best way to that goal is to adopt a new math and reading curriculum, while others might argue for requiring more standardized, district-wide teacher training. Both the goal and the strategy must be clearly set or the district will be beset by arguments between various factions over what to do. In every district, the strategy must be appropriate to the initial circumstances of the district. Before we consider the strategy, then, let's see where New York City started out with respect to student achievement, and what progress has been made.

Defining the Baseline and Recent Progress in Student Achievement

In 2002, the year that Mayor Bloomberg took office, the graduation rate in New York City's schools was 46.5 percent, an abysmal result from any point of view. On the National Assessment of Educational Progress (NAEP), run by the U.S. Department of

Education, only 19 percent of the city's fourth graders scored "proficient or above," the federal standard, in reading. Something dramatic had to be done. New reading books or an additional five days of teacher training each year were not going to be enough.

Five years later—after decentralization had begun, new principal training had been established, a host of additional changes had been made—things were improving. The 2007 graduation rate, including both June and August graduates, was 55.8 percent, an increase of 9.3 percentage points over 2002 (compared to a statewide increase of 3 points). The city's fourth graders had moved from 19 percent to 25 percent proficient or above in reading on the NAEP, though at the highest standard, "advanced," the progress was slight, from 5 percent to 6 percent. Not all students were achieving equally, though: 47.2 percent of black students graduated in 2007 (up 7.0 percentage points since 2005), and 43 percent of Hispanic students graduated (up 5.6 points).

Because every state uses different testing systems, it is difficult to compare results from one state to another. There is only one national test, the NAEP, which is administered by the federal government and tests about three thousand students in each state every other year, first in 2002, and then every two years since 2003. The sample is small because the intent of the NAEP is to measure the performance of each state, not of a single school district or school. However, eleven cities have voluntarily asked to have larger samples of their students tested, and some of those—including New York City—were among our eight study districts.[1]

The NAEP mathematics results show substantial gains for New York City from 2002 to 2007. New York City's fourth grade math scores rose from 21 to 34 percent at or above proficient and from 2 percent to 5 percent advanced, both very positive results.

As mentioned, fourth grade reading scores also rose, from 19 percent to 25 percent at or above proficient. These increases were slightly greater than for all large city districts and represented more than twice the improvement of the nation as a whole. New York's low-income fourth graders outperformed their national peers by 7 percentage points.

Eighth grade improvements, though, were so small as to be nearly invisible. In addition, black eighth graders in New York City, while scoring in the middle of the eleven city districts, nonetheless scored below 74 percent of the nation's black students in math, as was the case for black students in all eleven city districts. Hispanic students did only slightly better, scoring below 70 percent of the national sample of Hispanic students in math, while Hispanic students in all ten of the other districts also fell below the national average for Hispanics.

The annual New York State tests of students in grades 3 to 8 provide a more sensitive indicator, and they paint a brighter picture. These tests place students in one of four categories, from 1 (the lowest) to 4 (the highest). On the 2007 math state tests, 65.1 percent of New York City elementary and middle school students scored in levels 3 and 4, a gain of 27.8 percentage points since 2002. Black students made even greater gains, with 55.4 percent meeting the state standards, a gain of 29 percentage points since 2002, thus reducing their gap compared to white and Asian students. Hispanic students gained 29.6 percentage points, to 59.0 percent over the period, reducing their gap slightly. By comparison, 82.7 percent of white students and 88.4 percent of Asian students scored in the top two categories.

In summary, New York City in 2002 was failing its students, and badly. All ethnic groups were performing below the national averages, and the ethnic gaps were very large. Several previous administrations had attempted to improve things either by introducing new curricula, by requiring new district-wide teacher training, or by forming the schools into local community districts. Nothing had worked. When Bloomberg and Klein looked hard at the school district, they saw a huge monolith that was dying of its own mass and immobility. Initially they, like previous administrations, tried introducing new curricula and other traditional school district changes. Within their first year in office, though, they had decided to embark on the largest reorganization in the history of the school district.[2]

So now we have some benchmarks. We've compared New York City to other urban U.S. districts, and we've seen that by 2007 it had made strong progress in high school graduation and in elementary student achievement. It was still struggling in grade 8 and had yet to close the gap between black and Hispanic students compared to white and Asian students, though it was narrowing those gaps.

Klein and his team had initiated several changes that were working, even before decentralization had gone very far. But he could see that he was not yet able to bring poor students, black students, Hispanic students, and non-English-speaking students up to the level that would enable them to succeed. To do that, he concluded, he would have to find a way to get his 1,467 principals to make their schools individually successful, and that meant decentralization, finding skilled principals, and creating a choice system and an accountability system.

Defining the Strategy—Eric Nadelstern Takes the Stage

Eric Nadelstern just might be the most creative leader of urban high schools in America. While many districts have improved elementary school performance, few if any have managed to do so with high schools. Nadelstern is an expert in improving urban high schools that primarily serve disadvantaged students, from special education students to immigrant and low-income and minority students. He has had success after success in doing this, and he, more than any other person, was responsible for helping Joel Klein to develop the strategy of decentralization. He explains the genesis of his thinking:

"When I started teaching in the early seventies, I remember reading a piece written by Albert Shanker [former teachers union president] 'An American teacher,' where he suggested that the typical junior high school teacher with five classes of thirty kids, assigning 250-word compositions each week to each of the students, would need 156 full school days a year just to evaluate those compositions if it took seven and a half minutes to evaluate each one. That had a profound impact on my thinking about it, not to mention having been that teacher at a large, academic comprehensive high school with somewhere between 150 and 180 kids that I was responsible for, responsible but not accountable. It wasn't until I became familiar with Sizer's work that I understood that simply by doubling the instructional period, you could reduce teacher load by 40 percent and it didn't cost a plug nickel more! This is a matter of scheduling and how you conceptualize the curriculum. Well, essentially what we've done at the high school level in America is we've come up with an ingenious scheme, which was old when Henry Ford was making Model T's, to diffuse responsibility and accountability for kids so that at the end of the day nobody's responsible for any one student, but teachers are responsible for a portion of each kid." (Interview, March 31, 2006)

Eric Nadelstern is a teacher and a principal in spirit, though he now works in the central staff. Having founded several high schools in the city's toughest neighborhoods for kids who had dropped out, were kicked out, or had just arrived in the country, he became the leader of the more than five hundred Empowerment Schools, about one-third of all of the schools in the New York City school system. Nadelstern is soft-spoken and mild mannered, but at the same time intense, bright, ambitious, focused, and with a New York City edge—he is willing to push in order to make things happen. He's also a dapper fellow with a bushy mustache and eyeglasses and comes across as a natural contrarian who has a nice sense of humor to go with his independent spirit. Nadelstern has been offered the top job at large school districts elsewhere, with big raises in pay, but in the end, he's a New Yorker.

Nadelstern is a thinker as well as a doer. As is often true of innovators, he has thought through the most fundamental aspects of instruction and has developed a crisp point of view that enables him to chart a consistent course through the many complexities of this huge school district. For example, Nadelstern does not worry that focusing the curriculum on two basic courses, humanities and Math-Science Integrated, amounts to narrowing the curriculum, as many education experts feel. His view on curriculum is consistent with that of the Coalition of Essential Schools. As he puts it: "There aren't more than four subjects really that comprise not only the entire high school curriculum but the entire realm of human knowledge, and after seventeen years as a high school principal I had gotten it down to two, humanities on the one hand and math/science/technology on the other, and if I had a little bit more time, I might be able to figure out how to get it down to one." Nadelstern continues, "The reality is that the complexity in teaching is the relationship between kids and teachers in classrooms. And the challenge is to simplify the school structure so that it requires as little time and energy as possible in investment, and invest all of your resources into working with teachers to figure out how to better educate kids." (All quotes with Eric Nadelstern in this chapter are from interviews on March 31, 2006. In all, I met with Nadelstern approximately twenty times during this study). Not everyone would agree with Nadelstern's position on curriculum, but it is a well-thought-through position, and it complements his ideas on the other aspects of instruction.

Nadelstern developed his opinions through study and trial and error. As a new principal, he opened his school with eight periods of forty minutes rather than the traditional day of seven periods of forty-five minutes. From that starting point, "We moved in exactly the wrong direction, thinking that if eight forty-minute periods is good, then nine thirty-five-minute periods would be better. And then we fortuitously ran something called 'student for a day,' where every staff member followed a kid through his or her school day to get a sense of what the school was like from the student's perspective. And at the end of a three-month period after we'd all had a chance to do that, we filed into a room and the teachers were saying things like, 'You know, the most interesting thing that goes on in the school happens in the hall in between classes', or, 'If you change focus every thirty-five minutes, how can you learn anything?' The faculty committee came up with a brand-new schedule and we went from thirty-five-minute to seventy-minute periods and the kids went from seven subjects to five subjects a day. Teachers went from five classes to three classes, and so teacher load was reduced by 40 percent!" This, of course, was many years ago, when principals in New York City did not officially have the freedom to change schedules or curriculum, but Nadelstern was one of those renegades who did whatever worked best for his students.

From the outset, Nadelstern assumed more autonomy than other principals. His school, like the other "alternative" high schools for dropouts and failures, was ignored by the district, and he was left alone to create a different kind of school. After several years, his school had become so successful that it was attracting "regular" students instead of alternative students, and a new local superintendent ordered him to get back in line with everyone else. Moving quickly, Nadelstern converted his school into a charter school, thus escaping the heavy hand of local district office control. Two years later, after the threat had passed, he reconverted his school into a district school!

In order to make teachers accountable for the progress of specific students, Nadelstern implemented advisories of ten to fifteen students per teacher, and he organized students and teachers into the smallest units that were logically possible. Four teachers (math, science, English, and social studies) were given team responsibility for seventy-five to eighty students, along with two classrooms, access to laboratories and other specialized facilities, and a small budget. He left it up to each team of teachers to determine the best way to structure the curriculum to match the needs of their students and the abilities of the teachers. Their curriculum and schedule evolved into one of a minimum number of courses and maximum integration of material.

Nadelstern was later put in charge of the city's program to open small high schools for at-risk students under a Gates Foundation grant. This was during the years immediately before the Bloomberg-Klein leadership team arrived on the scene. Since the new schools reported to him, he used the opportunity to create small schools that had autonomy. He taught the new principals how to drive down teacher loads and improve student performance. The difference between these new schools and the city's traditional high schools was striking: "When we started the small-schools work in the Bronx in 2001–2, there were twenty-two Bronx principals, most of whom had large schools, and most of whom had never been in a small school. And so we started holding principals' meetings in small schools, and I remember a

Bronx principals' meeting at Banana Kelly High School [the school is on Kelly Street, which is shaped like a banana]. It's in the Hunts Point section of the Bronx, which is the poorest part of the poorest congressional district in the state. The kids coming to that school were all from that neighborhood and it was among the most educationally challenged, economically deprived student populations I've ever seen a school work with. And the principals, the large-school principals walking through that school couldn't understand two things. The first thing they couldn't understand was why the kids weren't angry. And so their first response was, 'These aren't our kids.' So we sat and we looked at the reports on who the incoming population was and disabused them of any notion that this was a specialized population. The next thing they couldn't figure out was why there were only fifteen kids in a class. 'They must have more money!' And so we sat budgets side by side, and my small schools didn't have any more money, but they were using their resources differently. A large school could have as many as eighty people that have something to do with security for all or part of their school day. A school with four or five thousand in New York could have as many as eighty people in that function. A small school has one— the principal. And that's a very small part of the principal's day, hopefully."

Joel Klein, meet Eric Nadelstern. Now Klein had both a goal and a strategy: the goal was to improve the academic performance and graduation rates of all students, and the strategy would be to do this by giving parents choice, giving principals autonomy, and holding principals accountable for the success of their students.

2. THE PREPARATION PHASE

Joel Klein took office in 2002. Eric Nadelstern opened the first twenty-nine Autonomy Zone schools in September of 2004. What happened in between was intense preparation.

The first step involved analysis of the existing state of affairs. This was time-consuming because the information systems then in place were designed to support a centralized district and thus did not provide data on individual schools. As Nadelstern noted ruefully, "We spent one hundred years creating a closed system populated entirely by teachers. I mean, the remarkable thing is that in a system as large as the New York City public schools, up until a few years ago everyone in it was a teacher, no matter what their assignment was. The accountants had been teachers. The business office was populated by people who'd been teachers. The people running transportation had been teachers. It was a remarkably closed and insular profession and the assumption was that—much like the army—you have to move up through the ranks—that the president of Ford Motors needs to be able to do a tune-up before he can be president of Ford. What most educators don't know is that that question [of what went wrong] has been decided—and not in their favor. And part of the reason is, I mean, we're saddled with the most bizarre IT data management system anyone could find. It's not even Windows-based. It's DOS-based, in 2006! And mainly because it was designed by teachers. Right. So principals have no data at their disposal, other than what they collect. We're reduced to collecting data by hand and saying to principals, '*You* tell us! Fill out the report and *you* tell us how your school's doing.'" Although the district has work to do on its student information systems, it did have in place a financial information system that each principal could address to find out just how much money they had left. That system, which had taken several years to develop, was a boon to the upcoming reforms.

The planning team included several newly recruited staff who had experience with policy analysis, and some who had experience in government and in politics. Several of these team members played valuable roles and then after their job was done moved out of the district to other challenges. The team was assisted by a group of between six and twelve consultants from one of the major management consulting firms, McKinsey & Company. They were knowledgeable about planning processes, organization, finances, budgets, and staffing ratios and performed a monumental amount of work in slightly less than two years.

Because Klein had concluded that he would likely need to implement a suite of several related changes including choice, school empowerment, Weighted Student Formula, budgeting accountability, and reorganization of the central office, he began to implement some of the changes as he was able, without announcing all of them at once. Early in his administration, for example, he implemented a district-wide choice program that invited every family to list up to twelve schools that they would like each child to attend. At about the same time, he opened the Leadership Academy to train future principals, as a freestanding nonprofit entity that raised its operating funds through donations from foundations and from New York City businesses. It was a great help to have introduced these two major elements of the overall change package ahead of the others.

Meanwhile, the team had to do extensive analysis to arrive at a set of weights that could be used in a Weighted Student Formula plan, and several sensitive political considerations had to be taken into account, such as the possibility that some schools would lose funds, while others would gain. Other planning tasks included setting out the elements of an accountability system, forecasting the number of new principals that would be needed over the next five years or so (the estimate was about eight hundred), defining the areas of freedom that principals would and would not have, planning for the reorganization of the central office to support empowered schools, planning a communications program to present these changes to employees and to the public, and hiring new senior staff.

There was a lot to do, and all of it got done. Time was short, because Mayor Bloomberg would "term out" at the end of 2009, if he were elected to a second term to begin in 2006. (In 2008 the term-limits law was repealed by the City Council, and the mayor announced that he would run for reelection in 2009.) Of equal importance was that Klein did not have to go over each detail of the change with his school board because he did not report to a school board—he reported only to Mayor Bloomberg. It seems unlikely that so many changes could have been implemented had New York City not adopted a system of mayoral control of the schools beginning in 2002. Mayoral control will expire at the end of 2009 unless it is renewed by the legislature of New York State. That surely would disrupt and might even reverse the progress that has been made.

Even as the planning processes continued full tilt, Eric Nadelstern opened the first schools that would pilot-test the coming district-wide reform. At the time, though, no one knew for sure whether these first schools would succeed and whether decentralization would even get off the ground.

3. THE PILOT PHASE

At the outset, the district did not announce an intention to decentralize entirely. Instead, the first cohort of schools, known at the time as the Autonomy Zone schools, consisted of twenty-six schools drawn from the district, plus three charter schools. The principals were asked to form four "networks" of their own, in order to have an informal source of mutual support and to learn from one another's experience. The support staff consisted of Nadelstern plus four additional staff. Once each month, Nadelstern met with the principals as a group, to share information and develop policies as issues arose. Educators will notice that this by itself was a major change. In most districts, principals spend only a few days each month in their schools because they are called away several times each week to attend endlessly dreary meetings that one or another central staff feels are essential. Nadelstern ended this practice and instead told his principals that they would be called out no more than once per month, that the meetings would take place after the end of the school day, and that their attendance was voluntary! The principals unanimously praised this change, which allowed them to spend their time visiting classrooms every day, working with their teachers.

Every school was required to ally itself with an external collaborator of its choice to assist in professional development for teachers, in developing effective advisories, and to help in other ways. The twenty-six schools ended up choosing a set of ten different external partners such as Bank Street College, New York University, and the Anti-Defamation League. At the end of the first year, twenty principals reported having used their autonomy to create innovative curricula, sixteen had altered the school schedule, thirteen had introduced portfolio or project assessments or other new ideas to supplement the traditional assessments of student progress, and seven had altered the school structure, using "looping," creation of thematic submits within the school, interdisciplinary teacher teams, and so on.

Klein had decided that the first Autonomy Zone schools should be nominated by the ten regional superintendents, to gain their support. Many of the superintendents nominated their renegade, difficult-to-control principals, the ones they were glad to lose—yet these were exactly the sort of independent leaders that Nadelstern wanted. Other area superintendents nominated struggling principals, and Nadelstern had to work closely with them. Every principal who wanted to join the Zone was required to sign a five-year contract that set out specific goals for attendance rates, course completion, and other measures of student performance. They were promised that they would have control over budget, curriculum, staffing, and schedule. In return, they had to agree that their continued employment would depend on their ability to meet specific targets for student performance. At the end of five years, a principal who had failed to meet his or her performance targets would be terminated.

Most of the schools that were nominated for the program were in the poorest neighborhoods and had the greatest achievement challenges, exactly the kinds of schools with which Nadelstern had experienced his greatest successes in the past. As a bonus, these schools were in neighborhoods that did not attract much media interest, and thus Nadelstern was able to test his ideas with nary a mention in the press all year long, which allowed his schools to make their mistakes and find their way without the additional pressure of media scrutiny.

Many of these schools were brand-new, start-up schools. Most of the new schools followed the pattern of admitting only one class, a ninth grade, in their first year of operation. That meant that the principal, who was usually a person with a very strong teaching background but no previous leadership experience, had to provide leadership to only about one hundred students, five or six teachers, and one office assistant. That was a near-perfect setting for a new principal to be able to learn how to be an effective instructional leader. Each year, these new schools added a new ninth grade, and as a result the principal's leadership experience grew each year as the school grew. In addition, Nadelstern's small staff and the staff of the Leadership Academy together developed a program that identified principals who would open new schools and put them through an intensive eight-month training program and then provided them with coaching support during their first year in their new school.

As a result of these positive conditions, the first-year Autonomy Zone schools, founded in 2004, prospered. There were problems, of course. One school, for example, did a midyear evaluation and found that its projected course-passing rate was a disastrous 20 percent. The school responded by creating a two-week makeup period at the end of the semester. By year's end, the school had achieved a course passing rate of 86 percent.

Overall, the first year of the Autonomy Zone was judged a success. The principals had embraced their autonomy and had used it in ways that were helping their students. They took their performance targets seriously. The external collaborations had enriched the schools and had given principals and teachers a sounding board and a source of friendly criticism. Zone schools employed a great variety of instructional approaches, but nearly all of them developed "differentiated instruction"—ways to tailor instruction to the needs and learning style of each student, and nearly all gave special emphasis to math instruction, a chronic weak point for most of their students.

Dr. Amy Liszt has performed an independent evaluation of the performance of the first group of Zone schools from the fall of 2004.[3] Comparing pre-Zone performance to that after two years in the Zone, Liszt reported that graduation rates rose from 65.8 percent to 74.5 percent and that the passing rate on the Regents math exam rose from 71 percent to 89 percent and on the English exam from 81 percent to 85.5 percent. Attendance rose from 88.7 percent to 90.9 percent, the annual dropout rate fell from 1.9 to 1.1 percent, and college acceptance rose from 80.3 percent of students to 93.1. All in all, a very strong record.[4]

Meanwhile, Joel Klein's staff was working full speed to prepare for a possible district-wide scale-up, though no decision had yet been made to go district-wide. Nadelstern received permission to recruit a second cohort of Autonomy Zone schools. The 2005–6 school year opened with a total of forty-eight Autonomy Zone schools, of which forty-two were district schools and six were charter schools.

Of the forty-two district schools in year two of the pilot phase, twenty-five were high schools, one was K–6, one was K–8, one was 6–8, and nine had unique grade level configurations. My data did not include five of the schools, because they declined to participate in my study, and participation was voluntary. By the end of year two, seventeen of the schools had adopted the combined courses of either humanities or MSI, or both, and twenty-two had adopted double-length courses, or block scheduling. All of the schools had implemented advisories. Although they had not yet been formally granted full control of their budgets, thirty-one of the principals had paid teachers an extra stipend for working extra hours as tutors, activity counselors, or in planning activities. In thirty-three of the schools, teachers served as advisors to various student organizations.

Our research found that eighteen of the principals had controlled their staffing mixture before the Autonomy Zone (some of these had been chosen by Nadelstern at an earlier time), and all reported having that control as a Zone school. Thirteen said they had controlled their professional development budget before the Zone, while all of them reported that they controlled it as a Zone school. Twenty-two had controlled their instructional materials before, and all had that control as Zone schools. Twelve had previously controlled the budget necessary to offer programs for parents, and thirty reported controlling that budget as Zone schools. One interesting observation was that almost all of the schools had arranged the students' chairs into circles, which encourage student interaction. Only one school had its chairs in the traditional straight rows facing the front of the classroom.

We also found that these autonomous principals followed a variety of strategies. Of the forty-two Autonomy Zone schools, only seventeen reported having implemented humanities and/or Math-Science Integrated classes. These schools had by far the lowest Total Student Loads in the Zone. All of the schools had eliminated most of their non-teaching staff and had instead added more classroom teachers. In time, more of the autonomous schools may take an aggressive stance in reducing Total Student Load, though not all of them had done so at the time of our study. If this does happen, TSL for this group of schools will drop below the average of 88 that we measured.

One additional observation is in order at this point. When it comes to freedom to design their own curriculum, the elementary schools of New York City do not have the same autonomy that middle schools and high schools have. Early in his tenure as chancellor, Joel Klein had apparently followed the advice of his senior staff to implement district-wide standard curricula for elementary schools in English and in math. At the time, schools were employing a great variety of curricula of their choice, but training for principals and teachers was inadequate. In order to improve instruction quickly, Klein opted for the centralized approach. Many argued that the standardized approach would actually harm student performance, while others who preferred standardization felt that Klein had chosen the wrong books. Fortunately, many of the city's principals have sufficient self-confidence to push back against the central office if they feel that their own curriculum is superior, and fortunately, the chancellor has been willing to let them do so. In the end, the district presented standardized curricula to its elementary schools but did not force schools to adopt them. This example illustrates one of the ways in which central office staffs naturally strive for control over the schools. It also demonstrates that no organization is ever 100 percent consistent, whether it strives to be centralized or to be decentralized. While it is true that all systems should be aligned for decentralization to succeed, it is also true that one should not be compulsively neat about how an organization is structured. Organizations are made up of human beings, and there is no one theory that can be slavishly followed in designing them.

4. GOING TO SCALE

It is now February 9, 2006, the winter of year two of the Autonomy Zone, and things are going well. Better than many had expected, in fact. Joel Klein reflects on what he's learned from the pilot Autonomy Zone: "The theory of the Autonomy Zone when we piloted it was if we look at public education today, the school is the unit that matters. We do not know what unit you are worrying about, but if it is not the school, you are going to get it all backwards, and when people say they are all bad schools and the public school system is no good—and our theory is 'Is the system focused on the right unit?'—and the obvious answer is no, not at all. The two necessary conditions for that are a thorough understanding of autonomy, or as we call it, empowerment—and accountability. The system has very little of both. The school leadership has multiple effects, many of which you have written about—one of which is that it actually deters good people from coming into the system. One of the reasons you see this outlet of charters is that some people feel their accountability is an empowerment, when in public education it has not been. We piloted this in a way to test some of these principles. For example, in public education, I get all the time this discussion with principals and assistant principals that if a school has three hundred students, they should have an assistant principal, and it is all kind of by the input numbers, which is preposterous. So what we wanted to see is: given discretion, given flexibility, how would people reconfigure the work that they are doing, and we wanted to see from day one what these performance contracts—what implications they would have to move schools to understand that accountability has to be at the level—accountability in America is a compliance system like all the other school regulations, so you get this disconnect between the work that your school leader is doing and the accountability system. If you do not integrate, then you are going to continue to have a lot of noise in the system."

Klein continued, "What we are going to do is beginning in the fall, we are increasing it by some two hundred schools—at that point, we will be close to 20 percent of the city. It will be larger than any of our regional structure zones in terms of number of schools. We are going to do many more middle schools and elementary schools, and we are going to do the kind of budgeting work that you talked about [in *Making Schools Work*]. In other words, if you take out the hard-core central cost, we are going to try to migrate the system to a purchaser model, drive as much of the dollar as you can into the principal and let her decide which professional development, and obviously hope that two things will come out of that—a more efficient allocation of the city's resources and second of all, frankly (and at the same time, we are thoroughly revamping, and Jim [Jim Liebman, Chief Accountability Officer] can talk to you about that), our approach to accountability. We are moving way beyond NCLB to have a richer quantitative and a very robust qualitative set of analyses—which will become a way to monitor performance— but more importantly, to change performance—and those are the core principles, and we are very excited about them." Reflecting on the pace of the scale-up, Klein later added, "I actually think that the organization will significantly tip. Maybe not irrevocably but significantly, after we add two hundred schools. Two things will occur: first of all, scale—remember, I will have two hundred sixty schools, and that is bigger than virtually every school district. And second of all, there is no question that this is going to stimulate a demand in the City. When it is a little pilot with fifty schools, most of them high schools, it is a very different perception. I believe the system will significantly move at that number. In my own view, and I have said this, I would like to increase the number over the next year and the following year and continue the migration."

Seven weeks later, Eric Nadelstern reflected on the coming, scale-up: "I think Joel's right. I think '06 is the watershed, interestingly. It may not be apparent widely until a year later, but if it could be done with 200 schools, it could be done with 1,400 schools . . . and the structures we're going to have to necessarily build around 200 schools which will look markedly different from the rest of the organization, as well as our ability then to push much more in the way of financial resources into those 200 schools, I would say are irreversible to the extent that once people experience that, and realize the potential benefit for creating circumstances where more kids are more successful, it is going to be hard to argue for something else." (Interview of March 31, 2006)

The pilot program was succeeding. The talk around the district was that the principals were enthusiastic, the teachers were happy, and student performance in the Zone was on the rise. Randi Weingarten, president of the City's United Federation of

Teachers, had this to say: "I was the first one who started talking about how schools should have autonomy, and we tried actually to do this during [an earlier] era, with school-based autonomy. And then the whole school leadership teams, the whole notion of school-based autonomy, we actually tried doing this within the context of a decentralized system, probably 1990–91, '92, '93. And it just didn't have, it had huge traction from teachers, but there was the same kind of opposition from the principals that you're starting to see now from the principals' union, and there was a lot of opposition from the superintendent level. But if you read our contract from 1990, we had this whole—we attempted to do this whole thrust of school-based decision making. The difference was, we tried to do it collegially—versus now, it's very, very top-down, meaning that the New York City experiment is very different than the others in that it is all premised on 'the principal knows best.' Some of the Zone schools are really happy with it, and some of the Zone schools are not happy. The majority are happier than they were before, because the system had become quite Stalinistic." Weingarten added, "We like the notion of allowing schools—we always think about schools as schools and classrooms, as the point of, as the pivotal juncture in education. Because ultimately, the place where kids learn is in the classroom. And so, when you look at the school and/or a cluster of classrooms as the center, what has happened is that you have not heard me—you've heard me raise some concerns, but you have not heard me say, 'No, this is a bad idea,' because this has historically been where the union has wanted to be, where the schools are the center, the schools are the pinnacle, and the rest of us are in support of that." (All quotes from Randi Weingarten are from an interview on May 10, 2006.)

Weingarten also expressed her thoughts on the subject of Total Student Load: "We used to say that the maximum load in secondary school should be eighty. So, what ends up happening in New York City, you're doing it by still having the same number of teaching periods, but by having block programming. In the private institutions they are reducing the number of kids you actually see and—how to explain it?—also reducing the number of kids in a classroom. So both of these concepts are important. You can't see 170 kids. I remember when I taught five periods in a high school. The rigor that everybody talks about—it's impossible to do. And anybody who says otherwise is kidding themselves."

At the time of this interview, the annual questionnaires in which teachers evaluate their principal had not yet been introduced, and this might have eased some of Weingarten's concern: "If you had that evaluation piece, so there was a check and balance, people would support having somebody as the ultimate arbiter. As long as they believe that ultimate arbiter is fair." Though Weingarten was often a tough opponent for Klein and Nadelstern, in the end all three of them proved to be big-picture leaders. All three shared the vision that Weingarten expressed: "What can help kids and adults and society and working people both dream their dreams and achieve their dreams? There's only one thing that can really do that, and that is a viable public education system."

The Autonomy Zone Becomes the Empowerment Schools—And Grows Fast

Letters went out to invite a new group of principals to join the reform, which was rechristened the Empowerment Schools. When the responses came back, it turned out that Klein and Nadelstern had been off in their estimate of 200 schools. Instead, they were about to have 332 Empowerment Schools, the equivalent of the sixth largest school district in the nation. Many of the new Empowerment Schools were large, up to about 2,700 students, and some of the principals had been in office for twenty years or more. The word had spread, and principals all around the city were ready to sign up to get their freedom and were willing to accept the risk that their continued tenure would depend on producing student achievement results. To those cynics who believed that principals were just going to work for a secure paycheck, this must have been a shock.

Now Nadelstern and his small team had to prepare to lead and support 332 schools. The principals were asked to form themselves into fourteen networks of their own choosing, with about twenty-four principals in each network. Each network was provided with a support team consisting of a network leader, typically a former successful principal; an achievement coach, who was expert on how to get hold of the available student data and district resources; a business services manager to assist in solving problems having to do with budget, contracts, purchasing, personnel, and grants; a special services manager to assist with the complexities of rules and funding for English Language Learners, special education, and related issues; and a one-year instructional mentor to assist with getting support funds for mentoring new teachers and providing ongoing professional development. Principals do not report to network leaders—it's the other way around. The principal is the client, and the network team is his service provider.

During the summer before the 332 Empowerment Schools began, there was planning and training for all of the principals. First the principals met in their networks with their support team. Each principal was then encouraged to create a school team, consisting of the principal and two to five teachers, through which all of the teachers could be connected to the planning process. In addition, each network of twenty or so principals elected a team of five of their own to represent them at an Empowerment Schools–wide set of meetings. Coordinating it all was Eric Nadelstern and his support team of five people at Tweed Courthouse.

The Empowerment Schools had a successful year after their big scale-up from 42 schools in 2005–6 (excluding six charter schools that were part of this group) to 332 in 2006–7. Ninety-nine percent of the 332 principals replied on a survey that they liked the Empowerment Schools organization and wanted to stay in. Thirteen of the fourteen network leaders said that they would return for the 2007–8 school year. The survey also revealed a problem in one of the networks. One of the network leaders received several neutral or negative ratings from principals. Nadelstern asked the principals for a private meeting, at which he discovered that this network was composed entirely of the most independent-minded principals, none of whom wanted to be part of any network. They just wanted to be left alone. After three years as a network, they had never met! At the end of their meeting with Nadelstern, they concluded that they had actually learned something and said that they might meet again.[5]

I had thought that this would be the last big jump in size for the decentralization effort for a few years, while these 332 schools became accustomed to empowerment. I was wrong. The clock was running on term limits for the mayor, and Klein was ever more convinced that this new direction was going to produce dramatic improvements in student achievement. The question now occupying his mind was how to keep it going after Mayor Bloomberg left office and he was replaced by a new chancellor. There was also the possibility that the legislature would turn down a continuation of mayoral control of the schools, so that a new school board might take office in January of 2010, one that might know very little about the decentralization effort and might well not support it.

Klein could count on having through 2009 before time ran out. Out of the district's 1,467 schools, 1,135 were still run in the traditional manner. If he decentralized another 375 or so schools each year, he could get all of them into the program before he left office, but they would still be unstable and in need of at least a few additional years of support before they could fly on their own. If he did not get all of the schools decentralized in time, Klein guessed that the next mayor or chancellor would have a good chance at undoing all that he had accomplished.

Klein had the option of scaling up the reform more quickly, thus providing more settling-in time and giving the decentralization more strength to resist a possible future political attack from traditionalists. That option posed a different risk: could he empower 1,135 schools over one or two years? Those principals who were most willing to accept the new accountability had already volunteered for the Empowerment Schools. How would the remaining principals respond? What should he do?

Principals Get the Power to Choose Their Own Provider of Central Services

On April 17, 2007, the *New York Times* reported that the ten regional superintendent offices would be abolished for the following year. Instead, principals would choose a School Support Organization (SSO) to provide services to them. Each school would pay an annual fee to its SSO, from a low of $29,500 to the Empowerment Schools organization, up to $145,215 per year to join a Baltimore-based organization, which was ultimately not included in the program. Critics of the change, according to the newspaper, "have urged the Bloomberg administration to halt its plans, saying that too much is changing too fast." It may have been the first time in modern history that a school district has been accused of moving too fast! The implication of the change from central office support services to SSO support was clear to everyone in the district—all of the 1,467 schools would now have to learn to operate in an autonomous fashion. The days of top-down central office directives were over. Moreover, the traditional regional superintendents were out of business. From now on, the principals would control the money for regional staff support, and the SSOs would have to compete with one another to offer better service to principals at a lower price. Joel Klein had decided that, once and for all, he needed to turn the monopoly of central office control upside-down and truly empower the principals. This change would be difficult for the next mayor or chancellor to undo, and thus decentralization would have stronger protection than it did now.

The plan was to grant to each of the 1,467 principals a total of about $200,000 per year with which they could buy their central support from one of three kinds of School Support Organizations. There were (1) four Learning Support Organizations (LSOs), each led by a strong former area superintendent and run by the district; (2) six Partnership Support Organizations (PSOs), each one a nonprofit outside of the school district, including the City University of New York, the Center for Innovation–Public Education Association, and New Visions for Public Schools, all of which had extensive experience working with New York City schools; and (3) the Empowerment Schools Support Organization, led by Eric Nadelstern and his team, and thus also part of the district. Nadelstern had already found that with his system of a team of five support staff for every twenty schools, he was providing as much or more support as the traditional area offices, and at a cost that was 80 percent less! That 80 percent was retained by each school, enabling them to hire yet more teachers and push down Total Student Load still more.

Klein had made his decision: an immediate scale-up was the lesser of the risks. Each of the support organizations prepared to market its offering to the 1,467 principals, who for the first time in memory were the units that mattered most. What followed was a process that at times looked like a bazaar, with some SSOs and PSOs giving out souvenirs such as pocket-sized computer flash memory drives to those who attended their information sessions. In the end, every school chose an SSO or PSO, and the Empowerment Schools ended up with by far the largest number, 521 schools for the 2007–8 school year. Klein did not simply want to replace one monopoly (the former regions) with another monopoly (the SSOs and PSOs), so he provided that at the end of each two-year period, the principals could choose a new service provider if they desired.

Fair Student Funding Becomes the New Way to Allocate Money to Students

While all of the preparations by principals and support organizations were taking place during the spring of 2007, Klein unveiled another of the major elements of his decentralization, a new budgeting system known as Fair Student Funding (FSF). We've noted before that once a district commits to decentralization, it must have a way to allocate money rather than positions to its principals, and that method is Weighted Student Formula budgeting. New York City's version of WSF is called Fair Student Funding. All schools were put on the FSF system starting in the fall of 2007.

Fair Student Funding, like any weighted student-based budgeting approach, has two objectives. First, by allocating money to students and then having the money, rather than formulaic positions, go to the schools, FSF is an integral part of decentralization. Second, FSF has been shown to greatly reduce the inequities in spending per child that develop in most districts. Inequities develop through two main routes. One is that parents who have clout always find ways to get special privileges and extra grants for their child's school. Second, teachers tend over time to migrate to upper-income schools by making use of their seniority rights. This causes schools in wealthy neighborhoods to end up with more experienced, higher-paid teachers, with the result that those schools spend more per student than schools in poor neighborhoods. It takes several years for a teacher to become fully skilled, as Randi Weingarten noted: "You start seeing skill levels, real proficient skill levels, third, fourth, and fifth year." If students who attend poor schools are denied equal access to these more skilled teachers, a fundamental inequity has been created.

Fair Student Funding redresses that funding inequity to a substantial degree. However, schools under FSF cannot dismiss a veteran teacher and replace her with an inexperienced teacher simply because the school is over its "salary cap." The district is phasing in the new process over several years so that schools that have primarily highly paid teachers can wait for the normal retirement process to create openings that they can then fill with teachers who are lower on the salary scale. Once parents and teachers become accustomed to FSF, they will for the first time be able to see clearly how much money their school has, and they'll have their own suggestions for how best to use that money. It will be difficult for a future chancellor who has centralizing tendencies to take that local budget control away from the schools.

Whether the ten newly created support organizations will match or perhaps surpass the achievements of the Empowerment Schools organization remains to be seen. Whether these reforms will erase the achievement gaps between the haves and the have-nots also remains to be seen. Whether New York City's graduation rates—55.8 percent at the end of the 2006–7 school year—will reach or exceed the 68 percent (and rising!) of Edmonton we will not know for several years. However, where student achievement is concerned, there are several signs that things are improving, and no signs that things are getting worse.

5. PREPARING THE CENTRAL OFFICE STAFFS FOR DECENTRALIZATION

Joel Klein has yet to reorganize the core of the central office staffs. While the support organizations have control over some functions, their main role is to serve as a liaison between principals and the central office staffs who decide how to spend special education funds, set personnel policies for hiring new employees, determine which schools will receive building maintenance, and so on.

Here's one example of the magnitude of the task that remains. It's April of 2007, the district-wide scale-up has just been announced, Fair Student Funding is in place, the Leadership Academy is training and providing coaching for new principals, and all systems are go. Sort of. The Council of School Supervisors and Administrators has asked to meet with Eric Nadelstern to discuss summer school for the Empowerment Schools. The principals thought that they were supposed to have autonomy, but they've each just received a detailed memo from a central office staffer telling them which teachers they must hire, when summer school must begin and end, what the hours must be each day, how the classes must be staffed, what buildings they can and cannot not use, and so on. The traditionalists in the central office seem still to have the upper hand, and these principals are discouraged. Apparently, the central office staffs have not gotten the word that the schools now enjoy freedom to make their own decisions. Nadelstern responds patiently to each question and then summarizes by telling the principals that they can start and end summer school whenever they want and that they can hire anyone they want as long as they respect the union contract, and he suggests that they experiment and try things in summer school that they've always wanted to try but did not have the freedom to do. In other words, it's their summer school, and they should run it as they see best.

Next, the principals want to know why they have to accept the children that the district sends them through the computerized choice system. They complain that some of these youngsters are on probation, others just got out of jail, and others have severe special needs. Nadelstern points out that the old funding system gave principals incentives to avoid these high-cost students, while the new weighted Fair Student Funding will instead give them incentives to want these children and to create specialized programs to serve these children, because they will bring much more money with them to the school.

The next topic they want to discuss is that of the Integrated Service Centers (ISCs). Joel Klein is preparing the central office staffs to support decentralized schools by reorganizing some of those staffs into five centers, one for each of the boroughs of New York City. Each will serve about 250 to 300 schools. Within each Integrated Service Center there are about eighty staff, all of whom report not to a regional head, but to their functional department head in central staff headquarters. These include, for example, the Division of Budget Operations and Review, School Food, Pupil Transportation, the Division of School Facilities, the Division of Instructional and Information Technology, and so on. If principals wish to make changes in their staffing pattern, they are supposed to receive approval from the various central staffs involved, and the ISC is supposed to provide liaison assistance. Increasingly, these requests from principals are routinely approved. However, the principals, who have lived through several previous attempts at reorganization, are concerned that as long as these central staffs remain in place, a new chancellor will be able to use them to reassert central office control and gut the decentralization.

At present, one person from each Integrated Service Center has been appointed to be liaison to a group of schools, so that the schools won't have to figure out for themselves whom to contact in the central office to get a question answered. While this is a step in the right direction, the problem of making the central staffs fully responsive to the schools is not yet solved. Central staffs are now supposed to exist to serve the needs of the schools. However, the central office still controls the budgets for the services that it provides, and in time it can convert that control over budgets into control over the schools. It's the golden rule of school districts: whoever controls the money gets to make the rules.

Klein might take his cue from Edmonton, as some other U.S. districts have. Edmonton faced the exact same problem. The central staffs told the schools when their roof would be fixed, their carpets replaced, and their buildings painted. If a principal called a central staff department for help or advice, he'd usually get an answering machine that told him the answering machine was full. To solve this problem, Edmonton's Mike Strembitsky divided the central office staffs into two sections. One section consisted of the essential governance functions such as legal, finance, and some personnel functions. These were retained as central staffs, though they were organized into teams that each served the needs of several schools. Each team was held accountable for the success of "its" schools. Remarkably, those central staffs almost overnight rushed to help the same schools that they previously had treated with disdain or worse.

The remaining half of the central staff, including special education specialists, school psychologists, curriculum development specialists, maintenance workers, and others, were each invited to participate in the process of developing a fair billing rate per hour for their service. Principals were then granted the budgets that had previously been granted to those staffs, and the principals were free either to buy services from the central staff or from any outside provider. As if by magic, those central staffs figured out how to be responsive, polite, and accommodating to the needs of schools. As a result, the principals developed a strong preference for buying services from the same people as before, but they received much improved service. However, some of the central staffs have had to cut personnel at some times and hire at others, as the demand for their services has fluctuated.

The central staffs in New York City are not yet fully committed to the new decentralized approach. It's a fair guess, though, that plans might be under way to change that. Chancellor Klein may have signaled that intention when he appointed Eric Nadelstern to a newly created position—Chief Schools Officer—early in 2009. In that position, Nadelstern will oversee all of the SSOs, the PSOs, and the Empowerment Schools Organization, as well as the Integrated Service Centers and Chancellor's District 79 for alternative schools and programs for students who are most at risk of failing to complete high school.

6. SELECTING AND TRAINING PRINCIPALS

Question: What do you look for in a principal?
Eric Nadelstern: Great teacher. I'm looking for our best teachers. I'm trying to convince those teachers that it's the same job. It's

just the students change. So instead of working with students, they work with teachers—with adults. (Interview of March 31, 2006)

The Leadership Academy was established by Mayor Bloomberg in 2003 as part of the Children First Initiative. It is a nonprofit entity, 501(c)(3), with its own board and staff, separate from the Department of Education, though the department accounts for virtually all of its business. In the fiscal year that ended June 30, 2005, the total budget of the academy was $20,795,700. This represented a 7.6 percent decrease from the previous year's budget. The academy offers four major programs, all of them for current or aspiring principals in the New York City schools.

1. The Aspiring Principals Program

The Aspiring Principals Program (APP) is a fourteen-month, full-time program that enrolls about sixty-five students each summer. APP begins with a six-week-long Summer Intensive that resembles a day-and-night boot camp for aspiring principals. In the most recent year, more than 1,400 aspirants applied to this program, of whom about 600 were generally qualified, and 66 were admitted. Most of the successful applicants were serving at the time of their application as assistant principals, though others had a variety of backgrounds. Successful applicants receive a salary that approximates their most recent pay.

I made three or four visits, each for two days, to the Leadership Academy over a period of four years. I interviewed APPers, as they refer to themselves, facilitators, graduates of the program, and the leadership of the academy, including the CEO, Sandra Stein. The APP is perhaps the best leadership training program that I have ever seen in any institution, period. I have visited the widely admired corporate training programs at IBM, General

Electric, and Hewlett-Packard. I've observed business school leadership programs at several leading universities. The APP is better than any of them. The APP has a focused mission: to prepare leaders for the New York City Department of Education, and it has an extremely dedicated staff. The staff plays a very unusual dual role. It acts as both instructor and evaluator. As one participant observed, "I'm in the middle school strand in a team of five. And in the room you have a facilitator but there's also an aide to the facilitator and sometimes there are other people in the room. And the first thing I realized is that although not everybody in the room is an APPer, they each have a notebook, and they're taking notes on everything that happens . . . they're pretty much watching everything." (Interview of May 2, 2007)

Although the story may be apocryphal, it is said that Chancellor Joel Klein once instructed the staff to ask the question, "Do I believe that this candidate will be willing to push the system, to confront his boss, to put his job at risk, in order to do what is best for his students? If the answer is no, kick him out of the program." Typically 10 to 15 percent of the members of a class are counseled out of APP. Eighty to 90 percent of APP graduates are hired as principals within one year. The curriculum is heavy on teaching the candidates how to interpret standardized test results to discover the precise areas of weakness in their students and then to know how to successfully move both a brand-new teacher and an old war horse to adopt new, more successful instructional approaches. They also practice, with professional actors, controlling their emotions in the face of an emergency, an angry parent, or a violent student. Their major assignments were described by another student: "What are the needs of the school? How do we change culture? How do we create strategies to change this school around? That was the basis for most of our projects. It's kind of like *The Apprentice,* where everyone takes a turn being the project manager every week. At the end of each project, there's a 360 feedback, where everyone in your group gives you honest feedback on you as a leader." (Interview of May 2, 2007)

Those who survive the Summer Intensive are assigned to work in a residency with a strong, experienced principal for the following academic year. The students are brought back together periodically for additional instruction. Several students said that the major lesson that they learned was how to accept honest feedback, really accept it, and improve. They also became comfortable with the idea that they would be held accountable, and that accountability in fact increases their autonomy, because a successful performer can be an independent decision maker. Others added that they also learned a great deal about how to give others honest feedback.

The facilitators and instructors pointed out that they assign students to teams with others who are the most dissimilar from one another. They point out to the students that when they go to a new school as principal, they will have to depend on a team of people who are not only unlike them, but may be resentful of them. Their job in the APP, as in later principal roles, is to learn how to successfully lead a diverse team. During the residency, the APPers observe classrooms, write evaluations of teacher practices, and then give feedback to the teacher. Later, they in turn receive feedback on how they handled that teacher contact and on how they might improve in giving feedback to teachers.

2. First Year Support

First Year Support (FYS) provides any first-year principals in the district with one-on-one coaching from a staff that consists almost entirely of successful, retired principals. Continuing support is also available for second- and third-year principals. During the 2006–7 school year, FYS provided coaching to 111 first-year principals, 94 second-year principals, and 39 third-year principals. First-year principals in the program participate in two retreats and five one-day training sessions in addition to the coaching.

3. New School Intensive

New School Intensive (NSI) provides all novice principals who are opening new, small schools with one-on-one coaching by retired principals who have small-school experience. Participants also receive leadership development and technical support. Although participation in NSI is voluntary, approximately 96 percent of first-year small-school principals participate in the program. During 2006–7, forty-two first-year principals participated, along with forty-seven second-year principals and thirty-one third-year principals.

4. Empowerment School Intensive

Empowerment School Intensive (ESI) was launched during the summer of 2006 in collaboration with the Empowerment Schools. ESI trains principals in three broad areas: (1) to analyze and use data to improve student outcomes; (2) to incorporate the Empowerment Schools performance targets and data into the work that is already under way at each school; and (3) to learn how to use the principal's autonomy to improve student outcomes. Each Empowerment School Intensive involves a team of teachers who choose a group of between fifteen and thirty low-performing students and devise strategies to assist those students in improving their performance. In the process of creating tailored instructional strategies for each of these students, the teachers gain experience in making use of the available data on students and in personalizing instructional approaches to fit the needs of each student. They then apply what they've learned to all students in their school.

Most school districts have annual principal turnover in the range of 10 to 15 percent each year. When a major reform takes place, that rate rises somewhat. When many new, small schools are launched, the need for additional principals increases further. The result, according to the Leadership Academy, is that about 45 percent of the principals in New York City have three or fewer years of experience as principals in the New York City Department of Education. Despite the relative inexperience of its body of principals, the city's schools have shown steady progress in student achievement since 2002. Some substantial portion of the credit for that success surely belongs to the New York City Leadership Academy and its staff.

7. SUSTAINING THE NEW ORGANIZATION OVER TIME

As of the summer of 2008, Joel Klein had served as chancellor for more than six years, a record for the city. Urban superintendents serve, on the average, for less than three years. Probably no single factor is more important in sustaining improvement than stability in the leadership of the district. Solidifying New York City's decentralization will take at least a few more years. If Klein serves as chancellor to the end of Mayor Bloomberg's current term, a total of eight years, the changes will have been fully developed, but they will need another four or five years of stability to be irrevocably in place. If Mayor Bloomberg serves a third four-year term in office and if the state legislature renews the current system of mayoral control of the schools, then New York City may permanently remake its school district.

Taking these uncertainties into account, Klein and his team

have put into place not only the Children First decentralization, but also other changes that will protect decentralization against the possibility of backsliding in the future. The first of these was school choice, which has empowered families to choose the school that they like best. In addition, the ten former area organizations have been abolished, and the administrative funds that they consumed have been allocated to schools. A return to area administration would have to take some of that money away from the schools, which would be politically difficult. Fair Student Funding, another major change, will ultimately enable teachers and parents to understand for the first time how much money their school has, and through the school councils and community representatives in each school, to have a say in how that money is spent. Taking that local flexibility away would be politically risky for a new mayor or chancellor. The annual surveys of parents, teachers, and students have brought out into the open new information about how satisfied people are with their schools, and if the district is recentralized, those survey results could plummet, which would be another deterrent to recentralization.

The accountability system and the user-friendly district website have enabled parents to get honest, unvarnished information about their child's school. That system provides principals and teachers with motivation for improving the schools and is also a defense against any future changes, such as recentralization, that might harm that performance. The Leadership Academy provides a strong source of skilled principals, and its continued strength will guarantee the success of decentralization for many years into the future. If the central office staffs are fundamentally reorganized so that the dedicated employees who work there are rewarded for assisting schools rather than for guarding the funds that they have been told to protect, the last source of an easy return to centralization will be gone.

Perhaps the best way to guarantee the continuation of decentralization in New York City's schools is to make sure that the public is well informed about the performance of the schools. In past years, that information did not exist. Now, it does. No one can guarantee that the next mayor or chancellor will even understand the decentralization of the district, let alone want to continue it. That's not necessary, though. All that is necessary is that the public have easy access to valid information about how the schools are doing. If decentralization produces good education, the public will demand it and guarantee that it will continue.

How to Identify a Superintendent Who Can Lead Change

School districts that want to achieve their own full-scale decentralization and that also need to fill their superintendency ought to take note of some of Joel Klein's strengths and weaknesses. Klein is not an experienced educator and he had never before worked in a school district. That was a disadvantage, because education on a large scale is very complex, and he had a lot to learn. Fortunately, this disadvantage was more than balanced by his strengths. First, he was able to recognize and attract talented people who either knew the school district intimately or had skills and strengths that would be valuable. Second, he was willing to grant freedom to those people, something that many leaders do not do. Third, he had a very clear vision of what he wanted to accomplish: empower schools and motivate them to enable poor, minority, and recently immigrated students to succeed at the highest level. It is impossible to overestimate the importance of this point. Some superintendents are careerists whose primary goal is to get to be superintendent and then to continue to be superintendent for as long as possible. Their idea of success is to keep the teachers union happy, the school board happy, and the parents in the dark. They have no idea what they'd like to accomplish as superintendent—they just want the big office with the private bathroom and the center chair at staff meetings. Pass them by. Look for a person who knows what he or she wants to accomplish for the students. Fourth, he had courage. On one occasion, when I explained that he could take a path that would deliver half a loaf, which would be a gain to these students—and avoid conflict with a powerful external faction—or he could go for the whole loaf and take a personal beating, Klein looked me in the eye with a grin and replied, "Now, why do you think I took this job?" Naturally, he went for the whole loaf. And in the end, he got it.

Fifth, Klein had experience working in large, decentralized organizations, including the U.S. government and Bertelsmann. He understood what it takes to change a very large organization. Sixth, Joel Klein is an unusually bright person, one who was able to grasp the essence of a very large number of complicated issues, and do it quickly. Finally, Klein had another advantage of inestimable value: he had only one boss, Mayor Bloomberg.

This may seem too large a task to ask of one superintendent and one school board or mayor, and it may seem that your school district will never get to where New York City is going. That isn't so. It does take a collection of unusually dedicated and talented people, and perhaps some luck, to find the Northwest Passage, to produce the first computer, or to get to the moon for the first time. Once the first pioneers have shown how to do it, though, ordinary people can learn from their example and get there, too.

What Are the Early Results in New York City?

Although more time is needed to tell whether this district-wide reform will succeed in raising the performance of all students, by the end of the first school year of district-wide reform, 2007–8, some positive results were apparent. In math, 74.3 percent of the students in grades 3 through 8, district-wide, met or exceeded the state standards, up from 65.1 percent at the end of the previous school year. In English, 57.6 percent met or exceeded the standards, up from 50.8 percent the year before. In both cases these gains exceeded those for the state as a whole. Black fourth grade students narrowed the mathematics gap with white and Asian students by 16.4 percentage points from 2002 to 2007, while Hispanic students narrowed their gap by 15.2 percentage points. Both black and Hispanic eighth graders also slightly reduced their gaps, and both groups slightly reduced their English gaps in both fourth and eighth grades.

Mayor Bloomberg announced the results of the second year of district-wide survey results. Overall, 806,539 surveys were returned for a response rate of 55 percent, up from 41 percent the previous year. Sixty-one percent of teachers returned completed surveys, an increase of 17 percentage points, and 40 percent of parents did so, up from the previous year's 26 percent. Ninety-two percent of parents were satisfied or very satisfied with the education their child received, up from 88 percent the previous year. Eighty-five percent of teachers said that their school leaders made clear what was expected of them, up from 79 percent the year before. Student results made clear some of the work that has yet to be done: only 53 percent said that students who get good grades at their school are respected by others, up from 51 percent the year before.

If New York City can do it, any school district can. Among

the inventory of types of school reform from performance-based pay to managed instruction, none is as challenging to implement as district-wide decentralization. On the other hand, no other solution can produce the same reductions in student loads or provide as much personal attention to each student. The larger the district, the more difficult it will be to decentralize. The good news is that every school district in America should find it easier to decentralize than New York City did.

5

THE FIRST GENERATION: BOSTON, HOUSTON, AND SEATTLE

Edmonton, of course, was the original pioneer, having begun its implementation of decentralization more than thirty years ago, learning by trial and error how to do it. Approximately twenty years after that initiative, the first generation of decentralizers appeared in the United States: Boston, Houston, and Seattle. Each of the three was aware of the Edmonton example, and both Houston and Seattle devoted substantial effort to visiting and studying what Edmonton had done and how they had done it.

Each of these cities approached school district decentralization in its own unique way, though all included our Five Pillars and Four Freedoms. Boston was perhaps the most unusual in its approach, because its decentralized schools developed as a renegade movement that was initially treated with indifference or worse by the central office staff, though that attitude eventually gave way to something more akin to a partnership. Houston and Seattle are very different in size, but they adopted implementations that were similar in many ways. These three districts deserve credit for their willingness to be pioneers, but they were also at what some call the "bleeding edge" of change—they made missteps that in some cases cost them dearly. In all three of these first-generation decentralizers, the catchphrase might have been "Leave it to the principals!" because that's what they did. Each of the three empowered their principals (in Boston, the twenty who ran Pilot Schools; in the other two, all principals were empowered), but none of the three realigned its central staffs to support them. As we will see, that and other elements of administrative infrastructure are necessary for sustained, successful decentralization.

Every school district that embarks on the road to decentralization will, in a real sense, be doing its own pioneering. It will be traveling in regions that are entirely foreign to it. Though the voyage will be full of surprises and challenges for any new travelers on this path, there are now charts that identify some of the greatest perils and mark some of the safe passages, as a result of the lessons learned by these three districts.

Boston Public—A Diverse Urban District

Boston Public Schools serves 56,190 students in 144 schools, of which 20 are Pilot Schools (including 2 state-chartered Horace Mann schools). Seventy-one percent of the students of Boston Public Schools are from low-income families and qualify for either a free or reduced-price school lunch, compared to 76 percent in New York City. Three of the schools are grade 7–12 selective admissions, or "exam" schools, including the oldest public school in America, the Boston Latin School, founded in

1635. Forty-one percent of Boston's students are black, 35 percent are Hispanic, 14 percent are white, and 9 percent are Asian. These proportions approximate that of New York City's schools.

Boston experienced significant "white flight" during the 1970s and 1980s era of forced busing. Enrollment in the district fell from about 90,000 to roughly where enrollment stands today, around 56,000. The school district was thrown into chaos as budgets were slashed and racial tensions rose. Today, 27 percent of Boston's students attend private, parochial, or charter schools or attend suburban schools through a cross-district program.

Boston, like New York City, has a school system controlled by the mayor, as a result of a 1989 referendum. Unlike New York, though, Boston has a seven-person School Committee that governs the district, with the committee members appointed by the mayor. The contract between Boston Public Schools and the Boston Teachers Union permits maximum class sizes of twenty-two in grades K–2, twenty-five in grades 3–5, twenty-eight in grades 6–8, and thirty-one in grades 9–12, among the lowest of any urban area in the nation. The four-year high school graduation rate for the class of 2006 was 59 percent, with 17 percent still in school for a fifth year.

In the NAEP eleven-city tests, Boston's fourth graders rose in English from 16 percent at proficient or above in 2003 to 20 percent in 2007. Those scoring "advanced" rose from 2 to 4 percent. Among eighth graders, English scores were flat or rose by one or two percentage points over the period. By comparison, math scores rose dramatically in Boston, from 12 to 27 percent at or above proficient, and from 1 to 3 percent at the advanced level. Eighth grade math scores on the NAEP also rose, from 17 to 27 percent at or above proficient, between 2003 and 2007. Boston's eighth grade math scores were slightly higher than those in New

York City, while fourth grade scores were in each case a few percentage points below those for New York City.[1]

BOSTON MIGHT BE THE BEST-RUN CENTRALIZED DISTRICT IN AMERICA

Boston had the benefit of a long-serving superintendent, Thomas Payzant, who served from 1995 through June of 2006, nearly eleven years. Payzant had previously served for about eleven years as the superintendent in San Diego, California. He was attracted to Boston in part because Mayor Thomas Menino offered him a five-year contract, longer than he had ever had before.

Superintendent Payzant had a deep belief in public schools as a source of cohesion in our society and of opportunity for those who are at the bottom of the economic ladder. He wanted his district's "choice" system to produce schools that combine middle-class with at-risk students, though that's not yet happened. He believes that good teachers in a stable system with strong principals are the key to success, and arguably he managed to create that. He also believes that effective principals are an absolute necessity: "I would say that one of the things that has characterized my work here has been really focusing on principal leadership. And one of the huge state policy decisions that was made, which I mentioned when we last spoke, was in the Education Reform Bill that goes back to '93/'94—principals were taken out of collective bargaining." After detailing the union situation in Massachusetts, he continued, "That was number one. The second was that when they were taken out of collective bargaining, they could only serve on one-, two-, or three-year contracts, and the superintendent is the decision maker with respect to who's selected and how long they serve. And beyond that, superintendents, particularly in Boston, were given control of all personnel. So there's no requirement to go through a school committee to get approval of personnel employment. In fact, I arrived in October, and in April I non-renewed the contracts of six principals and they've never been back." Payzant has also attended to the district's need to develop new, strong principals: "We've focused on creating a group of aspiring principals and then a solid development program for those who are going to become principals." He went on to describe Boston's training program: "The Principal Fellows Program that we have—now, thanks to Eli [Eli Broad, Chairman of the Broad Foundation], in its fourth year—is competitive and small: ten to eleven fellows each year in the program. They have a summer program which is curriculum-based. During the academic year they continue with their seminars and study and are four days a week, full time, with a very successful principal in the district." (All quotes from Thomas Payzant are from an interview on October 31, 2006.)

Despite his commitment to having a strong principal in every school, Payzant believes in centralized school districts, and not because he likes power—he appears to be ill-suited to that role—but because, as he puts it, "I don't believe it's possible, given whatever the recent number is—90,000 to 95,000 public schools in America—that in your lifetime or mine, or perhaps that of our children and grandchildren . . . there will be the kind of policy direction and resource allocation that will enable all of them to act as 'tubs on their own bottom' and figure out what needs to be done." What he means by this is that he doesn't see any way to create an accountability web that is reliable enough to give principals and their schools autonomy. At the same time, he is aware that unless every "tub," or school, sits solidly on the ground on its own bottom, if they are instead stacked one upon the other in a large vertical hierarchy, all of them are likely to fall over. Faced with this stark choice, Payzant has opted to keep a tight central office rein on his principals.

Payzant talks with enthusiasm about the systems that he has created—systems that have improved curriculum, classroom instruction, and data on student performance, all of which have been implemented across the board in all Boston public schools. Some observers of the district regard Payzant as the finest of the traditional district superintendents. By this they mean that they hold him in high regard because he brought Boston Public Schools from chaos to stability with a traditional, top-down approach, and because they universally regard him as thoughtful, open-minded, and very expert on just about every aspect of K–12 education. Boston, though, is a traditional, centralized school district that grants relatively little autonomy to its principals. If centralization can succeed in an urban district, Boston should be the best example. The district is relatively well funded, with smaller Total Student Loads than most, and it was led for many years by one of the most talented educators of our time.

Although Superintendent Payzant ran a centralized district, in retirement he acknowledges the drawbacks of centralization, noting that "part of the problem is that they want a one-size-fits-all solution." He had, after all, implemented a system of school choice, a move that decentralized a major decision to families, but since the schools have the same schedules, staffing, and curricula, the range of choices is limited. Payzant's traditional side emerges as he adds that "the challenge is, how do you take whatever seems to work with the most students? How do you take it to scale, and provide the kind of supports that are necessary, so that student achievement will improve and we'll make more solid progress in closing the gap?" By "take it to scale," Payzant meant his two major efforts, Focus on Children I and II, each a five-year plan to specify performance standards by grade and subject, to give all teachers at the beginning of each school year a curriculum calendar and pacing guides, and to enhance the diagnosis of student progress by adding district-wide tests "at the end of chapters," at midyear, and at year-end. In addition, deputy superintendents visit each school and meet with each department to ensure adherence to the district-wide plan. Though Payzant is anything but a rigid thinker, his approach to instruction clearly fits the category of a top-down, one-size-fits-all approach.

As he later reflected on those five-year plans, Payzant puzzled over how he might have introduced some flexibility into the standardized curricula, schedules, and staffing formulas that had served Boston so well: "I'm still not giving up on systems of schools, but I do think they've got to be more nimble in providing the kind of environment that a variety of schools can exist within them." Payzant had raised the district up out of its troubles through systems of testing, curriculum development, teacher coaching, and others. Although he had success with his systems, he still didn't seem confident that the systems on which he had relied would ultimately get Boston Public Schools where it needs to be.

Payzant knew enough to be skeptical that centralization was the whole answer, but he feared even more what might happen if he gave each school autonomy. That fear seemed to stem from the diversity that had rapidly overtaken Boston, with each newly arriving group becoming a political constituency with its own educational agenda, adding to the cacophony of unions, community organizations, and other seekers of self-interest. This overwhelming diversity, it seemed to him, had undermined people's willingness to sacrifice any part of their narrow agendas for the more fundamental common good: "I worry about that a lot and I've seen that over the years as I've sat through hundreds of hours of school board meetings, and what happens with every interest group coming in and the tendency to rather than have your budget be a financial plan that is aligned with the priorities of your educational plan, to have a budget that is chopped up by throwing a little bit to every special interest group that comes in." It apparently did not occur to Payzant that what he was attempting—a standardized solution for very diverse communities—might be impossible to achieve. Payzant did not appear to believe that if each school had substantial autonomy, it would find the specific instructional program that best fit its unique needs. One is tempted to see in the contrast between New York City and Boston a fundamental difference along the lines of McGregor's Theory X and Theory Y, that is, that most people, given freedom, will usually do the right thing (X) versus that too much freedom will likely produce chaos (Y).

The dual goals of producing standardized educational systems and allowing some flexibility led to visible tension and occasional confusion in Boston's non-Pilot schools. Some principals, for example, felt that they did have substantial autonomy: "Right now there is enough money for [this many] teachers. However, and we don't do it too often, were I to decide that I want one teacher less and with that amount of money I want more assistants or a guidance advisor or whatever—I would just write that into my budget!" (All interviews with principals took place during November 2006. Specific interview dates are not reported in order to maintain anonymity.) Another principal was more direct: "They don't even know what I have." As in every district, a few principals were simply inventive: "I try to be creative . . . so I will go and hire a counselor and I will say to them, 'You are the registrar, on paper.'"

For the most part, though, Boston's non–Pilot School principals acknowledged that they enjoyed very little freedom. For example, when it comes to scheduling the district-standard six-hour day, one principal remarked of Boston's centralized systems, "We are an 8:30 to 2:30 school. They have three tier schools. There are 7:40 to 1:40, 8:30 to 2:30, and then you have the 9:20 to 3:20 schools. You cannot change those tiers based on buses and the economics of what it would cost to switch unless you are able to link to another school that has the same tier, but even then it is difficult based on where the buses are coming from. So you do not have much autonomy in order to do that." Yet another principal, asked if he could convert some of his budget to hire an administrative person if he so desired, replied, "Impossible!"

Boston Public Schools have pursued a program of research, analysis, and participative dialogue that is admirable. It has stuck to a consistent approach for more than ten years, and as a result, it has made steady progress in student achievement. The district has made great progress since the relatively chaotic years before Mayor Thomas Menino and Superintendent Thomas Payzant took over. New superintendent Dr. Carol Johnson, who took office in August of 2007, appears to favor the creation of more Pilot Schools. Most Bostonians seem to be quite satisfied with this approach (though we can't know for sure, because Boston Public Schools does not make survey results public), in large part because of the high regard they had for their former superintendent.

Meanwhile, far away from district headquarters, a revolution was under way that would challenge the traditional district systems. This revolution was a result of the very diversity that Payzant feared would ruin Boston Public Schools, and its participants wanted to have the freedom to design their own solutions for their own situation. These Pilot Schools did not want to be force-fed the "one best solution" from headquarters.

THE BOSTON PILOT SCHOOLS

The Young Achievers Science and Mathematics Pilot School (K–8) is located in Jamaica Plain, Boston, near the Arnold Arboretum. Young Achievers is a member of the Coalition of Essential Schools. The 287 students attend each day from 9:15 a.m. until 5:00 p.m., for seven hours and forty-five minutes. The student body is 67.6 percent black, 22.0 percent Hispanic, 5.9 percent white, and 2.1 percent Asian. Seventy percent are from low-income families. Twenty percent are special education students, about average for the district. Daily attendance averages 96.3 percent.

Although Young Achievers has a diverse student body, it is often thought of as a school for African Americans, and it accepts that role with pride. If Young Achievers is a "black" school, it is a successful black school. On the state MCAS test in English for 2005, 87 percent of third graders received passing marks (versus 78 percent for all Boston Public Schools students), as did 100 percent of 7th graders (versus 80 percent for the district). In the math test, however, only 54 percent of fourth graders passed—for lessons unknown to me—(versus 73 percent for the district), as did 81 percent of eighth grade students (versus 52 percent for the district). The results for 2007 were even better, with 100 percent of third grade students achieving passing marks in reading (and 48 percent proficient or advanced), compared to an unchanged 78 percent for the district (with 32 percent proficient or advanced).

The school has fifty-four employees and six student teachers. Twenty-three of these (including the principal and the assistant principal) are credentialed teachers, and another twenty-three are non-credentialed teachers or paraprofessionals who assist the head teachers. Every classroom has two teachers. There are ten administrative staff, including a principal and an assistant principal (who doubles as a math coach), along with an IT specialist, a nurse, a custodian, two office clerical workers, and three student support coordinators, who arrange internships for eighth graders, schedule support services, and so on. The principal points out that "we spend our money on class size and on adult-child ratio." As a result, the school has no director of instruction, fewer instructional coaches than is standard, and lacks some of the other administrative positions that are standard in Boston. In fact, there is little if anything at Young Achievers that conforms to the systems of Boston Public Schools, other than the required standardized tests. As a Pilot School, Young Achievers does not have to conform to the district's systems.

We are in the K–5 building. It's more than one hundred years old, but it looks good—it's been well maintained, and it is very clean. The principal, Virginia Chalmers, is visiting a K–2 classroom that includes both four-year-old and five-year-old children. The first grade is visiting the Museum of Fine Arts today, so there are nineteen students who have the use of two connected classrooms, each with little child-size round tables and chairs, with a few Apple computers, a terrarium, a listening center with headphones, a bookcase with books, and cots for nap time. It's November 2, early in the school year, but student work is already on the walls. The first graders have put up displays about bees along with their projects on fruits, vegetables, and grains. The second graders are about to leave for a field trip to the arboretum. As we've said, every classroom in grades K–5 has two teachers on duty between 10:00 a.m. and 4:00 p.m.: a head teacher, who is credentialed, and a community teacher, who typically is not.

Down the hallway, a third grade classroom of eighteen students has a head teacher, a community teacher, and a paraprofessional who is required by the Individualized Education Program (IEP) of a special education student. So there are three adults for the eighteen children in this class. The room is equipped with four iMacs and a printer, with another three iMacs in a large coatroom, and the books are neatly arranged by category, including biography, poetry, realistic fiction, narrative nonfiction, humor, and Harry Potter.

In grades 4 and 5, one teacher teaches math to all of the fourth and fifth graders, for a total of two double-period classes of twenty students, or forty students. She may also have an elective course of five to ten students for a TSL of 45 to 50. The students also have physical education (soccer for all, at the moment), art, and music. Another teacher teaches science to all of the fourth and fifth graders. The third course is humanities.

In the middle-school building, students have a two-hour block of humanities (English language arts and history) and a two-hour block of math/science, plus advisory of eight to ten students that meets twice a week. The school has decided on single-gender advisories, so each grade level has separate advisories for girls and boys. The district allocation is not enough to pay for all of this staff, so Ginny Chalmers raises another $400,000 or so each year by applying for outside grants with the help of a parent/community committee.

Young Achievers is a happy and successful school, though the teachers and staff work hard and have long days. Everyone here is dedicated to the mission, and all are aware that the school enjoys a special position within Boston's African-American community. Ginny Chalmers is a hands-on principal who enthusiastically engages her teachers on the topic of instruction. With a sixth grade math teacher, for example, she observes that the school does not believe in "tracking" students into fast and slow math groups because, for example, a student might have trouble with number sets but be very comfortable with geometry. She doesn't want the school to lock any part of a child's mind into a slow track if it's ready for a fast one. Ginny continues, "So we might get a sixth grader new to our school who's four years behind in math and they just don't ever want to work on math. But then, if you say okay, . . . we're going to get there . . . it starts to feed on itself. It really does because human beings want to develop, they just do!"

Chalmers is a successful principal and knows it. She's willing to talk openly on the record about Boston Public Schools: "Tom . . . really was able to stabilize this district in a way that it never had been before. But I always used to say to him, you know, we had these two very different models of reform, and one was highly centralized and highly controlled, and the other was the Pilot School network. And I said, 'I don't get it. What's the deal? Do you really believe in both of them?' And he'd say something like 'Yes,' or 'I think so,' or something." (Interview of November 3, 2006)

DAN FRENCH AND THE CENTER FOR COLLABORATIVE EDUCATION SUPPORT A REVOLUTION

Boston has twenty Pilot Schools, the first of them founded in the mid-1990s, a few years after the state of Massachusetts first permitted charter schools. Pilot Schools are public schools that operate under the ultimate oversight of the superintendent of Boston Public Schools, but that enjoy great operating autonomy. Every Pilot School must have a governing board consisting of teachers, parents, and community members, and no one of these groups may hold a majority of seats. The boards have the authority to hire and fire the principal. They hire a principal by submitting one nominee to the superintendent. If the superintendent does not approve the nominee, the board must submit another name.

These powerful governing boards play a role that is quite different from the school site committees that we've seen in other districts. The crucial difference is that the Pilot School boards are accountable for the financial and academic performance of the school. If a Pilot School accumulates a large enough deficit, it will go out of business. If a traditional Boston school goes into a serious deficit, the superintendent will have to bail it out, and thus the school site committee is not really responsible or accountable. As a result, school site committees compromise the accountability system within a district, but they are the accountability system in a Boston Pilot School.

Boston also has fourteen charter schools, all of which are nonunion. The Boston Teachers Union and the Massachusetts Federation of Teachers have strongly opposed any increase in the number of charter schools, with considerable success. Nonetheless, Boston's charter schools have prospered. A 2006 study by the Massachusetts Department of Education found that, as a group, charter schools in Boston scored "significantly higher" than the district average each year from 2002 to 2005 in both English language arts and mathematics. The higher scores held for black, Hispanic, special education, and English Language Learner students.

Partly in response to the popularity of charter schools, the Boston Teachers Union approached the school district (before Thomas Payzant had become superintendent) with the suggestion that together they design a small group of schools that would operate within the district and that would have simplified union contracts and great autonomy as a way to compete against the charter schools, which were proving to be very popular with families. The teachers union and the district jointly retained Dan French, a former state education official, to help them to develop the contract that would create the Pilot Schools. In the end, the two sides agreed that the new schools would have very brief union agreements of two or three pages, that at least two-thirds of the teachers at a school would have to agree for their school to switch to Pilot status, and that teachers at each Pilot School would be invited to renew their Pilot School employment each year by signing a brief work agreement that set out working hours, duties, and pay. The Pilot Schools would be independent of the school district and would instead be governed by their governance committees. In return, the teachers union retained the right to veto any application for a Pilot School.

By all accounts, everyone who was involved had expected that only a handful of schools would want to make the switch, since it would likely end up meaning more hours of work for teachers, with fewer union protections. To their surprise, many teachers were enthusiastic about the idea, a large number of schools applied for conversion, and eleven conversions were approved in the first few years, between 1995 and 2001. Seven more conversion applications were subsequently approved, though the teachers union discouraged these. Two other schools joined the Pilot Schools through state rather than Boston applications, before the union exercised its right to veto every subsequent Pilot School application for the next several years.

The Boston Pilot Schools have enrolled a student body that almost, but not quite, mirrors that of the district as a whole. Of the Pilot School students, 57.4 percent are black (versus 51.2 across the district), 23.2 percent are Latino (versus 33.7 percent), 11.6 percent are white (versus 9.7 percent), and 7.3 percent are Asian/Pacific Islander (versus 5.1 percent). About 10 percent are special education students in the Pilot Schools, compared to 20 percent in the district as a whole, and some district officials feel that the Pilot Schools have been unwilling to take the special education students whose needs are the greatest, perhaps because neither the district schools nor the Pilot Schools have Weighted Student Formula systems, and thus the Pilot Schools have a strong financial incentive not to take students who are very expensive to serve. In addition, the ten Pilot high schools have a more selective group of students based on previous attendance in middle school: 7.2 percent of district ninth graders had attendance rates less than 80 percent in eighth grade, while Pilot Schools had only 2.9 percent such students. In addition, Pilot School ninth graders were less likely to have received warnings on their eighth grade MCAS math tests (48.0 percent) than district ninth graders (58.5 percent). It is likely that more of those Pilot School ninth graders had been educated in Pilot middle schools. It is also possible that the parents who chose to send their children to Pilot Schools were somehow better educated, more focused on educational achievement, or otherwise advantaged over their Boston Public Schools counterparts.

Pilot School principals do not receive coaching or training from the district. Instead, they receive administrative and principal coaching from the Center for Collaborative Education (CCE), a nonprofit entity founded by Dan French. French had the task of facing off against the central office staff to win budget control for the Pilot School principals. At the outset, before CCE existed, each Pilot School principal had to negotiate on her own with the district staff over her budget. Each came away with a different amount of money per student, depending on how well she negotiated. French wrestled that central staff over the budget, line by line, getting as much money and as much autonomy for the Pilot Schools as he was able. The district central staff seemed at times to be his adversary rather than his ally.

In 2007, the CCE published a four-year evaluation of the Pilot Schools. This evaluation found that Pilot Schools had an average attendance rate over the four years that ranged from a high of

95.3 percent to a low of 94.4 percent, while the district schools ranged from 90.6 percent to 89.1 percent over the period, a difference of about 5 percentage points in favor of the Pilot Schools. On the grade 10 MCAS exam in English, Pilot Schools averaged a 78.9 percent pass rate, compared to 59.3 percent for district schools, a large difference. On the grade 10 math test, the Pilot Schools averaged a passing rate of 64.8 percent, compared to 52.6 percent for district schools. It should also be noted that the Pilot Schools had a dramatic increase in their math passing rate, from 39.2 percent in 2002 to 52.0 percent in 2005. Finally, Pilot Schools had a four-year high school graduation rate of 75.7 percent compared to 52.2 percent for other district schools, also a large difference.

It seems likely that the relative success of the Pilot Schools was due at least in part to their lower percentages of students who previously had low attendance rates and low math scores. It also seems likely that many Pilot Schools were able to implement changes that brought real achievement gains to their students. While one cannot conclusively say from this evidence that the Pilot Schools outperformed other district schools with the same students, it is clear that the Pilot Schools have served their students at least as well as Boston Public Schools has done. Preliminary results from new studies now under way reinforce the conclusion that Boston's Pilot Schools are exceeding the gains made by district schools that serve similar student populations.

My research team performed its own independent analysis of student performance in the Pilot Schools. We did not attempt to compare these schools to all U.S. schools. Had we done so, it is likely that the Pilot Schools would have been standouts. Our objective was only to compare them to the other autonomously managed schools among our eight study districts, in order to learn which forms of decentralization have the greatest effect on student performance. Our evaluation shows how effectively the autonomous schools of each of the eight districts used their freedom. While our analysis found that reductions in Total Student Load made the greatest difference in student performance, we also evaluated several additional instructional changes that autonomous schools could have made. Not all of the autonomous schools in the eight districts acted to reduce TSL aggressively, and not all of them attacked as many other changes as they could have.

Overall, our results show that the Pilot Schools in Boston fell below the average score for the autonomous schools in our sample on improvements in "percent proficient," the federal standard. A recent (2009), carefully controlled study commissioned by The Boston Foundation arrives at a similar conclusion. That study also found that charter schools by far outperformed both Pilot Schools and district schools in Boston. (Atila Abdulkadiroglu et al., *Informing the Debate*)[2] Although Pilot School principals on average controlled 75 percent of their budget, some controlled a good deal less and others controlled more. For every 10 percentage point increase in budget control, Pilot high schools reduced TSL by 4 students, compared to 25 students in New York City. However, the Boston public high schools, which are not autonomous, had very low TSLs of 85.4 on average, well below any other district. Given those very low TSLs achieved by Payzant, perhaps there was not much room for the Pilot Schools to reduce TSL further. Our results also show that for schools that are similar in poverty level and previous student performance, Boston's Pilot Schools did not significantly enhance student performance, compared to the other autonomous schools in our study. (See Appendix 6.)

After the retirement of Superintendent Payzant, change continued, with some signs that are promising for the continued success of the Pilot Schools, though with a few concerns as well. For one thing, as of 2007, Pilot School principals have been required by the district to attend the same training and to receive the same coaching that is now required of all Boston Public Schools principals. The financial staff of the district has, by all accounts, accepted responsibility for seeing to it that Pilot Schools are fully and equally funded and is now acting to maintain the budgetary freedom of those schools. Other changes suggest that the administration is moving to embrace the Pilot Schools as an integral part of the district, rather than viewing them as an outpost of renegades, as they were previously felt to be by some.

Understandably, Dan French and the CCE may view these changes with a mixture of relief and of trepidation. Surely the additional support of the district's central staff must be welcome, but the Pilot Schools, founded on a Boston Tea Party–like taste for freedom, can be expected to guard with vigilance their continued independence. In the best of all possible worlds, the entire district may ultimately move away from its past centralized attitude and toward a new vision that embraces the idea of empowered schools.

WHAT WE CAN LEARN FROM THE BOSTON EXPERIENCE

What can we conclude from this study of the Boston Pilot Schools? First, we can see that real increases in principal autonomy are possible, as we've seen before. Real empowered principals are not a theoretical concept without real-world application. Second, we note that the Boston school district did not at first embrace the Pilot Schools but left them to fend for themselves with minimal financial or administrative support. The district did not take steps to guarantee that Pilot School principals were rigorously selected and intensively trained, nor did it provide new principals with coaching. The district did not reorganize the central office so that it would support rather than hinder the efforts of the Pilot Schools. Had the district been more supportive, the Pilot Schools might have become even more successful than they have been. Third, the Pilot Schools were meant from the outset to be independent of Boston Public Schools, and they have jealously guarded that independence. As a result, the reforms born in the Pilot Schools have by and large not influenced the other Boston schools. Fourth, the Boston Teachers Union, which had initiated the idea of creating the Pilot Schools, soon became hostile to them, and it has apparently not altered that negative posture. That hostile attitude has had the dual result of limiting the growth of Pilot Schools and of raising even higher the wall between the Pilot Schools and the other Boston schools, thus guaranteeing that the positive lessons of the Pilot Schools have not migrated into the district as a whole. We see once again that successful decentralization requires multi-pronged change and that all systems must be aligned if a decentralizing district is to reach its potential for increasing student achievement.

Boston Public Schools is an award-winning school district. It has achieved steady and sometimes dramatic gains in student performance. The Boston Pilot Schools have grown up largely outside of the district organization, and they have established a successful network of autonomous schools. It is remarkable that a district that has pursued an explicit and consistent path of centralized management has nonetheless permitted this independent entity to flourish. Perhaps the Pilot Schools survived in part because the community rallied around them and protected them.

Most centralized urban districts have found ways to sabotage or undermine local attempts to establish autonomous schools, while in Boston they had a chance to grow at least modestly. Without the support of important community organizations like the Boston Foundation, though, the outcome might have been altogether different.

Together, the centralized Boston Public Schools and the autonomous Pilot Schools make an odd couple. Perhaps only an unusually thoughtful leader like Thomas Payzant could have achieved this feat. Stay tuned, though, because there is a chance that the district will conclude that to continue its improvement it, too, should embrace the idea of autonomy for principals. On the other hand, it is possible that only a leader as dedicated as Dan French can sustain the Pilot School network, and that it will ultimately decline. Or perhaps the two systems will continue side-by-side as friendly rivals for decades to come. Only time will tell.

Houston Moves to the Top Among Large Texas Districts

The Houston Independent School District educates approximately 202,000 students at 306 campuses and programs. The student population is 58 percent Hispanic, 30 percent black, 9 percent white, and 3 percent Asian/Pacific Islander. Seventy-eight percent of the students are from low-income families, and 27 percent are Limited English Proficient students who, combined, speak more than ninety different native languages.

The Houston decentralization effort was launched by the school board in 1990, with *A Declaration of Beliefs and Visions*. This document, which the district continues to honor, called for fostering strong relationships between teachers and students, shared decision making through a decentralized system, a focus on performance rather than on compliance, and a common core of subjects for all students. In 2005, the board adopted its Board Monitoring System, which requires the superintendent to report regularly through quantifiable measures on academic progress, operational effectiveness, public and employee support, and facility management. In 2006, the board adopted a performance pay system under which teachers can earn annual bonuses of up to $3,000 for helping to improve student performance. Houston has long had a principal training academy that has been a point of pride within the district.

By 1999, the Houston Independent School District had made many changes that were revolutionary for the times. The school board had been entirely changed to a group that unanimously supported decentralization. Tenure had been eliminated for senior central office administrators and principals, who received in return the opportunity to earn annual performance bonuses of up to $5,000 in 2001 plus ongoing administrative stipends of $7,500 per year. Superintendent Rod Paige, a nontraditional superintendent who had never previously worked in a school district but had served as dean of the College of Education at Texas Southern University and had been a member of the Houston School board, had moved 254 staff from the central office out to one of twelve regional offices (now replaced by five regions) where they could better serve the needs of the schools. Student achievement had begun to rise.

Many of the board members were satisfied with the progress, but others worried that the changes had not been hard-wired into the district and that a new school board or a superintendent with a top-down leadership style could return the district to its former centralized ways.[3] Schools were still budgeted through the old enrollment formula system that sent positions rather than dollars to each school, and a principal of a typical elementary school with a total annual budget of about $2 million had control over less than $100,000 of it. In an attempt to give staying power to the decentralization that they had created, the school board in 1999 approved the implementation of a Weighted Student Formula system. They had closely studied this approach in Edmonton for several years and decided to adopt it. The Houston school district also oversees twenty charter schools that are operated by universities and various other organizations. According to the district, about 60 percent of the district funds are now allocated directly to schools for their discretionary control. Houston was included in both of our studies, in 2000 and in 2006. In the first study, district principals reported that they controlled on the average 59 percent of their budgets, while in the second study principals reported control over 74 percent, a substantial gain.[4]

Houston, like all school districts, has its critics. Many of these have taken issue with the focus that both the state of Texas and the Houston school district place on improvement in test scores. They argue that too much emphasis on test scores will create pressure for schools to "teach to the test," particularly when publishing companies sell both the test and the test preparation books to the same district. That pressure may produce narrowed curricula, repeated drilling on likely test items, and a false reading of student improvement, they argue. A few years ago a scandal erupted over falsified test scores in several Houston schools, clear testimony to the potential harm that can result from an overemphasis on test scores. The measurement of school performance might be more balanced if the district added site visits to each school and questionnaires filled out by students and teachers to its complement of accountability and performance measures.

Beginning in 1992, the Houston school district established Shared Decision-Making Committees (SDMCs) consisting of teachers, parents, and community representatives to advise each of its principals on budget, curriculum, staffing patterns, organization, methods for input by parents, staff, and the local community, and school improvement. About 46 percent of the 2,655 SDMC committee members responded to forty-four questions in an annual online evaluation of this process in 2007. Forty-three percent reported that their SDMC functioned as a decision-making body, while 33.5 percent said that their committee was advisory to the principal. Eighty-eight percent agreed that "I felt very comfortable and free to express my thoughts at our SDMC meetings," while 78.3 percent felt that "the principal implemented the majority of the SDMC recommendations." Although these committees do not have formal decision power, it is apparent that a large proportion feel that they are part of the decision process. In most cases, that perception among committee members likely stems from a healthy partnership between the principal and teachers at the school.

Another set of surveys of one thousand district households and three hundred parents of district students was taken during 2006. Fifty-one percent of the community respondents felt that the district is "on the right track," while 68 percent of district parents felt that way. Eighty-two percent of the community respondents said that the district uses taxpayer dollars wisely. Seventy-nine percent of parents said that the district treats parents as valued partners, while only 35 percent of parents felt that the district has enough computers in its schools. Sixty-nine percent of parents said they were satisfied with the board of education, 70 percent said that of the superintendent, 79 percent said that of principals, and 79 percent also said that of teachers. While these survey results are not as positive as the ones we reviewed earlier from Edmonton, they are good. Surely any elected public official would be pleased to have survey results as good as those of the Houston school district. All of the survey results are readily accessible on the user-friendly district website.

Every Houston district school receives three separate accountability reports. First is the report produced by the Texas Education Agency (TEA), which rates schools and school districts as exemplary, recognized, academically acceptable, or academically unacceptable, based on scores on the state test, the TAKS, on dropout rates, and on four-year completion rates. Test results for each major racial group and for economically disadvantaged students are broken out separately. Second is the Houston district's own accountability system, which rates schools both on progress over the last year and on performance compared to other district schools. These ratings are also based on standardized tests, including the state TAKS test and additional district-specific standardized tests. Third is the federal standard of Adequate Yearly Progress (AYP), defined in the No Child Left Behind Act of 2001. Every school in every state must have an annual progress goal that is set by the state.

Among these accountability reports, the district and the press pay the most attention to the state ratings. By this measure, the Houston school district has done well over the past four years since Superintendent Abelardo Saavedra took office. The number of district schools rated exemplary by the state has risen from 6 in 2005 to 38 in 2008, while recognized schools have increased from 29 to 118. Academically acceptable schools have declined from 212 in 2005 to 105 in 2008, and academically unacceptable schools have declined from 34 to 15. While some experts have criticized the TAKS for being an easy test, and while Houston was embroiled in years past in scandals related to the purported inflation of both graduation rates and test scores, there is no argument that whatever the standards, the district overall has improved substantially over the past few years.

In order to have a benchmark for comparison, we can compare these state ratings of district schools in Houston to the same ratings for Dallas schools. In the Dallas, Texas, Independent School District (about 160,000 students), the number of schools rated exemplary declined slightly from 16 schools in 2004 to 15 schools in 2007 (the latest year available on the Dallas school district website), while "recognized" schools declined from 55 in 2004 to 36 in 2007. At the lowest rating, Dallas had 2 schools rated academically unacceptable in 2004, a number that had risen to 26 schools by 2007. Dallas has not made any move toward decentralization. In this comparison, it appears that Houston is continuing to make very strong improvements.

Houston is one of our eight study districts that participates in the special NAEP sample test of eleven urban districts administered by the federal government. Among fourth grade students, the percent in Houston scoring at or above proficient in mathematics rose from 18 to 28 percent between 2003 and 2007. Advanced scorers rose from 1 percent to 3 percent over the period. Eighth grade students also had strong improvements in math, from 12 to 21 percent at or above proficient, and from 2 to 4 percent scoring advanced. While no one can rest on their laurels when only 21 percent of eighth grade students are at or above proficient (the federal government requires that 100 percent of students reach this level within a few years), the yearly progress has been strong. Houston's fourth grade black students are in the middle of the eleven cities in math, while Hispanic fourth graders are at the top, though still below 60 percent of the nation's fourth grade Hispanic students. Eighth graders seem to be consistently improving as well, unlike in many other districts, with black students scoring second-highest among the eleven cities and Hispanic students third from the top.

In reading, Houston's students did not do well. Fourth grade students scoring at or above proficient fell slightly, from 18 percent to 17 percent. Advanced scorers were flat, at 3 percent in 2002 and in 2007. Eighth grade reading scores were only marginally better, with a rise from 17 to 18 percent at or above proficient, and a flat 1 percent scoring advanced throughout the period. Among racial and ethnic groups, Houston's fourth grade black students were third highest in the eleven-city group in reading in 2007, while Hispanic students ranked fourth from the bottom. Eighth grade reading rankings put Houston's black students second from the top, while Hispanics were in the middle of the group.

Our study compares the Houston district only to the other seven study districts that are also decentralizing. It may well be that Houston, as the only major Texas district that has implemented decentralization, is indeed outperforming other Texas districts. Our analytical goal is to test whether one approach to decentralization is superior to another. We found that although Houston principals on average control 73.7 percent of their budgets, their average Total Student Load was 160 in high schools and 162 in middle schools. As we've said earlier, this might be in part because Houston has a smaller per-student budget than most of our other districts, but it is also true that Houston has not focused any of its reform effort on reducing teacher loads. As a result, we also found that for a 10 percentage point increase in principals' budget control, Houston schools on average did not reduce their Total Student Load at all, nor did increases in autonomy yield any improvement in student performance. Student performance did improve in Houston in mathematics, but that improvement was not statistically attributable to the increase in the autonomy of principals. The improvements might have been due to the incentive plan for teachers and principals or to improved math curriculum, or to more drilling on math preparation tests, but during the Saavedra years, principals' autonomy has not produced gains in student performance.

Consider, for example, the way that autonomy was used in one fairly large middle school, grades 6–8. The great majority of the students are Hispanic, of whom the principal estimates 30 percent are foreign born. More than 90 percent are from low-income families. The school is organized into traditional departments, and the typical teacher has a total of 160 to 170 students. The school has more than 100 employees, of whom about half are teachers. The principal says that he or she has the freedom to cancel certain things, such as the school band, the football team, or the arts program, and can use the money saved for other activities. However, he or she is not aware of the concept of Total Student Load. The principal does not control the special education budget—the district sends the number of special education teachers and paraprofessionals that it calculates are necessary.

Under Houston's approach to Weighted Student Formula budgeting, every school is charged about $45,000 per teacher, regardless of what that teacher actually earns. In other words, each principal pays the average teacher salary for the district, not the actual salary of that teacher. As a result of the steady outflow of veteran teachers from this school, these low-income, immigrant students have primarily new teachers who earn low salaries, and this means that the district is spending less per student in these schools than in the upper-income area schools that have primarily experienced teachers who earn much higher salaries. Most educators would argue that experienced teachers would have a greater impact on these students than on students who are already relatively well prepared.

The principal comments that the school's math scores are weak, and that these scores could improve if the school adopted double-period block scheduling for math classes, but that would mean making cuts in other areas like fine arts: "Instead of just getting kids every other day, I would give it to them every day, and that would cost me more teachers." It's a tradeoff that the principal has declined to make. The principal continues, "Am I willing to give up my hourly dance and my hourly piano and my hourly chorus and my karate man? And all my counselors? That's the difficult question. I know how I can improve my math scores, though, by double-blocking math." (Interview during 2006) None of the Boston Pilot School principals or New York City Empowerment School principals have simply double-blocked math or English. Instead, they have used the combined courses of humanities or math-science along with double-blocking to greatly reduce TSL. This principal could do the same without cutting any of his electives like music or art, but he or she hasn't been trained in the concepts of Total Student Load.

Next, we visit an eighth grade science class. The room has an old microscope that looks inoperable, a few mineral samples, and a chart of the human body. There are no useable microscopes, scales, or other laboratory equipment in view. Three of the work tables have running water, but none have gas for experiments. The students are looking up information in their textbooks and filling in the blanks—they aren't performing experiments or doing research outdoors. There is no student work on display anywhere. These are signs of an unmotivated and unimaginative school, one that would benefit from an active, engaged principal who has been properly selected and trained.

In another classroom, the teacher is using an overhead projector with the image projected onto the blackboard, spilling as low as the chalk rail and well above the top of the blackboard. The day is sunny, and the shades are up, as are the lights. No one, including me, can read anything that is being projected. The teacher could move the projector closer and pull down the screen but does neither. This is seventh grade science, and again, there is no student work posted anywhere. It's December, and there should be lots of student work on display both for parents to see and to reward and motivate the students. The teacher changes the transparency and again, with the window shades pulled up, the screen not down, and the projector too far away, no one can read any of it. The principal did not greet the teacher when we entered the classroom, nor does the principal say anything to the teacher as we leave. The school has a state rating of academically acceptable, which puts it in the bottom half of Houston district schools.

Houston has many wonderful schools, but this is not one of them. The principal of this school is subject to the same incentives as all principals for getting higher test scores. However, if the principal does not have the training or the coaching to know how to translate autonomy into lower TSL, the principal is limited to using the school's freedom to hire supplemental staff to teach arts, music, karate, and to provide supportive social services. Clearly, bonuses and threats are not enough. Weak principals cannot respond effectively to strong financial incentives.

Taken as a whole, the various evaluations of the Houston school district suggest that it has improved substantially compared to other Texas districts and that it has kept pace with the improvements made by other large urban districts across the nation, but that it could achieve greater improvement in student performance if it were to focus on TSL. The Houston district has made it clear through its accountability and performance pay systems that it wants improvements in student achievement, and it has granted a great measure of autonomy to its principals. However, the Houston school district has not yet developed a path that connects greater principal freedom to higher student achievement. Unlike the Coalition of Essential Schools or New York City, Houston has yet to develop a method that will enable each principal to navigate from freedom to achievement. Without such a point of view, the district is limited in its ability to train or coach its principals in how to use their autonomy effectively.

If the Houston Independent School District does not have a well-developed concept of instructional management to guide its principals, it will be in danger of backsliding in its commitment to the potential of principal autonomy. Decentralization, after all, is an unnatural state for any hierarchy. Decentralization will decompose over time unless the district knows exactly why principal autonomy is valuable and has a clear motivation to strive constantly to renew it. For example, the Houston school district now believes that principals do not have the time to become curriculum experts, and thus it is creating district-wide curricula.

One principal commented on the fact that his new small high school was required to adopt the instructional methods that are now standard for all schools: "If a school of three thousand has it, then we should have it for four hundred, and that's been the real struggle." (Interview of December 2006) The Houston district has moved away somewhat from its earlier commitment to autonomy for all schools, and instead, notes Superintendent Saavedra, "low performance schools may not—it may be best that they not have the level of autonomy that a high performance school has, for example, or the high performance principal." (All quotes from Abelardo Saavedra are from an interview of May 2, 2006.) The implication of the new policy is that schools that have high ratings will have more autonomy, but even that is not clear. The district acted in 2005 to add nineteen "feeder pattern" executive principals, each of whom oversees one or two high schools and the middle and elementary schools that feed into them. School principals now report directly to an executive principal, who in turn reports to one of the five region superintendents, which seems a hierarchical rather than autonomous organization. According to Superintendent Saavedra, the role of these additional supervisors is "ensuring that instruction is aligned along the feeder pattern. Ensuring that the weaker principals are getting the right staff development."

Keep in mind that in New York City, all principals report directly to Chancellor Klein rather than to area superintendents as in the past, while the extensive web of accountability acts to keep them in good order. In Edmonton, all principals also report only to the superintendent. There are of course assistant superintendents in both New York City and Edmonton, and they do give guidance to principals, but they are not authorized to tell principals what to do. A principal who cannot run her school properly in those districts is retrained or replaced. To declare that principals have autonomy and then assign supervisors to tell them how to run their schools only invites conflict and confusion.

It is not surprising that Houston's principals have in recent years become skeptical about what decentralization means today, compared to the autonomy that principals enjoyed a few years ago. As one said, "Well, with decentralization, there are some interesting caveats." Another commented, "In the beginning of decentralization, we had more freedom. Now, we have less freedom." Another commented wryly about the new process for planning next year's school budget: "The superintendent met with our ad hoc committee of principals and started talking to them about 'Is this working for you?' And no, it wasn't. And we need to make some changes here. We spent lots of time talking about what will those changes look like? Someone would say, 'Every school needs a counselor. Every school needs a nurse.' 'Okay, we can do that.' What that means is that we take the nurse and counselor and these other positions like a fine arts teacher, we'll take these out of the big pot of money we give to schools, and give everybody one, and now you're required to have it! That means your discretionary funds are gonna drop considerably because you've added to your requirements."

Still, in some cases, principal discretion remains strong. Remarked one principal who felt that he enjoyed considerable autonomy, "Instead of having three counselors I only have one counselor because no one said you have to have three counselors. Having three counselors would be ideal, then you would have one counselor per grade level. But instead of hiring three counselors what we have done is contracted through the communities in the schools and they send us two counselors. They have—they get federal grants and some of the charges that we get to have them are a lot less than—I have half a social worker. I split a social worker with another school. No one said I had to have a social worker, but I've felt that we needed one. This school definitely requires one. Just because of all the issues of poverty." Another principal also clearly felt that he still has responsibility for his school budget, as he noted, "It's yours now. It's here. You drive it. You correct it. If you're in the red, you need to figure it out. So, pretty much, I'm scared to death! At some schools you start with a deficit, and we did start with a deficit, so we're being pretty frugal . . . you have to pay it back. Textbooks—you have to pay it back. Missing textbooks—they hold you accountable."

Yet another principal explained the rather complicated system through which he creates flexibility with both his budget and his staffing pattern: "We had a science specialist advertised and we haven't gotten any good candidates so I closed it by December 1. You have to close it by December 1, or then you're charged—you lose it. So I closed a science specialist and some hourly lectures here, they will put it [the money] in the General, and from there I shift it wherever. I choose where to shift it. It could be used for materials or overtime or tutoring." As this principal explains some of the darker secrets of his craft, it becomes apparent that autonomy is hanging on among those principals who have tasted freedom and are fighting to retain it.

Yet another principal explained how he used his autonomy: "The first thing we did was change our counselor position and turn that into a social worker position. And so we saw that as more of a thing that will help [our school] is a person in that position who would reach out not only to the kids but support the families that needed that. And then, after that, as that position evolved, we kinda needed somebody that would be more academic—which the counselor had taken on some of those jobs. So, at first we hired a reading specialist. Over the last two years, our reading scores have been great! So what we saw the need for was math/science. Particularly science. So this year, we have a teacher specialist in the area of math/science rather than reading. And that's [*teacher's name*]. And we were able to make these decisions for ourselves. We're able to say, 'Here's what [our school's] needs are: here's the evolving need, and here are the changes we will make.'"

It's apparent that autonomy, which was once universal among Houston's principals, is now a hit-and-miss proposition. Some principals have managed to hang on to their freedom, while others have not. Struggling principals are not retrained, coached, or replaced—instead, they are given a strong boss who tells them what to do. What was supposed to be a performance-based bonus system that would drive all principals to improve has, in the eyes of the central office, failed to do the job. Instead the new central office leadership has ordered that many of the former freedoms be reined in, but it appears that many principals are successfully resisting the new regime, at least for the time being.

The central office staff is, as always, the most important device in taking back control from the schools. For example, in Houston the central office has taken back the management of student data, partly in response to the testing scandals of years past mentioned above. The district wants its principals to be able to interpret and make use of student data, but it now withholds from them the freedom to design their own student data management systems. The district has also taken back control over the custodial budgets that were previously run by principals, thus removing what for some schools might have been a precious opportunity to add one or two more teachers or paraprofessionals, while relieving less experienced principals of a task that to them may seem unrelated to the core task of instructing students.

Houston principals do have the freedom to purchase professional development programs either from the central office staffs or from outside vendors of their choosing, a freedom that is of crucial importance to almost all principals. The district charges less for its programs than outside vendors do, though, and most principals choose to buy their teacher training courses from the central office.

So, is school autonomy alive and well in Houston, or are the new school board and superintendent moving slowly back toward centralization? There is evidence for both points of view. There are also some other explanations for the variety of opinions that administrators and principals express on the topic, which is a major item of discussion. One explanation is that during the years of the rapid implementation of decentralization, some inexperienced principals received more autonomy than they were ready for, and the new superintendent is keeping closer watch over them. Perhaps in the future he will restore more autonomy to them. Another explanation is that the new regime does not, at least not yet, fully appreciate the power of decentralization and is seeking to rein in at least some of that freedom. But by now, the principals and the teachers have come to like their freedom, and they're not giving it up without a struggle. Once people have tasted freedom, it can be tough to take it away. One good sign is that people within the district aren't afraid to talk about decentralization or to express their opinions on the subject, whatever those may be. As long as that dialogue continues, and as long as the school board and the superintendent are listening, there is reason to be optimistic about the continuation of decentralization in Houston.

Stepping back, one must give Houston the credit that it deserves for what it has accomplished since the chaotic, conflict-laden days before 1990, when decentralization began. Houston is no longer a troubled urban district, as it once was. It is a stable district with experienced teachers, rising student results, and a positive public rating. The district has maintained its commitment to Weighted Student Formula budgeting and to local school autonomy for nearly twenty years, and it has risen to the top among urban districts in Texas.

On the other hand, only 18 percent of Houston's eighth graders scored at or above proficient in reading on the 2007 NAEP, and only 21 percent reached that mark in math. White eighth graders were in the 71st percentile nationally in reading, while black eight graders were in the 33rd percentile, and Hispanics in the 31st percentile. Overall, the Houston Integrated School District is rated academically acceptable by the state. In order to improve to recognized or even exemplary as a district, Houston needs to find a way to strengthen greatly its lowest-performing schools. It seems unlikely that a return to the traditional top-down method of management, under which the Houston schools suffered for decades, will achieve a turnaround. If we take what we have learned from our other study districts, we'd say that the most reliable way to do that is for Houston to double its efforts to put a skilled principal into every school, give that principal autonomy, and surround her with a world-class accountability system.

Urban school districts have been at the bottom of a very deep hole for a long time. Even after fifteen or twenty years of steady progress, a district like Houston still has far to go before it can declare victory. Houston got where it is today not through incremental change, but by pioneering in the implementation of decentralization. Now on its third superintendent since the implementation of decentralization, Houston seems to be moving away from decentralization. It's not possible to tell quite yet where Houston will end up, but it is clear that both interpretations are now alive and well. Houston's pioneering former superintendent Rod Paige was largely responsible for putting school autonomy on the map in U.S. education. Houston continues to break new ground in performance pay, and in other ways. Let's hope that the Houston Independent School District also continues to provide leadership in school autonomy.

Seattle

Seattle was one of the cities that was hardest hit by "white flight" after the adoption of forced busing to achieve desegregation. Enrollment dropped from nearly 100,000 students in 1962 to a low of 39,087 for the 1989–90 school year. Some families opted for independent schools, while others moved beyond the city limits to suburban school districts. As a result, the Seattle school district was left with lots of large school buildings that were half empty, and costs per student were high. The district was beset by conflict among various constituencies, and test scores were falling. The state legislature commissioned an external evaluation that was sharply critical of the leadership of the Seattle Public Schools, faulting the district for allocating money in a way that robbed the schools of the flexibility that would enable them to tailor their programs to the needs of students. Several reform-oriented groups, which included the business community, ethnic communities, and the teachers union, coalesced into the Alliance for Education, which supported reform-oriented candidates for the school board. The new school board went looking for a visionary leader for the Seattle schools.

In June 1995, the recruiters hired retired army general John Stanford from his post as county administrator in Fulton County, Georgia. General Stanford had no previous experience running public schools, but he understood leadership, and he knew how to bring about change. In short order, General Stanford hired a former banker, Joseph Olchefske, to be his chief financial officer, and the two of them decamped to Edmonton to talk with Super-intendent Mike Strembitsky. After what Strembitsky recalls as no more than a half day, the two would-be reformers returned to Seattle and launched their implementation program. These two intrepid agents of change were convinced by what they had seen and heard in Edmonton, and furthermore, the idea of empower-ing principals appealed to both of them as a practical, common-sense idea. Besides, they had already talked to the reformers in Houston, and there was no reading to do on the subject, and no other districts for them to visit or study. Unencumbered by les-sons from other pioneers, they went forward.

In retrospect, the reformers in Boston, Houston, and Seattle didn't know enough to be afraid of the high odds against them. Ignorant of the power of the status quo, Stanford and Olchefske proceeded to design the first Weighted Student Formula system to be implemented in the United States (Houston's was second in 1999) and to use it as a way to decentralize their school district. Later on, however, the isolation of these efforts would prove to be very important, not least because when the change agents re-tired, there were no "outside" candidates who had experience with decentralization to replace them.

After only three years as superintendent, John Stanford died of leukemia. He had been a charismatic leader, the sort who in-spired confidence in others, the sort whom others willingly followed into uncharted territory. During his brief tenure, General Stanford had fully implemented Weighted Student Formula budgeting and school choice and had raised principal autonomy to the point that Seattle's principals controlled, on average, 79 percent of school budgets. However, he had not had time to build infrastructure, to create adequate principal selection and training efforts, to establish a fully developed accountability system, or to reorganize the central office staff, which chafed at the idea of giving so much power to the principals. By 2006, just eight years after Stanford died, principals' control of budgets in Seattle had declined from 79 to 48 percent.

Following the death of John Stanford, Joseph Olchefske was appointed superintendent of Seattle Public Schools. Olchefske served for six years, during which time Weighted Student Formula budgeting was refined and decentralization of budget control to principals was increased. Total enrollment grew to 44,831 by 2002, and the district managed to regain some market share from the independent schools—a major achievement. However, Olchefske's tenure was marked by conflict with the teachers union, partly in response to his attempt to dismiss low-performing teachers from the district. Meanwhile, many of the state's technology companies suffered financial decline. The school district budget was cut, leading to an unexpected deficit. In June 2003, Olchefske stepped down from his superintendency.

Olchefske was replaced by a former banker, Raj Manhas. Among his foremost objectives was to restore fiscal soundness to the Seattle district. In order to achieve this goal, Manhas had to close some neighborhood schools, a task that he accomplished, but that left many community activists and parents with hard feelings toward him. By 2006, Manhas had managed to turn the previous deficit into a surplus approaching an accumulated total of $20 million. In the process, though, he had reversed John

Stanford's decentralization program. By this time, according to the chief financial officer of Seattle Public Schools, principals had discretionary control over only 5 percent of their school budgets (although the perception of principals was that they had control over 48 percent, perhaps demonstrating the power of wishful thinking, or perhaps instead showing that principals had learned to be clever in what they reported to the central office). As one senior official remarked, "Ten years ago I was an advocate totally of telling people, 'Whatever it is that you want to do!' and then find the resources to do it, and let them look at it their own way. I do believe now after those ten years, that there comes a time if there is too much chaos, and there has been too much freedom, and there is not enough cohesion at all, that you have to bring the system to some kind of congruency and expectation. So that is where I think Seattle is." This official has reached a conclusion: "In Seattle for right now, I believe we need some boundaries in autonomy and that we need to pull it back a little bit. I talked to the board, and one of the things we are about to do is starting out a K–12 Math Adoption, and we have gone through the polarization of which way to teach math, and I said I don't really care what the material is, I just want people to teach the same thing so I can build a support for this stuff, and so that you can have collaboration, that I can provide professional development, so I can provide the key support pieces, the 'cutting and pasting' guide, and those that support the system." (Interview of July 13, 2006)

Perhaps this central office executive was correct. Seattle had not built the necessary infrastructure, and thus it wasn't really ready to grant full autonomy to principals, although it had done just that. Perhaps Stanford and Olchefske hadn't asked about the extensive accountability systems or about the lengthy principal training programs in Edmonton. As one central office executive noted, "Principal leadership is key . . . I have to have principals that have that instructional leadership piece, so that they know what to do . . . At this point, I believe that in Seattle we need to pull it back together." However, the solution that they preferred was district-wide standardization. For example, the Manhas central office staff standardized the number of weeks that fifth grade teachers spent teaching fractions, and it mandated the balanced literacy curriculum in grades K–2. The reversal of autonomy in these examples might seem unnecessarily stark, but the policy change makes clear one underlying truth about management: there are two ways to achieve success in managing a large organization. One way is to carefully select and thoroughly train managers, grant them autonomy within an accountability system, and provide them with lots of real-time feedback about their performance. The other way is to standardize the way everything is to be done from the central office. Seattle flipped from the first method to the second almost overnight.

Teachers who had become accustomed to working under the decentralized approach resisted this return to centralization. As one central office staffer remarked, "I've already warned them we are going to pull it back a little bit, and then they start yelling at me about who am I telling them what to do!" It becomes clear that autonomy is now under regular attack in central office conversations: "And that is another thing about autonomy—I guess I am disturbed about the fact that the faculty vote about having a specific program or not. So, and again I understand that the choice is high level, but if you need more dual language programs to serve kids, then I think that as a district, centrally, with principal representation and teacher representation, we need to say 'here is an area in town that would really flourish with this program,' and we really need to look at that and decide where it goes, and then we offer options about whether you want to stay there and be a part of it, and if you don't, we have an option to get, you know, but we are getting strung up by people saying 'thank you very much, but no, we won't have that.'" (Interview of July 13, 2006) It appears that the independent spirit inculcated in Seattle by Stanford and Olchefske is still alive, at least with some of the teachers and principals, but one wonders how much longer they can hold out against a central office staff determined to recentralize.

The new central office financial staff seems to take the attitude that discretionary spending is for "extra" money, above and beyond what it takes to run a basic school. Because the budgets have been cut so much, one staffer said, "it only works when you have enough resources to put behind it that you have really flexible money, and we have not had enough flexible money to make this decision-making a valid process." (Interview of July 13, 2006) Once again, though, it appears that the loyal (or perhaps not so loyal) opposition among principals is alive and well, as this person continues: "We are giving the schools enough money through the student weighted formula to allow for eighty-plus, maybe eighty-five—depends on who you are talking to—of high school kids to take about six periods of classes, not five. When we get to a high school like [*name of school*], which is what we call a full spectrum high school, you've got AP kids and you've got needy kids, academically. The principal and the staff are trying to run a program, and they can't provide the AP classes unless they steal them from the classes they would need for remedial math, or vice versa. So then you have created, through a lack of funding, a huge problem for the principal and for the community, and they fight each other." In Seattle, it no longer appears to be the case that the central office thinks about replacing big schools with small schools and then giving each the freedom to choose the instructional approach that best fits its needs. Inevitably, it may be the centralization of the district rather than the size of the budget that creates conflicts that play out on each campus. Depending on your point of view, you might regard the continuing independence of the principals of Seattle as a good thing or a bad thing. Either way, the district staff was preparing to exert top-down power by switching from sending Weighted Student Formula money to principals and instead returning to the old system of sending them specified job positions instead.

Principals had heard that this return to staffing formulas was about to replace at least part of their WSF allocations, and they weren't looking forward to it. Said one principal, "Over the four years I maintained local control, almost entirely. It is not the coming year that is being taken away. What we are being told is that next year, in spring of 2008, when we are doing our 2008–9 budget, is when we are going to be losing some of the student weighted formula control and be going back to a staffing standard, with a little bit of Weighted Student Formula put in. I have not seen the actual mode. It is really dumb, which is embarrassing." (Interview of March 2007) Another principal added, "So it was kind of the head business manager . . . who sat in the meeting and is listening to principals say that ration makes no sense—we cannot possibly run a school on what you're saying. The response was, 'That's the ration we have to hit because that's what the state and federal government say.' Well, great, so who's out there advocating for us and saying, 'This isn't working! Give it to us in dollars and let us turn around and use it!'" (Interview of March 2007) The autonomy that John Stanford and Joseph Olchefske had created did not terrify most principals—most of them had by now embraced it. Down in the trenches, Seattle's principals and teachers aren't yielding their freedom without a struggle. A divergence of opinion of this magnitude is a danger sign in any organization.

Perhaps Seattle has no choice but to return to top-down management if it cannot train principals sufficiently in how to use their independence to reduce Total Student Loads and take other steps that will enhance student performance. As one central office administrator said of the lack of training for principals, "The only thing that we have, and it is not for us, is that the University of Washington has training over there, and it is funded by the Annenberg Foundation, and it's an internship/training program, but it is all outside of us—we just happen to benefit because it is in the city. And a couple of the other high end institutions also have some pretty good training programs—only because it is geographical. We are not doing anything internally and it is sad. Same problem with administrators and the same problem with others—we do nothing about professional development here." (Interview of July 13, 2006)

Despite this apparently determined return to centralization, at least one senior official seemed open-minded about the idea of a real decentralization: "That is what is fascinating to me about your description and about how they are doing this in Boston and New York. We are still thinking, maybe incorrectly—based on what you were saying this morning—in a high school you need to have a principal, a vice principal, a college prep counselor, a remediation counselor, two drug specialists, because that is where people have their minds. We haven't made that jump to that flexibility that you were talking about." (Interview of July 13, 2006)

If any more evidence of the failure of Seattle to support autonomous principals is necessary, that evidence is available in the previously mentioned report of the Cross City Campaign for Urban School Reform, *A Delicate Balance: District Policies and Classroom Practice*, published in 2005. The report says of Seattle, "Almost every Seattle central office department called the principals with questions ranging from discipline data, to bus schedules, to requests for payroll figures. Seattle principals had to exert considerable leadership to integrate multiple agendas especially when there was confusion . . . One principal, in deciding not to worry about the district's indecisions, stated, 'I'm just going to sit out until the district has figured out what its focus for the schools really is.' "

Our research revealed that Seattle high schools had an average Total Student Load of 126 students in 2005. When a principal enjoyed an increase of 10 percentage points in her control over the school budget, on average she was able to reduce TSL by 4.4 students per teacher, a meaningful improvement, though not as large as in some of our other cities. Unfortunately, that change typically resulted in an improvement of only 1.1 percentage points in student performance.

Seattle administers staff and student surveys, and the results are available on the district website. In 2007, on a scale of 1 (worst) to 5 (best), high school staff gave an average score of 3.80 to their principal's commitment to shared decision making, down from 3.91 in 2005. On the principal's willingness to be a strong leader in school reform, staff evaluations in 2007 averaged 3.72, also down slightly from 2005. These and other survey results are reported in a manner that is difficult for anyone to interpret, though.

In the fall of 2007, Dr. Maria Goodloe-Johnson replaced Raj Manhas as superintendent of the Seattle Public Schools. By that time, the district had 45,300 students, of whom 51 percent were Asian, 33 percent were African American, 8 percent were Latino, and 7 percent were Caucasian. Forty-nine percent were from low-income families, and 7 percent were in special education. Eighty percent of fourth grade students had achieved passing scores on the state WASL (Washington Assessment of Student Learning) test in reading in 2007 (compared to 63 percent in 2001), and 62 percent passed in math (versus 43 percent in 2001). In the tenth grade, 69 percent (versus 51 percent in 2001) passed in reading, while 46 percent (versus 35 percent in 2001) passed in math. The white-black gap in tenth grade reading was 48 percentage points on the 2002 state test and had been reduced to 33 points by 2005. In mathematics, that gap had gone from 46 points in 2002 (8 percent of black students met state standards) to 44 points in 2005. The gap for Latino students has also narrowed slightly over those years, a positive sign.

Despite this record of steady gains in student achievement, a January 8, 2008, memo to parents announced that the district had decided to adopt new district-wide curricula in literacy and math in grades K–12. By that time, Seattle had abandoned Weighted Student Formula budgeting, and schools were once again assigned the numbers of positions that the central office staff calculated they should have, according to standard enrollment-to-staff ratios. One of the lessons of Seattle is that decentralization can be completely reversed, even after the eight years that Stanford and Olchefske had devoted to implementing it. A second lesson is that if principals are granted great autonomy, but without the selection and training that is necessary and without the accountability infrastructure to support decentralization, then decentralization will fail. A third and perhaps more subtle lesson is that until school district decentralization becomes the norm in the United States, it will always be at risk and under attack by those who, intentionally or not, represent the thinking of the status quo.

From the start of decentralization in 1995 through the end of the Manhas administration in 2007, decentralization was the norm in Seattle. Over that period of twelve years, student performance increased steadily. However, it appears that the Seattle school board had experienced enough turnover that the understanding of decentralization had been vitiated. Given a lack of strong board backing, Manhas was easily able to rein in Weighted Student Formula budgeting, arguing that it had been responsible for the budget deficits of the Olchefske administration. When another new superintendent arrived in 2007, it was no surprise, given the nationwide dominance of top-down, centralized districts, that she returned the district almost entirely to central staff control. Through all of these changes in management approach, at least some Seattle principals managed to keep a measure of autonomy. That commitment to local autonomy is strong testimony to the basic, commonsense logic of decentralization.

At a more fundamental level, we can extract two major lessons from this story. First, a district should not implement decentralization in haste. Although it was wonderful that Stanford and Olchefske acted right away after their half-day visit with Superintendent Strembitsky in Edmonton, they should have gone back to visit his staff several more times before launching their own plan. Heads of large companies often have the same desire to rush into a reorganization once they see the need for it, but it's always a mistake to act before carefully thinking through the plan. Second, a school district should take the two or three years that are necessary to put into place systems for selecting, training, and coaching principals; for constructing a thorough web of accountability; for reorienting the central staffs; and for creating the budgeting and information systems that are necessary for principals to succeed in the Four Freedoms. Seattle, as a first-generation pioneer, did not know those lessons. Any school district that follows, though, has no excuse if it repeats those same missteps.

Boston, Houston, and Seattle: The First Generation in Perspective

The school districts of Boston, Houston, and Seattle have improved over the past several years. Whether that improvement has been large or small is a matter on which experts as well as parents disagree. All three allow families to choose their school. Beyond those similarities, there are few others. Boston has implemented a partial decentralization by creating twenty Pilot Schools, and the district staff has recently exhibited more enthusiasm for them than in the past. Houston decentralized all of its schools but now appears to be moving back toward recentralization, though it's too early to know for sure. Seattle also decentralized all of its schools, but it seems that without the infrastructure to cement those changes, Seattle has moved back to a more centralized system, though it remains more decentralized than the typical urban district in the United States. None of the three has reorganized its central staff into a form that can receive rewards and high praise for assisting schools, though Boston appears to be moving in that direction, and Seattle did make some early moves in that direction, before it turned the opposite way.

The three districts vary in the degree of autonomy that they grant to their schools when it comes to budget, staffing pattern, curriculum, and schedule. More importantly, neither Houston nor Seattle has developed an internal point of view or philosophy that links these Four Freedoms to Total Student Load and to student achievement, though several of Boston's Pilot Schools have done so. Perhaps the most obvious lesson, clear now to us with the benefit of hindsight—but surely not visible at the time— is that decentralization of budget control to principals is not enough to bring about noticeable improvement in student performance by itself. Two additional steps must be taken. First, a district must employ all of the Five Pillars: choice, empowerment through the Four Freedoms, effective principals, accountability, and Weighted Student Formula budgeting. All three of the districts implemented choice, and all used some form of WSF budgeting, but none of the three developed the infrastructure of a full-blown accountability system, and none of them developed a strong method for creating effective principals.

Second, only the Boston Pilot Schools enjoyed all of the Four Freedoms that principals should have. Without all four, a school cannot drive down Total Student Load to the point that student performance responds in a dramatic fashion. Third, decentralization can be sustained only if the governance apparatus—be that an elected school board or a mayor—has a deep understanding of decentralization and why it is important.

All three districts can legitimately claim success, at least on some measures. In all three, overall test scores rose strongly during the years of decentralization, and among the Boston Pilot schools, that growth continues today. However, because Boston and Houston participate in the eleven-city special NAEP test, we are able to see that they have not substantially reduced the gaps between whites and Asians as compared to black and Hispanic students, and we can see that gains have been more consistently achieved in the fourth grade than in the eighth. In Seattle, the state test results led to a similar result for the Hispanic and black gaps. This consistent inability to reduce the achievement gap between races is a source of frustration to these districts.

What gives them hope is the great success of schools like Young Achievers and Lilla G. Frederick in Boston. If these schools can succeed with primarily black and Hispanic students from low-income homes, then any urban public school district should be able to succeed. If it is indeed autonomy that has made these successes possible, then it may simply be a question of time before more schools with similar student bodies begin to succeed as well. On the other hand, educational researchers should look much more closely at exactly why these few schools are succeeding, so that their successes can be multiplied.

Our own analysis shows that all three of these first-generation pioneering districts have much to do when it comes to reducing Total Student Load. Still, these three districts deserve to be celebrated for what they have achieved rather than criticized for what they have not. All of them were pioneers, charting foreign waters. They are still experimenting, learning, and trying, because they care about the children whose education has been entrusted to them. Most importantly for us, we have learned valuable lessons from each of them.

Houston and Seattle ventured out alone, led by visionary superintendents but surrounded by nonbelievers. Both were able to demonstrate the power of the idea of school autonomy, and both were able to learn from the experience of Edmonton, but neither had the time that it needed to build strong fortifications against backsliding in the future. They cannot be faulted for their deliberate pace—each had to move slowly, because they were pioneering, picking their way and solving every problem for the first time as it appeared, not knowing what to expect or when to expect it. When the visionary leaders retired, the first great flush of excitement went with them, though the DNA of decentralization remains. Vision and style, we might conclude, can work wonders in the short run, but organization and infrastructure are essential for long-term sustainability.

The story of the Boston Pilot Schools is a more positive one, and it supports our argument because the Pilot Schools did have a more complete infrastructure system in their nonprofit partners, Dan French and the Center for Collaborative Education. Most of the twenty Pilot Schools are now more than ten years old. By all accounts, they are continuing to improve. From the outset, these schools have been in an organizational cocoon of sorts, nestled in the protective embrace of CCE.

In similar fashion, New York City has some seventy schools that have chosen as their support system the Center for Educational Innovation–Public Education Association, which has provided a protective environment for some of its schools for more than thirty years, while that city's New Visions nonprofit partner has done the same for approximately sixty schools for about twenty years. Within these educational hothouses, the schools are encapsulated within a friendly environment that understands ideas like choice, principal autonomy, accountability, and Weighted Student Formula budgeting. They are building their own infrastructure over time, providing training and coaching for principals and teachers, developing accessible student data systems, and protecting above all the autonomy of the schools. Boston, like New York City, has had more than its share of top-down superintendents, but even they have at least tolerated these renegade organizations, perhaps because their schools produced good student achievement and because students and parents loved their schools.

It may be that the future is now catching up to these three districts. As the idea of decentralization has now established itself firmly in other venues, public understanding and support for the idea is growing. Increasingly, large and medium-sized districts that go this way will be in the company of numbers of districts that have made a similar choice. Perhaps in the near future, the tide of decentralization will again return to Houston and to Seattle, and perhaps it will raise all of the ships in Boston. If so, it appears that all three cities have principals who will know just what to do.

6

THE SECOND
GENERATION: SPEED
AND INFRASTRUCTURE
IN ST. PAUL AND
SAN FRANCISCO

The next two cities in our study approached decentralization
with strategies that at the outset were similar but developed in
crucially different ways. The implementations in these second-
generation pioneers reflected their knowledge of what had gone
before. Both superintendents had studied the reforms in Boston,
Edmonton, Houston, and Seattle. As a result, both superintendents moved with self-confidence and speed to implement the
vision of decentralization that was so clear to them. Both of them
also made substantial investments in developing the infrastructure of decentralization, including changes in the organization

198

of their central office staffs and investments in developing the managerial capacity of their principals.

Both of the districts had been beset by public criticism and perceptions of failure before they embarked on their reforms, and both achieved considerable success through decentralization. Both determined from the outset that they would have district-wide school empowerment, and both accomplished that goal. Both adopted school choice, Weighted Student Formula, and principal budget control, though they differed in their implementation of certain aspects of these changes.

In addition to moving with much greater speed than their predecessors, both made substantial changes in the organization of their central staffs to encourage them to be supportive of empowered schools. None of the first-generation decentralizers had attempted central office reorganizations on the same scale. The leaders in St. Paul and in San Francisco were more intimately familiar with the central office reorganization that had taken place in Edmonton, and both attempted to move in that direction, though neither was able to go quite as far.

In order to develop their principals, both districts created new training and development systems. St. Paul put into place a lengthy development and training regime for prospective principals, while San Francisco created a new position, Instructional Reform Facilitators (known as IRFs), which created an internal training route with an external partnership with the neighboring University of California, Berkeley. Both of these development systems were more thorough and more elaborate than anything that had taken place in the first generation.

Both also inherited powerful school site committees or councils that had been born out of the site-based management movement twenty-five years before. Neither one managed to create a fully developed accountability system, perhaps because neither of their primary points of reference, Houston and Seattle, had done so. In both St. Paul and San Francisco, the reforms were opposed by local teachers unions that appeared to have been caught off guard by the speed and intensity of the reforms. Both of the superintendents left office shortly after our study was completed, after about six years in office.

In both cases, the school board experienced substantial turnover while the reform was under way. In St. Paul the new board members did not understand or support the idea of decentralization, while in San Francisco they did. As a result, in St. Paul the pioneering superintendent was replaced by an "outsider" who did not have experience with a decentralized district and who managed to undo much of what had been created, while in San Francisco it appears that the new superintendent will maintain the decentralization reforms.

St. Paul and San Francisco each had to invent creative solutions to the kinds of problems that other districts will face if they choose to go down this same road, and we can learn from both of them. Both of the districts made significant improvements in student performance through decentralization, and learning how they did so will be of help to others. Just as important are some of the situational differences that each of the new superintendents inherited, for no two districts are identical in history or circumstances.

St. Paul Decentralizes with Speed, Then Retreats

St. Paul, Minnesota, is a district of 41,444 students in sixty-six schools, including seven senior high schools, eight junior or middle schools, forty-nine elementary schools, one K–12 school, and one special education school. Within the district, 29.8 percent of the students are African American, 29.3 percent are Asian (with a large population of Hmong immigrants), 26.1 percent are Caucasian, 13.0 percent are Latino, and 1.8 percent are native American. A total of 39.7 percent are Limited English Proficient, 69.5 percent are from low-income families, and 17.1 percent receive special education services. The district attendance rate is 92.5 percent, and graduation rates range from a high of 87.3 percent for Asian students and 87.1 percent for Caucasian students to a low of 51.1 percent for native Americans and 60.5 percent for Latino students. The City of St. Paul also has about thirty charter schools, many of which enroll fewer than two hundred students.

THE PREVIOUS HISTORY OF SITE-BASED MANAGEMENT IN ST. PAUL

During the 1980s, the concept of site-based management (SBM) was stirring up attention among Minnesota educators. The University of Minnesota had partnered with the Minnesota Association of Secondary School Principals to sponsor a series of workshops for principals around the state. Out of that experience, a group of principals from St. Paul went off to visit the Edmonton Public Schools, after which the principals held a series of planning meetings on how best to proceed. After a few years, the ideas had coalesced, and St. Paul Public Schools invited its principals to apply for authorization to create their own SBM approaches. The district aired out the idea at a series of parent meetings. The chief concern that emerged was whether the members of a school site council might be held legally liable if a school under this system were sued. The answer to that question was no—members of a school site council cannot be held accountable. Once that question had been resolved, enthusiasm for the idea of autonomous schools that involved parents, teachers, and community members in a shared-decision process gained steam. Eight schools had established school site councils by the late 1990s.

DR. PATRICIA HARVEY BECOMES SUPERINTENDENT

The district hired a new superintendent, Dr. Patricia A. Harvey, who came to St. Paul in 1999. Superintendent Harvey, who was also an admirer of the Edmonton district, soon told her staff that they were going to take site-based management district-wide. By doing so, she appeared simply to be encouraging a popular idea that was already under way both in St. Paul and around the nation, though in fact she had in mind a much bolder plan—to implement the Five Pillars and the Four Freedoms, as in Edmonton. In exchange, Harvey was endorsing and thereby strengthening the hand of the school site councils, unlike in Edmonton, to the consternation of some St. Paul principals who did not relish the idea of having yet another boss in the form of these councils. According to a senior member of the staff, "And then as Pat [new superintendent Patricia Harvey] came on board, it was more of a brushstroke saying, okay, we are going to go to this—seventy-plus schools site-based. I think the reaction was mixed. There was a good track record with those eight schools, so folks had a sense that it was working in those schools, but they certainly weren't without problems. For some of the veteran principals, I think there was a sense that this is a threat to their decision-making authority. Some to this day have that idea, coupled with a sense that it is a lot of work for the building principal, that the preparation, the level of informing, the level of collaboration is, you know, 'you've just doubled my job here.' Now I have to report up, I have to report down, I have to report sideways." (All St. Paul central office interviews took place on March 16, 2006.) Although the councils are advisory to the principals, some principals anticipated that the community-based, shared-decision-making fervor might not increase their school's autonomy, but might instead consume the principal's attention and slow down the process of making changes.

Under Superintendent Harvey's leadership, aspiring school administrators were trained in the district's Leadership Institute for Aspiring Leaders, which included a three-week intensive summer program, monthly training during the school year, and regular meetings with an experienced principal mentor (each mentor advised four or five fellows and received a nominal stipend). After twelve months in the program, each fellow presented a capstone project to the senior staff, and the successful graduates then had their names circulated to those school councils that were seeking to fill positions for a principal or assistant principal. Each council interviewed as many candidates as it wanted, and then it submitted three names to the superintendent for her final decision. After six years, the Leadership Institute had graduated about 137 fellows, of whom about 50 were serving as principals, with many others serving as assistant principals. Each year, about 70 to 80 aspirants apply to the institute, and about 20 of these are chosen.

DECENTRALIZATION COMES TO ST. PAUL

Principals in St. Paul control, on average, 87.2 percent of their school's budget, the highest in our study group of districts. They also control their staffing pattern, schedule, and curriculum. The St. Paul district also adopted Weighted Student Formula budgeting, although they did it the hard way. First, they attempted to arrive at their own set of weights, based on their own analysis of what it should cost to educate a child. Said one senior staff person, "We had a committee of probably fifty people that worked for I want to say three years—and we couldn't come up with the weights. We looked at what Seattle was doing. We looked at what Edmonton was doing. You know, those districts who've been doing it for a long time. We couldn't come to agreement across the district, so we said, okay, the way the state funds us is to send revenue based on the characteristics of the child and therefore we will send revenue to the schools based on the characteristics of the child . . . and so that was our formula!" (Interview of March 16, 2006) This approach, to simply mimic the state weights, is what virtually all districts now do in creating their own versions of WSF.

Schools are cross-charged by the central office for their expenses, most of which are salaries. Rather than charge schools for the actual salaries of employees, they use the average of all elementary, middle, or high school teacher or staff salaries as the amount to charge each school. The central staff created a software program that automatically shows each principal all of their funding sources and enables them to do "what ifs" to see how they can give up something in order to get something else. For example, a principal can decide to have one less teacher and instead hire two educational assistants, or vice versa. Because it would have been very expensive to create a system that principals could use online themselves, the district instead asks them to come in and sit with a finance specialist, who helps them with their budget work.

A separate, online system allows principals to see where they stand on total spending versus budget during the year. A principal who has a deficit at the end of the year must repay that amount to the district during the following year. Because projected enrollment, on which the school budget is based, often differs from actual enrollment, the central office makes corresponding adjustments to school budgets twice each year, once in the fall and again during the winter. St. Paul has found that the school site councils take a great interest in budgets, and often the site councils will request budget data for other schools, in order to see how much money other schools are getting and how they are allocating their budgets.

In addition to reorienting the central finance staff to develop a school-friendly organization and attitude, Superintendent Harvey reorganized the hierarchy that supervised and supported the schools. Previously, the district had an assistant superintendent for teaching and learning, who in turn supervised two directors, one for elementary schools and the other for secondary schools. Dr. Harvey eliminated those positions and instead created three area superintendents, each of whom was accountable for the success of twenty to twenty-five schools. The accounting staff, which had mirrored the instructional hierarchy, now had to reorganize, too, and it assigned one accountant to support each of the three areas. Previously, these staff accountants had each done work in a specialized function, such as special education or English Language Learner budgets. Now, some of the accountants had to wear two hats, one as specialist in a set of accounts, and the other as general accountant for twenty to twenty-five schools. A principal who wanted to discuss a problem with her special education budget no longer had to find the special education accountant. She only had to contact her area accountant, who would find the special education accountant and iron out the problem for her. The new organization worked so well that the district's chief financial officer, Lois Rockney, sometimes worried (though with a smile) that the accountants were "going native": "Sometimes they're, to my consternation, looking out for the principals and not looking out for the district-wide budget!" The other crucial area of central office support or opposition to principals, human resources, adopted a matching organizational structure, with the result that the principals were now supported by the key central office staffs, headed by an area superintendent who looked after their needs.

At the time of our study, the central office was formally allocating about 50 percent of its total funds directly to the schools. The other half of the money was still officially controlled by central staffs, including, for example, funds for English Language Learners and for special education students. The central staff would calculate how much support each special education student had coming and then allocate the requisite positions to the principals who had those students. The financial staff was working on a plan to allocate more of its money directly to the principals, based on WSF. However, the finance staff had become very responsive to the desires of principals for budget flexibility and, as noted earlier, would welcome any principal who wanted to come in to discuss ways to use those centralized funds in a flexible manner. Thus, principals responded to our interviews by saying that, on average, they controlled 87.2 percent of the school budget.

Custodians, who seem to have powerful unions everywhere, are also centrally funded, presumably so that principals cannot eliminate any of their jobs. Utilities are also centrally funded, though Edmonton found that when they sent the utilities money to principals, everyone started turning off the lights and turning down the heat whenever they left a room! Other funds, such as professional development money, are allocated to principals, but under state law that money can be spent only on professional development. The principals have leeway, though, in deciding on the kinds of professional development activities they want to fund. Overall, the staff at St. Paul Public Schools implemented decentralization in a manner that was friendly and helpful to principals, though they did not attempt to wring out every freedom that principals could possibly have.

Every principal is required to submit a School Continuous Improvement Plan for improving their school each year and to show how their proposed budget will achieve the elements of that plan. The plan and budget are discussed with the site council before being submitted to the area superintendent. Although the planning process and the oversight of principals are clear, it's nonetheless difficult to dismiss a principal in St. Paul. The principals union, like other similar such unions, has negotiated a long and complex process that protects principals from unfair treatment but that can also be used to prolong the employment of ineffective principals. By comparison, Boston, Houston, and New York City can more quickly dismiss a nonperforming principal, though they cannot take such a step without due process.

St. Paul and Dr. Harvey are proof that change can be accomplished in good times or bad times. Each year since Dr. Harvey arrived in 1999, the St. Paul school district has had its budget cut by the state. The cause, in part, has been declining enrollment, as home prices have risen in the area and families with children have not been able to find affordable housing. But the state itself has been under budget pressure for several years. In any case, Patricia Harvey wasn't going to wait for financial surpluses to bring about change.

SOME ADDITIONAL CHANGES IN ST. PAUL

Another element that was central to the changes in the St. Paul schools was the Project for Academic Excellence (PAE). PAE was focused on workshops for teachers, especially in the skills of teaching writing and reading. Schools could voluntarily participate in PAE, and their teachers would be coached in how to improve their skills at analyzing student performance, determining what development each student needed, and providing feedback to each. Yet another effort was a task force on school choice, which found creative ways to expand school bus service to all students, so that choice could be a reality for all families. The district also paid close attention to class size reduction, going so far as to publish annual reports on average class sizes by subject (in 2005–6, average class size for high school English was 27.7, while in mathematics it was 30.1) as well as a Teacher Load Report, which reported the TSL for every middle and high school teacher and showed both the total number of students and the total number of unique students per teacher for each quarter. Curiously, though, these TSL reports did not stimulate any consistent efforts to reduce Total Student Load.

St. Paul transformed itself, as one of its publications said, "from a top-down, one-size-fits-all school organization, to a system of schools and programs that has the flexibility to represent the best interests of its constituents." ("Impact of leadership initiatives in St. Paul Public Schools," St. Paul Public Schools, November 2004, p. 1.) Training was provided to school councils, principals, teachers, and central staff, and systems were developed to implement WSF budgeting, school choice, and principal autonomy.

Among the key Four Freedoms, principals did get a large measure of budget control and partial control over their staffing patterns. They had less control over curriculum, particularly since the PAE program dictated one specific approach to the teaching of reading and writing. Principals did have the freedom to control their schedules. In sum, though, principals knew that the direction was toward more autonomy, and some of them, such as Jan Hopke-Almer at Phalen Lake Elementary, used every bit of their autonomy to create truly great schools.

Our analysis of the data on the 442 schools drawn from our eight study districts revealed that St. Paul high schools had an average TSL of 129. We found that district principals did not consistently use their freedom to reduce student loads and that they were below the average for our study districts in improving student performance. This may be due to the fact that principals had to satisfy their site councils in making changes in how they spent their money. As a result, we found that in St. Paul, principal autonomy did not produce meaningful overall gains in student achievement compared to our other study districts. It seems likely that the failure to reduce TSL was related to the relatively small improvements in student performance. Student performance for the district did rise strongly over the period, though not compared to our other study districts. In addition, those principals who had greater autonomy did not outperform principals who had less autonomy.

BATTLE CREEK MIDDLE SCHOOL CREATES SINGLE-GENDER CLASSES

Even without reductions in TSL, some St. Paul schools found they could do a lot with the freedoms that they had. Consider Battle Creek Middle School, with 675 students. The school is on Adequate Yearly Progress, or AYP, warning for having failed to make sufficient improvement under federal No Child Left Behind standards, but the principal intends to change that. Beginning in September 2006, Battle Creek offers single-gender classes in the four core subjects for boys and girls in the seventh grade. Next year, they plan to take single-gender core classes to the eighth grade as well. Each day starts with advisory, followed by seven periods of forty-five minutes each. More than 80 percent of the students are from low-income families, so the school serves free breakfast and lunch to them each day. The students are in uniform, a white shirt with either dark blue or khaki pants or skirts, and they may add a dark blue sweater if they wish. The floors are carpeted and the building is immaculate. A seventh grade history teacher says that he has five classes of about twenty-five students, for a TSL of 125, plus a coed advisory. Advisories are ubiquitous in decentralized school districts as one way to encourage the development of a sense of community. In empowered schools, that sense of cohesiveness seems stronger than in the schools of centralized districts. At Battle Creek, though, the larger TSL means that advisories are large, at about twenty-five students, about double the number in some other cities. The principal encourages every teacher to visit their advisory students at home and meet their families. As a small recognition, he pays the teachers twenty dollars for each home visit. The history teacher is pleased with the single-gender classes, noting, "it eliminates a lot of the elements of boys and girls together. Plus for things like grouping, it just takes a whole part of the problem out that I do not have to worry about. Having just boys or just girls in a group, I have it all set to go. I find the girls in particular are working faster. They seem to be less distracted—whatever the reason is, it has been very effective." (All interviews at Battle Creek Middle School took place on September 22, 2006.) Another teacher saw it in the opposite light, observing, "The girls are a lot easier to deal with, and I think it's dependent on the maturity level, and sometimes it is the skill level."

It's now seventh period, and one team of seventh grade teachers is meeting together, all of the teachers who share the same 170 or so students. The teachers like this team responsibility, noting, "it is a built-in way of dealing with any problems with a student. You can disseminate information about a kid, if there is, you know, some problem at home or whatever is going on with them, we have that network." Another continues, "A lot of the communication between the families and the teachers comes through the advisory teachers. So, that might be the first person who is going to make contact with the parent. That person is like a liaison between the parent and the rest of the team in general, and then based on whatever comes up in that conversation, then other steps may be taken. We have had times when we have had parents come in and talk to the teams because we have had issues." Another teacher added: "The first contact might come before the school year even begins, and we may call home to just welcome the family and ask them if they have any questions about the things we are doing." The principal decided to have one assistant principal to work with each of the four teacher teams. The assistant principals also serve as teaching coaches. For one thing, they hope to persuade teachers to get rid of their traditional rows of desks and replace them with tables that encourage dialogue among the students. For another, they encourage each teacher to visit other classrooms, to see how others handle one or another topic or situation. This new organization is taking effect, and it reduced the number of disciplinary referrals to the school office by a thousand compared to the year before. Now every student is known by at least four teachers and one assistant principal.

In a traditional, centralized district, a change to single-gender classes would require school board approval. More than likely, that would lead to the mobilization of various constituencies both for and against the change, a major uproar, and a silent vow by other principals never to attempt such a change. That's one of the many advantages of school empowerment.

STUDENT RESULTS IN ST. PAUL

Between 1999, the year that Dr. Harvey became superintendent, and 2005, the year she resigned, third grade reading scores on the

Minnesota Comprehensive Assessments rose from 32 percent proficient or above to 62 percent. Math scores for third graders rose over that time period from 32 percent proficient or above to 61 percent. In the eighth grade, which uses a different reporting system, reading scores rose from 49 to 65 percent, passing the district standard, and math scores from 44 to 48. Tenth grade writing rose from 63 to 80 percent passing. While the St. Paul district did not participate in the eleven-district NAEP special testing, the state measured gaps in test scores for African-American versus Caucasian students and reported that they were reduced slightly for reading in grades 3 and 5, while the math gap held constant for third graders and was slightly reduced for fifth graders. Both African-American and Caucasian students raised their scores sharply, but the gap between them was reduced only slightly or not at all. Hispanic students saw their gaps either hold steady or increase slightly, although they, too, sharply improved over the period in third and fifth grade test scores.

In high school, where Total Student Load can be most important, the test score improvements were much smaller (in single digits) for all groups of students, and African-American and Hispanic students either reduced their gaps slightly or lost a little bit of ground.

LEADERSHIP SUCCESSION PRODUCES
INSTABILITY OF THE REFORMS

Patricia Harvey resigned in June 2005. Only one of the members of the school board that had hired her in 1999 was still serving, and observers say that the new board did not have the same depth of understanding of decentralization or of the other aspects of reform at St. Paul Public Schools. Given the tremendous amount of work that Harvey had put in to bring the district to success, she must have found it dispiriting to have anything short of full, enthusiastic support from her board. She was succeeded by two interim superintendents, each of whom served for one year, and then by a new permanent superintendent who took office for the 2007–8 school year. The changes that she had put into place and the goodwill that she had created far and wide did not survive her departure.

Between the 2005–6 school year and the 2006–7 school year, the gaps in reading scores on the state test grew for African-American, Asian, Latino, and native American students. In the eleventh grade, the percent of students who met their improvement targets in both reading and math fell for every group except Caucasian students, who exceeded their targets. On August 5, 2008, SPPS Superintendent Meria Carstarphen announced that the district had been notified by the state that it had failed to meet its state targets for AYP for the second consecutive year. Under the federal NCLB law, the district had eighteen schools identified as in need of improvement for the 2007–8 school year, a number that increased to twenty-seven schools for 2008–9. The district sent fifteen thousand letters to the families whose children were enrolled in these schools, informing them that, under federal law, they had a right to transfer to other schools. Rumors circulated that many veteran educators and district staff, discouraged at this turn of fortune, were seeking jobs elsewhere or were planning to retire.

THE LESSONS LEARNED FROM ST. PAUL

The moral of this tale is complex. One conclusion is that a dedicated leader like Dr. Patricia Harvey can, with total devotion to duty, bring about top-to-bottom change in a school district of medium or small size within five or six years. A second conclusion is that if the leader is succeeded by others who do not share the same vision, the changes can be undone within a year or two.

A third conclusion is that six years is not long enough for a change as major as decentralization to take hold and to become strong enough to withstand leadership succession. A fourth conclusion is that elected school boards are not always a reliable governance mechanism if continuity is needed. Voters tend not to be aware of arcane subjects like decentralization, and they've surely never heard of TSL. They cannot be expected to hold their school board members responsible for continuing a pattern of successful reforms.

Another conclusion is that some improvements, such as those involving teacher training, are relatively easy to purchase through outside consultants and can be implemented widely. Other improvements, particularly those that involve major organizational change, are difficult to implement but, once in place, they have staying power. An additional conclusion, one that has been repeated in several fields of endeavor, is that when a school district embarks on a change that makes it a maverick or an isolate, it can rarely sustain that change over time. Once the new pattern has become more widely known and understood, though, the same changes come more easily and have greater sustainability. Finally, the concept of site-based management should be discouraged. A school district is a single, hierarchical entity that should be encouraged to operate in as decentralized a manner as possible. Decisions should be decentralized to principals, who should be held accountable for improving student achievement. If outside parties are introduced and granted influence within that hierarchy, as is the case with SBM, they will inevitably attenuate the effectiveness of the management system of the district and introduce superfluous personal agendas into the goals of the schools. It is easy for them to do so because they are not accountable, as is the top management of the district.

San Francisco Implements Decentralization under Trying Circumstances

It's June 7, 2006, and the San Francisco Unified School District is in turmoil. Earlier this year, Superintendent Arlene Ackerman announced that after six years in office she would resign at the end of the current school year. The newspapers have been full of stories of conflict between the superintendent and one or another local constituency. Some have praised her for insisting on high standards for all students in all schools, while others have criticized her for what they feel has been a "drill and kill" emphasis on test preparation to the exclusion of all else. To make matters much worse, the school district has been embroiled since 1983 in racial tensions that stem from a consent decree that resulted from a desegregation lawsuit brought by the NAACP. Leaders of the city's Chinese and Latino communities were angry at their exclusion from the negotiations and objected to the explicit "caps" on nine specified racial and ethnic groups on schools that had been found to be segregated. The district has, as a result of the decree, committed to allocating additional funds each year to the affected schools, thus raising more objections from the parents who felt that their schools needed more money, too. To top it off, Ackerman's predecessor had reconstituted ten failing schools, thus forcing their teachers to apply for jobs elsewhere and producing a tough conflict with the teachers union. While she contended with a situation that would have fully occupied the attention of most superintendents, Ackerman instituted sweeping changes in the district, including a substantial decentralization, that brought about steady, continuing gains in student achievement. Fortunately, Ackerman did not have to take the time to invent her decentralization plan from scratch, because she had been part of John Stanford's Seattle team and she subsequently had worked with Edmonton's Mike Strembitsky in an educational consulting firm. She was familiar with the work at Edmonton, Houston, and Seattle, and she had a clear and strong vision of what she wanted to accomplish in San Francisco.

HOW SAN FRANCISCO COMMUNITY ALTERNATIVE SCHOOL RAISED ITSELF UP TO SUCCESS

Meanwhile, at the San Francisco Community Alternative School, K–8, the end of the school year is approaching, and it has been another very good year for the 288 students and fourteen teachers. The school has a racial balance that many other California schools would envy, with 37.8 percent Latino students, 24.3 percent Asian, 16.0 percent African American, 10.8 percent white, and 6.3 percent Filipino. About 65 percent are from low-income families. Insulated by its autonomy from many external issues, San Francisco Community Alternative School has been working hard to produce gains for its students, and the results have been very positive. On the California Standards Test, the school-wide rate of proficient or above in English language arts has risen from 31 percent in 2003 (the first year of the test) to 48 percent in 2007. In mathematics, scores have risen from 23 percent proficient or above in 2003 to a very strong 59 percent in 2007. The improvement during Ackerman's tenure was dramatic, and it continued, though at a more modest pace, after the announcement of her resignation. During that time, the gaps have been reduced materially for African-American students in both subjects, while Latino students have reduced their gap materially in math but have seen their ELA gap increase slightly.

Community Alternative School has outperformed the district as a whole. Comparing Community Alternative School to others statewide with similar student bodies, the school's state ranking has risen from 6 (out of a possible 10) in 2003 to a ranking of 9 in 2006, the most recent year for which data are available. Community Alternative School is not one of the schools that receives extra funds, but it has nonetheless made gains by using its autonomy in creative ways, as do most San Francisco district schools.

Each of the classrooms combines two grade levels in one class, either K–1, 2–3, 4–5, or 6–7, but grade 8 is by itself. Principal Timothy Nunez refers to himself as the "lead teacher," because the school is "teacher run and project based," meaning that teachers make the decisions by consensus and that students work on major projects that last for several months or even a full year. The lead teacher position rotates among the teachers every three years.

One teacher has this to say about the rationale behind project based learning: "Project based learning is always, as you saw, a very engaging way to get kids motivated." Another teacher explains the combined classes as follows: "The teacher will have the kid for kindergarten and first grade, and that's a huge benefit in terms of being able to know the kids, develop a relationship with the family, get to know their learning style—and the kid's comfort with you." Following a description of the history of combined classes, the teacher continues, "Another huge advantage of the combination classes is that it's much easier for teachers to maintain a consistency of classroom culture. Classroom culture is really, really important, in terms of establishing a positive learning environment, and if you get twenty or twenty-five new kids each year, then you spend the first six to eight weeks of school establishing a classroom culture. And with the combination classes you have half of the class who already carries that culture and who will be able to help you establish that, and there's also a difference because it's not just the teacher establishing that culture, it's the peers doing that." Advisories provide another source of cohesion in the school. Grades 6, 7, and 8 have advisory for twenty minutes each day on Monday through Thursday and an hour on Friday. Each advisory consists of ten to fifteen students with one teacher and enables the advisors to strengthen connections both to the students and to their families.

The teachers at Community Alternative School continue to refine the way they organize their instruction each year. Recently, for example, the grade 4–5 teachers concluded that math instruction would work better for their students with single grade level instruction, so they have separated their 4th graders from their 5th graders into separate classrooms for math instruction. One of the two teachers of 4–5 takes the fourth graders for math, while the other teacher takes the fifth graders. For next year, the grade 6–7 teachers have successfully advocated for adding a math specialist who will teach math to sixth graders in one class and to seventh graders in another. Another half-time teacher will be hired to teach eighth grade algebra. In order to make these staff additions, the teachers have decided to replace the full-time physical education teacher with a half-time consultant who will cost less than half as much and to make other sacrifices. Although San Francisco Unified mandates district-wide curricula, its schools have learned to take good advantage of their remaining three freedoms of budget, staffing, and schedule. A creative educator can achieve a great deal with even a little bit of official freedom.

Once the teachers have agreed on the changes to their budget, they submit their proposal to the school site council, which in San Francisco has authority to approve or deny the school plan and budget for each year. The site council, in turn, will present the proposed budget, school plan, and staffing plan to the central office staff team that supports them. Ackerman and her then chief of policy and planning, Myong Leigh (since promoted to deputy superintendent), have organized the central office staff into five teams of eight or nine specialists each, representing all of the key functions of the central office, including budget, human resources, academics, special education, parent relations, and so on. Each team supports about twenty schools through the annual planning process, providing technical advice and eventually reviewing the final set of plans. In all, the district educates about 55,000 students in 110 K-12 schools and 34 preschools. As a result, the central office staff members get to know their schools well, and they take an interest in seeing their schools succeed. The process seems cumbersome at times, but it means that teachers, parents, central staff, and principals are united in their goals and plans when they go before the school board for final approval each year. It's much better, the teachers at Community Alternative School feel, than the old system in which they had to send a plan directly to the school board—whose members would have no idea whether the plan that they were asked to approve had broadly based support or not.

The teachers at Community Alternative School know their school budget intimately, and they spend whatever time it takes in planning so that they can use every penny for the benefit of their students, a necessity in an era of shrinking budgets. "We still feel like we're short-staffed. We still feel like there are places where kids can fall through the cracks because there's not an adult there to hold them up." The teacher continues, "It would be helpful to have a counselor on site who could work with those kids and specifically have skills with connecting them to the classroom. We don't have very many people who are outside the classroom, and those people that we have are stretched extremely thin . . . It would be really nice to have more than six thousand dollars in our supply budget for the year, but that's the stuff that makes it nice but not what actually does the work—that's people." So the all-important decisions about how to allocate scarce instructional resources originate with the teachers at each school, not in a faraway central office staff office.

Community Alternative School is not K–8 by chance, not in a district where most schools are either K–5 or 6–8. As one teacher says, "One of the advantages of being a K–8 school is that you have continuity of curriculum from K–8 and you can have accountability within your own school. In a K–5 school if the fifth graders are unprepared, you send them somewhere else. You never have to care about it. Here, if you send an unprepared fifth grader to sixth grade, the teacher sitting next to you at the meeting will look at you and say, 'Why aren't these kids prepared?' "

Another of the autonomies that is important to the teachers at Community Alternative School is professional development. As one teacher puts it, "I don't know if you call it a luxury or whatever, that we actually get to do all of our professional development in-house. So, we don't have to go through district professional development . . . I think that sensibly, the district says, 'Okay, if you're doing it this way, it may be different from the way that other schools are doing it, but you're getting results, so keep doing it that way.' So we get to design all of it! The teachers at school actually make those decisions . . . so it's very closely connected to the needs of classroom teachers." Professional development occurs periodically during the week, for one to two hours. The lead teacher and a team of additional teachers research and present the topic each time, while their students are taught by a visiting artist or musician. In addition, the teachers go away together for a few days before school begins and again during January or February in order to work intensively together as a staff. However, the budget in recent times has been pinched by other more pressing needs, so professional development has been irregular.

San Francisco Community Alternative School has found a way to maximize its autonomy within the constraints of the district's limited but consistent decentralization system. Our research shows that principals in San Francisco on average controlled 23 percent of their school's budget in 2005, well below the average for our eight study districts. According to the district, principals' budget control increased to about 45 percent of all district spending for 2008–2009. It doesn't seem to principals that they have quite that much autonomy, though, perhaps because the very tight district budget means that most schools are limited to hiring the necessary minimum number of classroom teachers and not much beyond that. Under those circumstances, staffing freedom is more a theoretical concept than a reality to many principals. In addition, the special education budget of about $90 million (which is separate from the general fund budget of about $480 million) is controlled directly by central office staff, who assign the necessary positions to each school, rather than sending the money to principals and letting them decide how best to spend it.

THE RESULTS OF DECENTRALIZATION IN SAN FRANCISCO

In San Francisco Unified, the average high school Total Student Load is 143, third highest among our study districts. The district does not have a local nonprofit partner like Boston Center for Collaborative Education or New York City Center for Educational Innovation, and it does not have the DNA of the Coalition of Essential Schools. As a result, reducing TSL has not yet been a goal of the district, though that could change in the future. Nonetheless, San Francisco principals make good use of the freedom that they have, producing a reduction in TSL of 7 students per teacher in high school for every 10 percentage point increase in the principal's budget control, the second best among our eight study districts. In the early years of decentralization, the principals and school site councils decided to eliminate large numbers of paraprofessional positions, using the money instead to hire more classroom teachers. In many cases, those paraprofessional employees had been used as hall monitors or lunchroom and playground monitors, while others were kept busy running the school copying machines. The union that represents these paraprofessionals immediately attempted to place pressure on the superintendent to countermand the decisions, but they were reminded that they had been part of the process that had established the school site councils and that had agreed to delegate the budgeting and staffing decisions to the schools. In the end, the grassroots legitimacy of the site councils was too strong for even the unions to overcome, and change went forward.

Our research also reveals that in San Francisco, the result of increasing school autonomy is an increase of 3.4 percentage points in student achievement (percent proficient or above) for every 10 percentage point gain in a principal's budget control, the second best result in our study. In other words, San Francisco has a nuanced decentralization that has been carefully crafted to match its unique historical and political situation. The central office holds back a large portion of the money to be allocated to struggling schools, especially schools with high proportions of low-income students, thus reducing the budget autonomy of all of its schools to a degree. At the same time, Superintendent Ackerman and her central office staff were committed to supporting the efforts of principals to seize the initiative and to use the autonomy that they do have to maximum effect in producing gains in student achievement. The result is a district that has become successfully decentralized and one in which principals, despite the absence of the Ted Sizer influence, effectively reduce TSL and raise student achievement.[1]

In addition to decentralization, San Francisco implemented

school choice, with 40 percent of families choosing a school that was beyond their normal zone by 2005. Ackerman also brought with her the idea of surveys of students, parents, teachers, and principals. In 2001, the first survey year, for example, 13,554 parents (23.2 percent) answered a Parent Satisfaction Survey, and the results for each school were posted on the district website. The full battery of surveys has been repeated twice since then, most recently in 2008. The district would like to make the surveys annual and plans to do so once more money becomes available. The principal accountability system is embodied in annual School Accountability Report Cards, which are posted on the district website and are user-friendly. The Report Card includes extensive information on everything from the suitability of physical facilities to average teacher salary for the school, administrative staff positions, and a variety of standardized test results, state evaluations, and progress on the federal No Child Left Behind requirements. Another important part of the principal accountability system is the annual evaluation of the school and of the principal by each school site council.

Although San Francisco has not created a New York City–style Leadership Academy, it maintains a close relationship with the master's-degree-granting Principal Leadership Institute at the neighboring University of California, Berkeley, and regularly hires about ten graduates of that program each year. The district has also developed a second, equally valuable source of new principals. In San Francisco, the highest-need schools are designated as STAR (Students and Teachers Achieving Results) schools. Each of the several dozen STAR schools is assigned a full-time, on-site instructional reform facilitator, or IRF. The IRFs, as they are known, are master teachers whose responsibility is to teach, coach, and provide leadership to the teachers at their assigned STAR school. Those responsibilities just happen to perfectly describe the critical skills of a successful principal, and thus many IRFs become assistant principals or principals after their STAR tour is complete. Sitting principals receive annual training through a variety of activities, one of which is the annual site council conference, to which every principal brings three to five members of their school site council for training and planning. San Francisco also puts a great deal of effort into training principals to make thoughtful use of student performance data as a basis for making changes in their instructional programs.

Arlene Ackerman felt that if she was going to give autonomy to her principals, she had to provide coaching and professional development to the schools that were in trouble. She, like the other superintendents in our study, was not in favor of a sink-or-swim attitude toward principals. As a result, a portion of the district's effort was directed to 43 of the district's 117 schools. These designated STAR schools each receive, in addition to one IRF, a full-time substitute teacher to enable teachers to attend training sessions, a half-time parent liaison, a part-time nurse and student adviser, and visits by art and music teachers who temporarily take over classes, also to permit teachers to attend training (although Community Alternative School had for years used art and music teachers for this purpose, the school did not receive financial support for those activities).

San Francisco's achievements in student performance are hard to quantify because the state of California changed its standardized tests during the years between 2000 and 2007. However, both the old and new tests use the same standard of "proficient or above." Between 2002 and 2008, the percentage of students scoring proficient or above in English language arts had risen from 35 to 49 percent, and in math, from 37 percent to 58 percent (grades 2–7), both strong results. Although San Francisco still had far to go to reach its federal No Child Left Behind objectives of 100 percent proficient or above, as is true for virtually all urban school districts, it clearly had made substantial progress during the years of decentralization.

REFORM IN SAN FRANCISCO SURVIVES AS SUPERINTENDENTS CHANGE

Superintendent Ackerman spent two years after her resignation teaching at the university level and doing other work. In the fall of 2008, she accepted an appointment as the superintendent of schools in Philadelphia. We can make an educated guess about what is likely to happen in the Philadelphia schools, and they're probably going to like the results. In San Francisco, Ackerman was succeeded in July 2007 by Carlos Garcia, who had served in Fresno, California, and in Clark County, Nevada. The Clark County school district had begun to try autonomous schools while Garcia was serving there, and the early indications are that he is supportive of the reforms that are under way in San Francisco.

It is tempting to say that Arlene Ackerman had walked into the middle of a political combat zone and that the combatants continued their war throughout her tenure, with some of them ultimately declaring war on her, too. Despite these harsh conditions, she pressed forward with her vision of a decentralized, more equitably funded school district. Two years after her departure, the indications were positive for the sustainability of her work at San Francisco Unified. San Francisco's system of Weighted Student Formula budgeting was completely intact and continuing to work smoothly, the school site councils continued to play a positive governance role within the decentralized system, and most important of all, the seven members of the school board, by all accounts, had accepted decentralization and were continuing to sail a steady course. Occasionally, one or another school board member might enthuse about an idea such as adding more paraprofessionals to every school, but others would remind him that those decisions should be left to the principals and the school site councils. After all, when budgets have to be cut, it is the principals and the site councils, and not the school board or the central office staff, that decide what each school can best afford to do without.

St. Paul and San Francisco, Different yet Alike

St. Paul and San Francisco both had powerful, visionary superintendents who knew what they wanted to accomplish and managed to do it over a six-year period. Both superintendents were familiar with the work in the first-generation districts of Boston, Houston, and Seattle, and both knew Edmonton and Mike Strembitsky personally. Indeed, Patricia Harvey and Arlene Ackerman were and are close personal friends. As a result of being in the second generation of innovators, both were ready to move quickly. It seems that the speed and focus with which reform took place in these two districts overwhelmed the school boards, the unions, and the central office staffs, at least at first. The risks of rapid change can be overstated, though, because even first-generation Seattle moved quickly to implement decentralization under John Stanford, but even there, he might have outrun his infantry and gotten so far ahead of them that they felt lost at times.

One of the most striking comparisons between the first and second generations is the extent to which the second-generation districts reorganized their central staffs into teams that were supportive of the empowered schools. Although both Houston and Seattle had made some changes along the same lines, and Boston's central office seemed to have accepted the Pilot Schools as deserving of their attention, none of the first-generation pioneers had gone nearly as far in reorganizing their central staffs as St. Paul and San Francisco did right from the start.

In both cities, the community seemed ready for decentralization. The site-based management movement was largely responsible for recruiting Harvey to St. Paul, just as the school site council advocates had found Ackerman. It's likely, though, that even the St. Paul leaders who had visited Edmonton were surprised at the extent of the changes that Patricia Harvey had in mind, and the combatants in San Francisco likely had mutually incompatible agendas when they agreed on Arlene Ackerman as their leader. When a radical new idea crops up, it is necessarily the case that very few people will know what to expect of it.

Another observation is that decentralization seems to produce positive effects for student achievement even where Total Student Load does not decline. The firing up of principals to be creative and to adapt their instructional programs to local needs is, by itself, beneficial. It is more beneficial by far if principals use their autonomy to drive TSL down, but that step requires systematic training of principals. In the case of San Francisco, the superintendent had previous experience working in Seattle and encouraged her principals to trade in administrative and non-teaching classroom aides for more credentialed teachers and instructional assistants. In St. Paul, that did not happen.

Today, at least eight districts are following that path, and the publication of *Making Schools Work* in 2003 prompted a variety of surveys of teachers and evaluations of the ideas of WSF and of decentralization, such as those by the Fordham Foundation[2] and by the NEA, the largest national teachers union.[3] As a result, there is at least a slightly growing acceptance of this new approach to organizing and managing school districts.

The idea of decentralization now seems to have become permanently part of the culture in San Francisco and St. Paul. Although decentralization seems to be on hiatus in St. Paul, it may come roaring back there, too. That will require a superintendent who will once again be a decentralizer, as Dr. Patricia Harvey was. In San Francisco, the new superintendent appears to be supportive of continuing the decentralization, though only time will tell how deep that commitment to decentralization is. Every school district that is now decentralized, and every district that contemplates taking that path in the future, will learn a great deal from these pioneers of the second generation.

Another important lesson that these examples teach us is that decentralization is anything but a monolith. There is an unlimited number of variations on the theme and many ways to implement change. In the end, though, every decentralizing district is betting that if it gives more autonomy to its principals, they will each find the unique path that will improve their school. Three other urban districts, the third generation, have recently chosen this path.

7

THE THIRD GENERATION: CHICAGO, OAKLAND, AND NEW YORK CITY

The third generation of implementers learned a great deal from the experiences of their predecessors. One of them chose to move more slowly, with greater care and deliberation than those who had gone before, while another did the opposite, moving with extreme speed to fully implement its changes. New York City was also part of this third generation, but we will mention it only briefly in this chapter, because it has already been discussed. None of these most recent decentralizers can be said to have yet achieved full realization of school empowerment, but all three show signs of building the kind of change that will be sustained for many years to come.

In Chicago, School Autonomy Is Taking Root

Chicago Public Schools educates 408,601 students in 655 schools, which makes it the third-largest U.S. district, after New York City and Los Angeles. Mayor Richard M. Daley runs the schools under a 1995 act and appoints the seven members of the Chicago Board of Education. The student enrollment by race is 46.5 percent African American, 39.1 percent Latino, 8.0 percent white, 3.3 percent Asian/Pacific Islander, 2.9 percent multiracial, and 0.2 percent native American. A total of 84.9 percent of students are from low-income families.

The Chicago Public Schools, as we noted earlier, have been through ups and downs over the past forty years, as have most urban school districts. In 1988, U.S. secretary of education William Bennett visited Chicago and declared that its public schools were the worst in the nation. Mayor Richard M. Daley was first elected in 1989. His campaign was based in substantial degree on a promise to take over the schools and bring them back to health. After his election, he was granted control over the schools by the state legislature. In 2001, he appointed Arne Duncan, then thirty-six years old, as Chief Executive Officer of Chicago Public Schools, a position that Duncan held for more than seven years, thus giving the district stability of leadership. In January of 2009, Duncan was chosen by President Obama to become U.S. Secretary of Education. Duncan, who had no previous experience leading an organization of any size, inherited a district that had been alternately centralized, decentralized, and then recentralized. Teachers and principals were generally discouraged and angry about their treatment, and parents and the press were very critical of the district. Under Daley and Duncan, Chicago Public Schools has had stability, and things have improved.

SUPERINTENDENT ARNE DUNCAN
LAUNCHES AMPS IN CHICAGO

The process of improvement had begun under Mayor Daley's previous superintendent, Paul Vallas, who adopted a school choice program and launched a great variety of new schools, including uniformed military schools, test-in schools, and small schools. While some of these schools enjoyed a measure of autonomy, the district was still centralized, through area offices and the central staffs. The result was that many principals were confused and frustrated about what was expected of them when Duncan took office. Many principals complained that although the district talked decentralization, the reality was the opposite. Despite the centralizing tendencies of the old CPS system, principals in Chicago have long had control over their curriculum at least in principle, though that freedom has been compromised by various curriculum initiatives from central office staffs. They have also long had control over school poverty funds from both the state and the federal government. As a result, Chicago's principals are accustomed to making some instructional decisions on their own, and most of them yearn for the additional freedoms that decentralization could give them.

In September 2005, Superintendent Duncan launched eighty-five AMPS (Autonomous Management and Performance Schools). The eighty-five schools were to be granted greater freedom than other Chicago public schools, based on their superior performance on standardized tests of student performance. By implication, Chicago had determined that autonomy was a privilege to be earned by demonstrating high student performance, rather than a tool that would enable all schools to improve—though it later reversed that stance. Why, the initial logic ran, should the district grant freedom to a school that was failing? The other seven districts had granted autonomy primarily to underperforming schools, based on the idea that without autonomy, no school could improve. Chicago is the only one of the eight decentralizing districts to have adopted the opposite philosophy. In practice, the difference between the two schools of thought is not as stark as it may appear, because all of the districts supervise low-performing schools more closely than they do high performers, but the Chicago approach to granting autonomy was nonetheless distinctive.

Critics of Chicago's autonomous schools point out that many of the original AMPS either were selective-admissions schools or were located in upper-income neighborhoods, and they assert that their high student performance is more a result of a privileged upbringing than effective schooling. If autonomy is good for the rich, they argue, should it not also be good for the poor? Initially, the AMPS were granted exceptions from district-initiated curricular initiatives in reading, math, and science and from centrally sponsored professional development courses for teachers.

These freedoms were meaningful to the schools, as evidenced in a 2005 study by the Cross City Campaign for Urban School Reform, which reported that Chicago teachers "were very critical of the central office's professional development offerings." In addition, the report observed that the central office had attempted to improve the way reading was taught by assigning the schools reading specialists who, while working in the schools, reported not to the principals but to the central office. Not surprisingly, the report found "teacher resistance" to these outsiders who had been imposed on them. By contrast, AMPS principals were to be allowed to alter their school schedule, create their own professional development programs, and transfer some funds from one program to another without prior approval from the area instructional officer, Chicago's version of regional assistant superintendents. Even though the defined freedoms were few at the outset, the first cohort of AMPS principals expressed great enthusiasm at being part of the program. The greatest benefit, they reported, was that now they were being left alone to work with their teachers and run their schools, rather than having to leave their school several times each week to attend one or another mandatory meeting called by a central staff or Area Instructional Office. In the fall of 2006, the number of AMPS was increased from eighty-five to ninety.

Beginning in the fall of 2007, the AMPS program adopted a major change in its original philosophy by creating the opportunity for any school, not only those with top student scores, to apply for AMPS status. Applicants were required to file a plan that described how they would use the additional freedom to improve student performance. The total number of AMPS increased to 108 in September of 2007 and to slightly more than 130 schools in September of 2008. AMPS have the option of continuing to report to their old area or of withdrawing from the area and reporting to the central AMPS organization instead. About 55 of the 130 AMPS have chosen to remain with their area; the other 75 have opted out. Those who opt out report instead to the central AMPS officer, Melissa Megliola Zaikos. Zaikos and her small staff serve as the central source of support for the AMPS, as well as going to bat for them when the central staffs attempt to place bureaucratic barriers in their way. Each year, Zaikos assigns a team of AMPS principals to visit each AMPS campus and evaluate it. She also provides a coach for every new principal, as the district does for all new principals.

During the second year of the reform, the AMPS received the additional clarification that they would enjoy six freedoms, including the original freedoms and in addition gaining the Chicago district's version of budget autonomy. Beginning in the fall of 2007, a subset of twenty AMPS principals were put on a trial "per student" funding system based on Weighted Student Formula, which gives them still greater control over their budgets. In time, it appears likely that this Weighed Student Formula approach will spread to all AMPS institutions.

RENAISSANCE 2010 SCHOOLS, CHARTER AND CONTRACT SCHOOLS, AND ADDITIONAL AUTONOMOUS SCHOOLS

Chicago Public Schools also initiated a second program, Renaissance 2010, under which it aimed to open or "turn around" one hundred small schools by the year 2010. This program, begun in 2004, had reached a total of eighty-eight schools by 2008. Renaissance 2010 includes forty-three charter school campuses, twenty "contract schools," and twenty-five "performance schools" that are almost indistinguishable from the AMPS except that all of the performance schools enjoy the benefits of WSF budgets. At the outset, the Renaissance 2010 Schools were intended to be small schools, but the idea of giving them autonomy had not yet arisen. Soon thereafter, Chicago committed itself to creating autonomous schools, and both the AMPS and the Renaissance 2010 Schools became autonomous.

The state of Illinois, under pressure from teachers unions, has a very restrictive charter school law that permits a total of only thirty charter schools in Chicago. The superintendent saw that charter schools were succeeding, and he wanted to be able to offer more schools that enjoyed the same kind of autonomy. As a result, several charter schools won permission to operate multiple campuses, and Chicago Public Schools also approved several contract schools, which are nearly indistinguishable from charter schools in their freedom but are not counted within the state-established cap of thirty charter schools, because they operate with contracts from the district rather than under state charters. Charter schools and contract schools are not required to have units of the Chicago Teachers Union, as are the performance schools and AMPS.

Counting the 88 Renaissance 2010 Schools and the 130 AMPS, the superintendent had by 2008 created a total of 218 autonomously managed schools. This amounts to 33 percent of Chicago's schools and may well have put the district beyond the tipping point, headed inexorably toward district-wide decentralization.

On the other side of the ledger, Chicago has moved gradually to develop the kinds of principal selection, training, and accountability systems that full autonomy requires. No district can grant full autonomy to its principals until it has in place the management systems that are necessary to guarantee that the principals are properly selected and trained and that the financial and student performance data are properly designed to provide accountability. Charter schools and contract schools are required to define their own accountability and governance provisions. At some point, it seems likely that the district will want to supplement these school-based accountability provisions with a robust district-wide web of accountability. That step has not yet been taken because it might conflict with Chicago's long-established and powerful local school site councils. Holding Renaissance or AMPS principals accountable is complicated because the local school councils have long had the authority to appoint and renew or not renew their own principals to a series of four-year contracts. They also have the power to approve school budgets. As we've observed, this type of system compromises accountability, because the teachers, parents, and community representatives on the school councils cannot be held accountable by the superintendent or by anyone else. On the other hand, these councils tend to be strong, even fierce, supporters of school autonomy, and they may prove in the future to be an important source of political support for the continuation of the decentralization of Chicago's schools.

Overall, the Renaissance 2010 Schools are outperforming traditional Chicago district schools, according to the district's data. Attendance in the Renaissance 2010 high schools averages 93.3 percent compared to 86.0 percent for traditional high schools, and the graduation rate averages 89.9 percent compared to 73.4 percent at traditional Chicago high schools. The AMPS by far outperform all other Chicago public schools by every measure, but this is likely a result of the selection process for the original AMPS, which chose the eighty-five district schools that had the highest student performance results. In time, Chicago Public Schools will be able to evaluate AMPS institutions by the gains that their students make from year to year.

Chicago has made changes in the central office staffs by creating Business Service Centers (BSCs) that assist all schools in learning how to manage their own budgets, though the traditional schools do not enjoy as much freedom in this regard as the autonomously managed schools. The BSCs have created an online system through which all principals can track their spending against their budget throughout the year, and they offer a host of training programs for principals in managing a school budget. All schools may also elect to pay an annual fee ranging from five to ten thousand dollars for "premium services" that include on-site training and support in budget management, periodic Web-based training, and other services. About one hundred schools currently subscribe to these premium services.

SOME RESULTS OF DECENTRALIZATION IN CHICAGO

On the NAEP tests administered by the federal government, Chicago, like almost all of our eight urban districts, finds itself making steady progress, albeit from a very low base. Fourth graders made solid gains in mathematics, from 10 to 16 percent at or above proficient, but they held steady at 1 percent who were advanced. Eighth grade gains in mathematics were similarly positive over the period. In reading, fourth graders also made good gains, but eighth grade NAEP reading scores were nearly flat over the period. Chicago's black and Hispanic fourth grade students ranked third from the bottom among the eleven NAEP cities in math, with black students scoring below 82 percent of the nation's black students and Hispanics scoring below 77 percent of all Hispanic students. The results for eighth grade math were similar among black students but slightly higher for the national comparison of Hispanics. In reading, Chicago's black students again ranked third from the bottom among the eleven cities, while Hispanic students ranked fifth from the bottom. In the eight grade, black students in Chicago ranked fourth from the bottom, while Hispanic students were the top ranked among the eleven NAEP cities, but 60 percent of the nation's Hispanic students outranked Chicago. Overall, Chicago's schools have made solid gains, though not in all respects. The performance of black and Hispanic students is very low and much in need of improvement. The central reform strategy consists of AMPS and Renaissance 2010 Schools, both of which are still too new to have yielded meaningful performance results, though the early indications are positive.

Our own analysis relied on data collected during the first year of the AMPS program and thus does not tell us much beyond what the initial picture looked like. We found that AMPS principals on average controlled 13.9 percent of their budgets after they had joined the program, compared to 10.8 percent for principals of nonautonomous schools, a barely noticeable difference, but this will presumably grow sharply as Weighted Student Formula funding is implemented.

During the first year of AMPS, the central staff had not implemented any kind of WSF funding process, as we've noted above. Nor had it set forth for principals a clear statement of just what they did or did not control. The gradual approach to decentralization in Chicago had the virtue of enabling the district to take one step at a time in this new direction while teachers, principals, and the public grow comfortable with the implications of decentralization. As a result of this deliberate pace, Chicago may be able to avoid some of the resistance that ultimately hurt decentralization in Houston, St. Paul, and Seattle.

Chicago has a contract with its teachers union that limits the flexibility of principals more than in most cities. It seems unlikely that Duncan could have succeeded in a New York–style fast implementation, given these restrictions. By now, however, Chicago's teachers should have developed confidence that decentralization is their friend rather than their enemy, and perhaps the pace of change will quicken in the near future.

On the other hand, the gradual approach to change has also meant that the commitment to decentralization has been inconsistent within the district. While some principals had been told that they now have autonomy, many of the central office staff still behave in the old centralized ways. One elementary school principal remarked that "you really aren't autonomous . . . They don't give me $X million and say, Go do what you want to do." Instead, she continued, "you're entitled to this many teachers." (All Chicago school interviews in this chapter took place during November 2006.) The gradual approach can succeed, but ultimately all of the elements of the district's management approach must be aligned for autonomy to realize its potential for student success.

Some Chicago high schools are very large, with more than three thousand students. One of these, Curie Metro High School, has decentralized itself into three self-contained schools, an International Baccalaureate school of about two hundred students, a vocational arts school, and a performing arts school, each with about 1,350 students. However, all of the teachers have five classes of twenty-eight students, for a TSL of 140. There are more than seventy non-teaching staff in each of the three schools, including administrators (assistant principals, deans, and counselors), custodians, security guards, and office staff. About one-third of the students meet the state standards on the required annual tests. We can see that there is great potential in Chicago to reduce Total Student Load and to improve student achievement as decentralization takes hold.

Our analysis shows that for a 10 percentage point increase in budget control, the AMPS reduced Total Student Load by an average of 1 student, well below the reductions of 4 students in Boston and 25 in New York City. As a result of this small improvement in student loads, Chicago AMPS were below average for our sample in raising student achievement as budget autonomy increased, though budget control had barely changed at the time of our study. The evidence from our other study districts suggests that if Chicago perseveres in its implementation of decentralization, these results will become much more positive.

A NEW TEST-IN HIGH SCHOOL USES ITS AUTONOMY

One positive development is that the creation of AMPS has sent a clear signal to AMPS principals that if they want to be creative, they are free to do so. One inspiring example of what an AMPS can do with its freedom is the Walter Payton College Preparatory High School, founded in 2000. Walter Payton is one of Chicago's selective-admissions high schools (its namesake was a much beloved player on the Chicago Bears football team). The founding principal, Gail Ward, had asked the district for permission to name her school after Payton, who was widely admired. In its first year, Payton admitted only a freshman class, adding a new freshman class each year until it was fully enrolled after four years. That way, the school was able to establish a brand-new culture. Payton has about 835 students, about twice the enrollment of the other autonomous schools that we studied. A total of 40.4 percent of Payton's students are white (compared to 8 percent citywide), 27.5 percent are black, 22.8 percent are Hispanic, 8.8 percent are Asian/Pacific Islander, and 0.6 percent are native American. One-third are from low-income families, and one-half of one percent are Limited English Proficient. In 2005, 93.8 percent of Payton's students met or exceeded the state standards on reading, math, and science. The school is thought to rank second in student achievement among AMPS institutions just behind Northside College Preparatory High School. Most teachers have five classes per day of twenty-eight students, for a TSL of about 140—right at the average of 141.9 for all AMPS high schools. English teachers have an average TSL of 120, well below most other AMPS, while math teachers average 115. In addition, each teacher has an advisory of about twenty-eight students that meets for ten minutes each day.

Admission to Payton Prep is based on seventh grade test scores, grades, attendance, and other factors, all of which applicants must submit during their eighth grade year. Some of the students travel as long as ninety minutes each way, and they have to get to the school on their own. The students see each of their teachers for class three days a week rather than the usual five days, in a complex modified block schedule. On Monday and Friday, students have eight periods of forty-six minutes each. On Tuesday and Wednesday, there are alternate blocks, for science labs, math projects, and English. All of the courses are either honors or AP. On two Thursdays each month, students come to school for the morning only, for a forty-minute advisory and for non-credit seminars in topics as varied as DNA crime scene investigation, vegetarian cooking, zulu, latin dancing, and wall climbing. Teachers don't have to be certified in these seminars, and students love them. The seminars are not permitted within the teachers union contract, but the teachers all waive that portion of the contract each year. On those Thursday afternoons, the teachers work together on planning and professional development. Another feature of this schedule that teachers like is that they have two free periods each day in addition to their lunch break. That's unusual, too.

The four college counselors are busy, because everyone at Payton goes to college, many of them to places like Carleton, Middlebury, and Harvard. Payton is able to maintain teacher loads below the district maximum of 150 and to offer extensive college counseling because it focuses its money on those objectives. Unlike most Chicago schools, Payton receives no federal poverty funds, so it has to choose what it will do. One teacher is "freed up" to perform non-classroom duties as the school technology coordinator, but that's it. The school has three assistant principals, one of whom handles scheduling and curriculum and is also in charge of renting out the parking lot and the gym on weekends, money that the school is allowed to keep. Another serves as admissions director and also oversees everything from student clubs to sports teams and proms. The third assistant principal is responsible for hiring, checking teacher credentials, and for student discipline.

Walter Payton, along with the other selective-admissions AMPS, has succeeded at what some thought impossible: 30 percent of Payton's students are coming from parochial and private schools. Payton has created a positive, intellectual culture for some of Chicago's most able students. It's an important symbol, standing as it does right next to the infamous Cabrini-Green housing projects, which are now being demolished for redevelopment. Not only has this school changed the future for hundreds of students, it will now be an important part of changing the character of the city, as middle-class and professional families increasingly move into the neighborhood, because the schools are excellent here.

LESSONS FROM THE CHICAGO EXPERIENCE

Chicago declared its intention to pursue decentralization as early as 2002. It followed through by creating the Renaissance 2010 Schools and the AMPS. The district has now created 218 schools that have autonomy. This large number of schools may put pressure on the entire district to convert to school autonomy, both because the autonomous schools are popular with families and because it will be difficult for the central staff to simultaneously run two very different administrative systems, one to support autonomous schools, and another to support centralized schools. As long as Mayor Daley remains in office, it seems likely that the current direction of change will continue. With former CEO Duncan now in Washington, it remains to be seen whether or not Mayor Daley will pick a new schools chief who is pro-decentralization.

It is apparent that Chicago's approach to implementing decentralization is more deliberate than the process in New York City, and with good reason. In New York City, term limits totaling eight years forced Mayor Bloomberg and Chancellor Klein to complete their implementation program rapidly, especially to give it at least two or three years to mature before they leave office, if decentralization is to last. (As of 2008, term limits had been changed, and Mayor Bloomberg was expected to seek a third term.) In Chicago, though, Mayor Daley does not have a limit on the number of his terms. When he completes his present term, Mayor Daley will have surpassed his father's record as the longest-serving mayor of Chicago. Given the inherited complexities of the local school council system and the Chicago Public Schools union contracts, it may be that Chicago is pursuing just the right pace of change.

When it comes to the substance of decentralization, Chicago and New York City are very similar. Both cities are employing the Five Pillars and the Four Freedoms, though neither district is adhering to every detail. New York City has taken school autonomy city-wide, and Chicago seems to be headed in that direction, too. Every school board and superintendent will need to weigh the advantages of faster change against the risks of change that is too fast. No matter what the future may hold, there is no question that Chicago Public Schools under Mayor Daley and former CEO Duncan has made major strides in a bold new direction.

Oakland Shows What Can Be Achieved in Just Three Years

Oakland implemented decentralization, Weighted Student Formula budgeting, school choice, stakeholder satisfaction surveys, and reorganized its central staffs, all within three years. None of our other study districts even thought about moving that fast. It did so in large part because its leader knew from the outset that his term would be short, and because he inherited a district that had been moving, although slowly, in this direction even before his arrival. It was able to do so because the school board had been suspended by the state, and thus the state administrator in charge of the school system did not have to answer to anyone but the state superintendent. The question is whether the changes begun in Oakland can be sustained over the long run.

Oakland, California, educates 38,982 students in 109 district schools and 32 charter schools; 36.8 percent of the students are African American, 33.3 percent are Latino, 15.4 percent are Asian, 6.8 percent are white, and 1.2 percent are Pacific Islanders. A total of 66.9 percent are from low-income families, 9.3 percent qualify for special education, and 29.9 percent are English Language Learners.

Beginning in the 1990s, young professionals who were priced out of the San Francisco housing market moved into Oakland, causing a rise in home prices there and driving out the lower-income families with children. The resulting declining school enrollment reduced the district's revenues, creating unrelenting financial pressures. In 2000, the school board agreed to a 24 percent pay raise for teachers over three years. The district staff subsequently discovered that the money simply was not there to meet these obligations, and in 2003, the Oakland Unified School District was found by the state of California to be insolvent. The state gave the district a $100 million line of credit, replaced the superintendent with a state administrator, Dr. Randolph Ward, and suspended all powers of the school board. Dr. Ward had his work cut out for him, to put it mildly.

ENTER DR. RANDOLPH WARD, AN AGENT OF CHANGE

Dr. Ward had previously served as the state administrator in Compton, California, in similar circumstances. He was a proven turnaround leader. He's a compelling person—physically strong, mentally bright, optimistic, and in constant motion. His approach is to provide strong leadership direction and to build a staff that can work cohesively together long after his job is done and he has moved on to his next assignment. Dr. Ward is also very direct. He looks for the toughest issues and engages them head on. A state administrator has no school board to slow him down, but neither does he have a board to hide behind. Ward likes that trade-off. He had to restore fiscal soundness to the Oakland district, and he addressed that issue by taking on the teachers union in a dramatic confrontation that lasted for two years and that came within hours of a strike. He insisted that teachers pay at least some portion of the cost of their medical insurance. In the end, the union complied, but Ward bore the brunt of their anger.

Fiscal health was important, but more important to Dr. Ward was educational soundness. He was a student of the Edmonton approach. He recalled telling his staff, "Our fiscal management, for example, started on the first audit—the baseline was 0.73 on a scale of zero to ten. Now if you look at that, then you understand what others believe is the risk of going to a [decentralized] model, they would say, 'Your fiscal situation is at 0.73—what are you thinking to decentralize?' Some of the fiscal and, more important, the academic—how the fiscal and academic person felt. And I come back to those folks and say, 'Over-centralized models sure didn't work here! Not to mention fiscally it bankrupted the district, but academically things weren't happening as well, except through some of the small schools stuff." (All quotes from Randolph Ward are from an interview on July 17, 2007.) Ward has another important strength—he's not a know-it-all. It's typical of strong leaders who can confront tough problems that they aren't good listeners, but Randy Ward was looking for help, and help was right under his nose, in the form of BayCES.

BAYCES BRINGS THE INFLUENCE OF TED SIZER'S COALITION OF ESSENTIAL SCHOOLS

BayCES, the Bay Area Coalition for Equitable Schools, has its office right down the block from the Oakland school district headquarters. In a real sense, it's the northern California equivalent of Boston's Center for Creative Education, which supports that city's Pilot Schools. Like the CCE, BayCES is a spin-off of the Coalition of Essential Schools, and it remains an affiliate of the CES. In fact, the original name of BayCES when it was founded in 1991 was BARCES, the Bay Area Regional Coalition of Essential Schools. Steve Jubb became executive director of BayCES in 1998 and served in that position until his retirement in 2007. Under Jubb, BayCES had been growing steadily, working with one or two schools in each of several northern California districts, such as Berkeley, Emeryville, Fremont, San Francisco, and Vallejo. A year before Randy Ward's arrival, the Oakland district and BayCES had opened their first new small schools in Oakland. Both BayCES and the Oakland district believed in the power of school autonomy, and they made a perfect match. Ward especially liked the idea that, long after he had moved on, BayCES would remain to continue the school autonomy that he planned to implement. Ward recalled a lunch with Melinda Gates of the Gates Foundation at which he told her, "I think you've got something here, because too often they make these relationships or have these relationships with just the school district, and the leadership changes, and you know, something happens in the governance structure, whatever, and things fall apart. And I think that the BayCES of the world that are far and few between—get some as committed and competent as the one we have here and as their executive, the CEO is Mr. Jubb— I think plays a critical role. In Compton, I had the same Gates small schools monies as they had up here. I couldn't find a legitimate, competent, outside organization. I ended up going with somebody from Illinois, Washington, or something . . . that had no connection. I mean, they came in here and they had to figure it out just like everybody else! BayCES and their people, I mean, they've got ex–board members, school board members that are on their board. And their commitment is in the right spot. So, I think that is also the future. I think that whoever comes in here and replaces me as the State Administrator, and eventually a superintendent, would be wise to continue that kind of relationship and would be very unwise to let some of the politics or the authority issues—that you know are always a part of these partnerships—get in the way."

Before Ward's arrival, Oakland had brought in Katrina Scott-George from BayCES to join its four-person Office of School Reform (OSR). The OSR had been created to oversee the development of small schools. As part of its work, OSR had been doing some analysis to determine whether the small schools were receiving the proper funding. They found gross inequity. Oakland serves a small community of very-high-income families in its hillside neighborhoods and a large population of low-income families who live in the flats. In Oakland as in most districts, teachers have a collectively bargained right to take a job opening when it appears, based on seniority. In many cases, teachers use their seniority to move to the wealthier schools.

OAKLAND IMPLEMENTS WEIGHTED STUDENT FORMULA BUDGETING FULL ON, USING "ACTUAL SALARIES"

Many parents do not realize that schools in wealthy neighborhoods have some teachers who earn up to twice as much per year as the less experienced teachers in the low-income neighborhoods. That's because in most districts, a teacher's pay is based mostly on the number of years of service. Thus, the hillside schools in Oakland were spending up to twice as much per student as the flatland schools. This result turns the state's policies upside down, because virtually every state allocates money to districts based on formulas that have the goal of spending more money on low-income students, in the belief that it costs more to bring those students up to state standards than it costs to do the same for wealthier students. Almost no school district wants to confront this issue, however, because wealthy families have political clout. The result of this maldistribution of educational funds is that the gap in student performance between middle-class and low-income students continues year after year.

Randy Ward was not afraid of this confrontation. After completing a thorough analysis, and having sent teams to visit Edmonton to see their implementation of Weighted Student Formula budgeting, he set Results-Based Budgeting (RBB) in motion. RBB did not attempt to perform its own analysis of how much should be spent on each kind of student, as St. Paul had done at first. Instead, like most districts that now use WSF, he simply adopted the existing state amounts for each student characteristic, such as English Language Learner or special education. That formula, though, is only half of Weighted Student Formula budgeting. The other, more sensitive half, is whether to charge each school for the average salary of its employees or to use actual salaries. If a district uses average salaries, as all save New York City and Oakland have done (Houston has expressed its intention to use actual salaries but has not yet done so), the existing funding inequities will continue. In that case, WSF budgeting will still serve the important function of giving budget flexibility to principals, but the achievement gaps are unlikely to be reduced.

If, on the other hand, the district decides to charge schools for their actual payrolls, as Oakland did, some schools, mostly those in wealthy neighborhoods with long-serving teachers, will be over their budgets. As Ward put it, "Well, it is a salary cap. There's no question about it."

The effect of a salary cap, if it is implemented suddenly, will be to force the schools that are over their cap to dismiss some of their mostly highly paid teachers and replace them with lower-paid teachers. That kind of requirement would play havoc with schools and create an outcry among principals, teachers, and families. Fortunately for Ward, Oakland's voters had approved a three-year parcel tax for the district right before his arrival, and that additional money had not yet been allocated. The state administrator was able to use that as "hold harmless money." He gave extra money to the schools that were over their salary caps, with amounts from $2500 down to $500 per student as each school's budget required. He warned the principals that this "hold harmless" money would be available for only three years, and that they'd better start planning to replace retiring, veteran teachers with lower-cost young teachers. The hillside principals were satisfied that the plan was a fair one. The flatland schools were happy, because Results-Based Budgeting gave them—for the first time—all of the money that the state had intended them to have, and their budgets rose. Most principals looked forward to having greater flexibility with their funds. Ward expected that it would take a few years for principals to learn how to use their budget flexibility in ways that would help students. For example, he expected that principals in the toughest schools would invent ways to keep their teachers: "Here's what we're working on, and I think this is part of the evolution. One is, our principals just haven't yet figured out good techniques for keeping people, whether through their budget abilities—even though you can tell me, you know, there's a way of keeping people. You can pay them extra stipends for mentoring. You could, okay? We haven't figured that out yet. But that takes time. It's not something you can put on a formula and say, 'Do this.' The other piece is that we're doing this grant. You may have heard about it. It's a federal grant that is out there for making sure we are really on this one. It'll bring up to $8 million over five years or so to put the right teachers in the right school. So it's some kind of incentive, stipend, something that, with the help of this grant and RBB, we can actually work out with the unions to keep and retain people in these tough schools. All of this is part of what has to happen. You just can't recipe this and expect it to stick." Although it's unlikely that either parents or the public understands the courage that it took to implement RBB using actual salaries, other decentralizing districts understand. The Oakland staff was proud that their district had done the right thing. One senior staff member recounted with relish a meeting with her counterpart from the Houston district: "He said, 'Well, what's unique about what you're doing in Oakland?' I said, 'We're doing actual salaries.' He goes, 'Okay, you win.'"

Results-Based Budgeting had other, more immediate benefits, as Randy Ward noted. "Substitute teachers were free! If a principal had someone absent, they just called central, and central sent them a substitute. They didn't pay for that substitute teacher. So I took all of my budget for substitute teachers and sent it to the principals. I said to them, If you need a substitute, hire one, but don't ask me if you run out of money, because I don't have any. I sent all of it to you." In the first year, Oakland's spending on substitute teachers fell by several million dollars, and principals were free to use that money on other school needs. Now, if a teacher told her principal that she had in-laws coming for a visit and she'd love to have Friday off, the principal was likely to tell her that she could do it, but it would take money away from other school needs. Before, the principal would have been likely to tell her not to worry, to go ahead and take the day off.

In the end, Results-Based Budgeting was implemented successfully. As of 2008, Oakland principals controlled on average about 84 percent of the money (compared to 60.5 percent in our study in 2005). The salary cap had the expected effects, except in one respect. Some had expected that the flatland schools would be able to hire teachers with long experience, but that did not happen. Nonetheless, Ward was satisfied, because flatland principals had more money than before, and they were able to use that money to hire a larger number of new teachers than before, thus reducing class sizes and student loads. Although the idea of Results-Based Budgeting had been gestating for a year or so before Randy Ward's arrival, he seized on the incipient effort and implemented it with what, in education circles, was blinding speed. Ward did not have to explain RBB to the school board, and thus he could move fast. The central office finance staff did not like RBB, though. Under RBB, they had to spend months developing budgets for each school, while under the old centralized system, that aspect of their duties could be done in a few days. In addition, the school board and some in the community felt left out of the process, and the teachers union did not feel that it had been adequately consulted. Because of Ward's strong support from the Gates Foundation and the Broad Foundation, some critics accused Ward of attempting to turn Oakland Unified into a business corporation. (Interview of July 17, 2006)

SANKOFA ACADEMY SHOWS HOW TO DRIVE DOWN TSL IN OAKLAND

Whatever the remaining issues might be, Oakland has provided enough leeway, and Dr. Ward provided more than enough encouragement, for an entrepreneurial principal to accomplish a lot. Consider Sankofa Academy, K–5, a new small school. The principal, Danielle Neves, is a Boston native who attended Yale University and graduated later from Southern Connecticut State University. She was a Teach for America teacher at a Los Angeles school in Watts before coming to Oakland. Neves designed her new school by meeting with her team each Friday for a year, putting together their plan for Sankofa. Part of the process involved meeting with parents in the community. As she remembers, "I spent time in big meetings where people yelled at me . . . it was, like, 'Welcome to Oakland.'" (All interviews at Sankofa Academy took place on April 6, 2006.)

Neves describes how the plan evolved over that year into a plan to open with grades K, 1, 2, 3, 6, and 7, and then grow from there into a full K–8, although she ultimately decided on a K–5 format instead. She developed her curriculum in partnership with a nonprofit organization, Facing History and Ourselves, which had begun by developing a curriculum that deals with the Holocaust, and which had subsequently added curricula organized around the Armenian genocide, American slavery, and other major human rights issues. She explains, "Our students are 98 percent African Americans. Seventy percent are low-income. We want our kids to be empowered to not just look at an incident or look at a situation and feel 'I'm just the victim,' because even if that's the role I chose, or is assigned to me, there are still choices I'm making that then impact how this all works out, and so what we wanted to do is to start to build that consciousness for kids, starting in kindergarten." After more enthusiastic detail about the basis of the school's curriculum, Neves continues, "And then eventually moving to a place where students do service-learning projects, because they're choosing to participate. ('So, based on my learning about myself and how I interact with the world, I want to choose to interact with the world in a particular way.')"

Neves also paid close attention to how her new school would enter an old, established community that had strong feelings about its schools: "Mostly the older African-American families are moving out, actually out of Oakland, to places where they can buy—they can sell their home here for a good chunk of change and buy a less expensive home somewhere else. And young white families or young white single people are moving into the neighborhood, into those homes. And so the demographics are changing and the schools are changing, so there's hurt in this particular community about that, and part of the demographic of the school not changing has to do with that, a lot of those folks who are moving in don't have kids, or they have very, very tiny kids. So all our hope is involved in developing this new school, and we'll also start to change the perception of public schooling in this area, so that those families will then send their students here. The low test scores and low achievement of our students, the high dropout rate, you know, the violence that happens in schools—all of those things have become such the norm that there's sort of a built-up hurt about that. There's a built-up hurt from families who went to Oakland public schools and didn't feel like they were served, and yet feel they don't have a choice about where their children can go to school, except the Oakland public schools. And also feeling often very shut out of the school. So not having a place or a voice in the school, what we've found is that we, as we encourage our families to have a place and a voice, they don't know what to do with themselves. So, the first half of this year, we had two camps of parents: the parents who would never come, except they'd come to a dinner or a meeting and look very perturbed, like they weren't sure what to do, or the parents who got over-empowered, who I had to rein in and say, okay, you can't discipline other people's children! You know, they were just, they were on it! But it was really a completely new thing for us to say, 'this is your school as well, you can—we expect you to be here, we want you to be here.'"

Grades 6 and 7 are cored and blocked. "One sixth grade teacher teaches English/social studies, the other teaches math and science. So, a humanities block and a math/science block. All teachers also teach an intervention class, for example for kids who need extra help in math or reading. Total Student Load is forty-eight—twenty-four and twenty-four. Intervention is usually with your own students . . . usually five to ten students." In addition, every teacher has an advisory of about twelve students. During advisory, several of the sixth and seventh graders help out in the elementary classrooms. The Coalition of Essential Schools is alive and well, and living in Oakland, California, thanks to BayCES and to the Oakland school district.

Listening to Principal Neves plan for next year's eighth grade start-up is like listening to New York City's Eric Nadelstern. "One of the things that's really important is that all of our eighth graders take algebra. Our theory is algebra for all. . . . We wanted to hire a math expert, to teach both pre-algebra and algebra to seventh and eighth grade students, so their load would increase. . . . They wouldn't have another content area to teach, which would also make science a single subject—one person teaching science in the seventh and eighth grades." Neves is also worrying about the No Child Left Behind law, which requires that every teacher be credentialed in every subject she teaches: "We're not sure that . . . we're going to get to keep seventh and eighth grade as a core humanities subject, unless we can bring in teachers who have a single-subject English and a single-subject social studies credential." She's also thinking, though, that most teachers could get their second credential in either one summer or, at most, one year of evening courses.

Neves likes her budget control: "Because we have complete budget autonomy, we create our own staffing structure. So we actually try to think out of the box about it." She has an administrative assistant who runs the administrative part of the school; a full-time family coordinator; a full-time instructional coach, who works with teachers; a contract consultant to deal with disciplinary issues; a school security officer; one full-time and one part-time custodian; and a food service person who comes in for two hours a day at lunchtime. This year, Neves has a tight budget because three people have been out on extended medical leave, "so we're way over on subs from what we thought we were going to spend. . . . My goal is, I will spend all of my money, and then I'll have some of everybody else's that they didn't spend!"

In the early grades, the official Oakland Unified curriculum is Open Court—a version of scripted instruction which has both strong critics and strong proponents—but Neves uses a different curriculum, Guided Reading. All of her elementary teachers have been trained in the same strategies for literacy. The teachers are encouraged to use Open Court to the extent they'd like. Some of the teachers use it a lot, while others never touch it. In order to get this flexibility on curriculum, a principal has to select a curricular approach that has been approved by its school community.

Neves faces challenges, for sure. Among her new sixth and seventh grade students, for example, none tested as advanced in math, and only 1 or 2 percent were proficient. She also comments that principals have been warned to stop the "dance of the lemons" by passing bad teachers on to other schools. Instead, they've been encouraged to be sure about a new teacher before approving her for tenure. Weak teachers aren't likely to want to work at Sankofa, though, because, as Neves says, "We have a longer school day, we require more hours for professional development, we require our teachers to all do five home visits a year . . . just building relationships with families, not to talk about student progress." On the other hand, every day, every teacher has someone else take her class for one period, so that she can grade papers and work on future lesson plans. The union contract calls for only one such period each week. Teachers also have a longer lunch period than standard, forty-five minutes versus the usual thirty.

A LOT HAS CHANGED AFTER ONLY THREE YEARS

Three years after Dr. Ward's arrival, much had changed in the Oakland Unified School District. A poster outside the superintendent's office announces that Oakland Unified has had the most improved test scores of any K–12 urban district in the state for each of the last three years. The number of high school students enrolled in Advanced Placement courses is up 50 percent over the last two years, half of the high schools are making their daily attendance goal of 94 percent, and average high school attendance rose 5 percent in just the last year. Another poster announces: "A new management and budgeting approach is transferring control of resources from the central office to the individual schools. . . . The district is changing central office operations and culture to provide more reliable, high-quality and cost-effective services to the schools."

The changes in Oakland happened fast by design, as Kirsten Vital, chief of community accountability, remarked: "Dr. Ward, as state administrator, made a conscious decision as a district to redesign quickly . . . rather than do it incrementally and slowly, in which case it would have taken years. . . . The clock is ticking, and we are in an emergency . . . we do not have another five years for kids to fail." (Interview of July 17, 2007) Oakland Unified quickly implemented a school choice program in which about 80 percent of families got their first choice. The remaining 20 percent of families were invited to visit the principal of their neighborhood school so she could find out why they hadn't wanted to go there. "We found out things—that, you know, some families did not want to go a school because it did not have a preschool program, or it did not offer the kind of wrap-around services after school that parents were expecting." She continues with an example of one school: "So families who have two- and three-year-olds are now engaging in the school, knowing that they are going to work toward whatever the problems might be, so that by the time K comes, they are going to commit and go to that school." It's not surprising that Vital, a native of Brookline, Massachusetts, is a former teacher at a Coalition of Essential Schools affiliated school in Whittier, California, and her mother once worked for CES founder Ted Sizer. As a teacher, Vital had two double-period blocks of humanities each day with twenty students per class, plus a large elective in a next-door school with thirty-five students, for a Total Student Load of 75. Most high school teachers in Oakland have TSLs of about 123, which is low for California.

Other changes include the introduction of annual surveys of students, parents, teachers, and principals; the creation of eight network officers, each of whom works with between eight and fifteen schools; and a complete reorganization of the central office staff into one that supports autonomous schools. As Randy Ward noted, "The infrastructure behind the change—if that doesn't change, then the change gets squashed eventually, or it ceilings out . . . If we're ever going to get central office to support the kinds of things you're doing in the schools . . . central office has to change."

OAKLAND SURVIVES LEADERSHIP SUCCESSIONS

Dr. Ward resigned his post in August 2006, three years after he had arrived. His job was done, and he was moving on to become superintendent of the San Diego County schools. Three years wasn't much time, not enough for the changes in Oakland to have become stable. However, Dr. Ward had demonstrated how much a leader can accomplish in a deeply troubled urban district if he does not have to deal with the politics of a school board. He created a benchmark of sorts, a standard that other superintendents, who do have school boards to bring along with them, can likely not match, but against which they can judge their rate of progress. Dr. Ward had known from the outset that this would not be a permanent assignment for him, and thus he had created a team of top staff, empowered them, and seen to it that they became cohesive. Ward was succeeded as state administrator by Dr. Kimberly Statham, his former chief academic officer. Statham kept the revolution going for one year and then resigned to rejoin her Maryland-based family. Statham, in turn, was succeeded by Vincent C. Matthews, former Oakland Unified chief of staff.

Could Oakland Unified survive its third superintendent in three years? In St. Paul, it was just this kind of instability in the leadership that had caused the decentralization reforms to disintegrate. Dr. Ward, though, had created a cohesive management team, and Dr. Statham, who had been an integral part of the change, continued to empower and encourage them, as did Matthews. As a result, the district leadership team redoubled its efforts during the transition period, increasing to about 84 percent the portion of the budget that it allocated to principals through Results-Based Budgeting. While many principals took to their new freedom with enthusiasm, others weren't sure just what to do with it. On the whole, though, student achievement continued to rise strongly in Oakland, and the changes seemed to be on track.

When the state of California had taken over the Oakland Unified School District, it had pledged to monitor five areas of operation, from pupil achievement to financial management, and to return each of the five to control of the school board when it had made sufficient progress. By April 2008, the state had restored local board control over three of the five areas of operation, and the board was preparing to once again assume full control of Oakland Unified. In addition to the state administrator, the board hired an interim superintendent, Dr. Roberta Mayor, who for the past five years had headed the state team that had oversight of Oakland Unified.

A month later, the state of California released its annual school district evaluations for the 2007–8 school year. Oakland Unified extended to a fourth year in a row its standing as the most improved urban K–12 district in the state. The graduation rate reported by Oakland Unified was 85 percent, and average daily attendance was 93.1 percent. On Oakland district surveys, 77 percent of teachers felt safe at school, and 74 percent of students and 42 percent of parents agreed. Ninety-two percent of students felt they were being held to high expectations, while 69 percent of parents and 72 percent of teachers agreed.

However, the Oakland Board of Education was about to reassert local control over the Oakland Unified School District, and they had not been included in Dr. Ward's change process. There were signs that some board members resented the treatment that they'd had, and few if any of them were well informed about Results-Based Budgeting or decentralization. The board of education had stated in its 2008–9 strategic objectives for Dr. Mayor that they wanted her to review the key reforms of the past few years. Perhaps the board wanted Dr. Mayor, the former state oversight leader, to delve deeply into what had been going on at Oakland Unified, in order to tell the board whether any of it was really worth keeping.

Now on its fourth superintendent in as many years, the Oakland Unified School District is once again at a crossroads. While the staff is as convinced as ever that the reforms that they initiated are having a strongly positive effect on student performance, the approach is still unusual in California and unknown in most of the United States. It's not clear that the new board and whomever they select as the new permanent superintendent will understand and appreciate decentralization, which is now ingrained in many of Oakland's schools, school site committees, parents, teachers, and principals. If the examples in other cities are a reliable indicator, Oakland will not return to its former decentralized ways fully for many decades, if ever.

OAKLAND UNIFIED LOOKS TO THE FUTURE WITH OPTIMISM, BUT CONCERNS OVER SUSTAINABILITY LURK

As the Oakland Unified School District prepared to begin its sixth year of decentralization in the fall of 2008, the pace of change was still fast. The staff had learned that while principal budget control was the linchpin, all of the Five Pillars and Four Freedoms were necessary if student performance was to continue to improve and the race gaps to be reduced. They had also reached the conclusion that they needed to develop a complete system for hiring and developing principals, and that they needed to enrich Oakland's accountability system. To start with, they engaged the same firm from Great Britain that has been providing annual school visits and evaluations to the New York City school district and asked them to visit each of the district's charter schools. If that experiment works well, perhaps those outside evaluations will be extended to all Oakland Unified schools. To ensure that central office staffs serve the schools rather than command the schools, Oakland also implemented surveys of principals to evaluate the quality and responsiveness of service that they receive from those staffs, much as Edmonton has done for nearly forty years. The district staff also took over responsibility for launching new schools, a role previously played by a joint BayCES/Oakland Unified team. BayCES shifted its role to providing leadership training to the district principals and staff.

The decentralization and many other reforms that Randy Ward and his team had begun seem to have survived through three new state administrators. Oakland Unified had steadily improved for five years by the summer of 2008. Despite these gains, Oakland has far to go because, like most urban districts, it started out at the bottom of a very deep pit. Forty-two percent of second grade students and 35 percent of fifth graders scored proficient or above on the 2008 California Standards Test, while 21 percent of eleventh graders made that standard. In similar fashion, 50 percent of second grade students and 10 percent of eighth grade students scored proficient or above in the state math test. Our analysis shows that Oakland Unified has not used its decentralization to focus on reducing TSL. Average TSL for Oakland high schools in 2005 was 123, and our study showed that, compared to schools in the other seven study districts, Oakland principals were below average for the sample in using their autonomy to reduce TSL and increase student performance, despite their rather high principal budget control of 60.5 percent. Without a doubt, though, Oakland has made very strong improvements in student performance, and there is no sign of abatement.

The Oakland school district has a valuable asset in its cohesive and committed senior staff. One hopes that they will be able to convince the school board that giving control to skilled principals and holding them accountable is Oakland's best hope for providing a good education to all students.

New York City Takes the Third Generation to a New Level

We've already covered the changes in New York City in detail, but here we can briefly put New York into the context of the third generation of pioneers. Mayor Michael Bloomberg and Chancellor Joel Klein anticipated that they would have eight years in which to carry out their reforms, compared to the three years that Dr. Ward was given. On the other hand, they did not expect to have twelve or more years to get their job done, as Mayor Daley and CEO Duncan must have imagined was at least a possibility. Thus, New York City had to move quickly but had the time to be deliberate as well.

It appears that New York City has gone about implementation in a particularly effective manner. New York's implementation of the Five Pillars and the Four Freedoms was more consistent than that of any of our other study districts. When we performed a statistical analysis of each of the eight cities, we found that the full array of changes was more consistently applied in New York than elsewhere, and that the autonomous schools there displayed a greater reduction in student loads and the largest improvements in student achievement. Of particular note are the great efforts that the New York school district put into the selection, training, and coaching of principals, largely through the Leadership Academy. None of the other districts has gone as far in focusing on the readiness of its principals to handle autonomy. New York also managed to avoid hard conflicts with its unions, although it did have confrontations over several issues, most of them unrelated to the decentralization.

Finally, New York devised the most complete web of accountability of any of our eight districts. The effort put into those changes, combined with the continuity in leadership, make the decentralization effort in New York City the standout in our analysis.

The Third-Generation School Districts in Perspective

The leaders of the decentralization efforts in the third-generation districts, Chicago, New York City, and Oakland, did a lot of homework before they started. They visited and studied the five U.S. districts that had gone before them, as well as Edmonton. All three received substantial foundation money and advice from the Broad Foundation in Los Angeles and the Gates Foundation in Seattle, among others. These foundations had become part of the national network of institutions that understood change, helped districts to change, and increased their odds of success. While it seems to take ten or twelve years for decentralization to mature fully in a school district, and while even that much time is no guarantee of sustainability, it looks as though all of the third-generation districts are moving in a direction that will have staying power.

It's also noticeable that all three of these districts welcomed help from outsiders, including charter schools, nonprofits such as BayCES, the Coalition of Essential Schools, the Center for Educational Innovation–Public Education Association, New Visions, and local universities. That was not always true of the earlier innovators, many of whom were wary of charter schools, and most of whom did not have access to local nonprofit organizations that had long experience with autonomous schools. New York City and Oakland were particularly fortunate in having local nonprofit organizations that had long ties to Ted Sizer's

Coalition of Essential Schools. It seems unlikely that these districts could have moved as fast or as surely in their reforms without access to that knowledge.

The teachers unions in the three cities responded to decentralization in some ways that were systematic. Two of the three superintendents chose not to directly challenge the unions nor to insist on broad revisions of their union contracts. The third, Oakland, had a major conflict, but over health benefits for teachers rather than over decentralization. Unfortunately, that conflict cast a pall over the entire relationship between the district and the union.

All three superintendents moved without hesitation to adopt changes that they felt were essential even though the contract did not explicitly permit the new arrangements. The union leaders were initially standoffish without being hostile to the new direction, possibly because decentralization has the effect of bringing instructional decisions closer to the schools and thus to the teachers, which unions typically favor. Overall, these third-generation examples suggest that decentralization and the accompanying Five Pillars and Four Freedoms are not incompatible with unions.

These three districts differ greatly in size. New York City is the nation's largest district and Chicago is third largest, while Oakland has less than 4 percent of the student population of New York City. School district size does not seem to matter much where the Five Pillars and Four Freedoms are concerned. The same initiatives matter just as much in large and in small districts, and they have similar positive effects on student performance.

All three of the superintendents led the decentralization effort with enthusiasm, and all proved themselves courageous and determined when faced with opposition from one quarter or another. In most other ways, though, they could hardly have been more different from one another. Chicago's Arne Duncan was a young man who had no experience as a teacher, a principal, or an official of a school district when he was appointed CEO. Many observers at first doubted that he would have the mettle to shake things up, but he has proven them wrong. New York City's chancellor, Joel Klein, also had no experience working in public schools, though he had decades of experience running large and complex organizations of other kinds. Klein was known to be a tough-minded and determined leader before he was appointed chancellor, and he has run true to form. Oakland's Randolph Ward was a deeply experienced educator, and he was also experienced at turning around failing urban districts. From the start, Ward acted with the self-confidence and focus that his previous experience had given him.

Although all three of these superintendents have more than ample inner strength, none of them is usually characterized by their staffs or by outsiders as a "know-it-all." Instead, all three instinctively reached out for help, welcoming it from every possible source. All three became serious students of decentralization and soon became expert on the topic. Perhaps inner self-confidence enabled these three, who occupied positions at the top of institutions that were among the most important in their city, to ask others for help. If so, then every school board should seek leaders who have the strength to admit their areas of ignorance and the humility to accept advice. The superintendency of any school district, large or small, is a physically, emotionally, and mentally demanding job. These men were unusual in their qualities, but they are not unique. Every school district can find a good leader, if it knows what qualities it seeks.

There is, of course, one additional similarity among these three districts that cannot be overlooked: none had a school board in charge while the reforms were under way. In contrast, the school boards in Houston, St. Paul, and Seattle all experienced substantial turnover during the years of our study. In each case, the result was a board whose members did not provide consistent support for decentralization. On the other hand, the San Francisco school board did manage to orient its new members quite thoroughly, and the result has been continuity of support for decentralization even with board turnover. That might be in part a result of the close involvement of San Francisco's board members in the annual planning and approval process with the many school site councils, a form of involvement that seems to have had the result of familiarizing every school board member with the nuances of decentralization. We should add that Edmonton operates with an elected school board but without strong school site councils, and it, too, has provided continuity of support for decentralization since 1977. Edmonton's pioneering superintendent, Mike Strembitsky, served as the district's leader for twenty-two years, though, and that likely was enough time for the idea of decentralization to have become "normal" rather than "experimental" in the city.

More can be said about the lessons to be learned from this third generation of decentralizers, and more still can be learned by comparing all eight of the districts.

8

SEVEN LESSONS LEARNED THROUGH EXPERIENCE

Lesson 1: Big Districts Need Small Schools

Scholars who study the structure of organizations have long held that any organization that has more than about 150 professional employees will suffer the negative effects of bureaucratization. That means that any school district with more than about two thousand students will likely begin to feel the problems that come with large size. If organizations remain centralized as they grow, they develop more and more standardized rules and procedures as a means to maintain control over all of their parts. The tradeoff is that increased standardization leads to reduced flexibility and limits the ability of subunits to adapt to their local needs.

In a centralized school district, all teachers may be required to use the same set of books and materials to teach reading and math, but not all students will learn or be motivated to learn equally from the same standardized approach. All schools in a centralized district are typically required to hold classes for the same number of minutes per class and for the same number of classes per day. Those restrictions will deny schools the flexibility to tailor their instruction to the needs of their students and the strengths of their teachers. If all college football teams had to use the same percentage of running and passing plays and had to employ identical defensive and offensive strategies, one team would be unable to take advantage of a talented passing quarterback and receivers, while another would be unable to emphasize its running game. That would lead to a much worse performance than each team is capable of producing. The same goes for schools. All schools within each state are required to cover the same ground, or standards, but should all schools be required to achieve their coverage of the required material in the same way?

Small schools of about five hundred students each are not only desirable for large school districts, they are a necessity. Many studies have emphasized the strong sense of community that can develop in a small school, compared to the anonymity that is typical of large schools. It's literally possible for the principal to know every student by name in a school of three hundred or four hundred students, and it's almost always the case that the teachers know all of the students in their grade level. Being known as a person, as an individual, is very comforting and also very demanding to students; they know that they are cared for and they know that their misbehavior will be spotted by their teachers.

Some of the districts in our study had opened small schools but initially had managed them from the central office in the same centralized, top-down fashion they applied to all schools. What they found after a few years, to their dismay, was that student performance in the small schools was no better than in their traditional large schools. Their conclusion was that if you divide a large, failing school into several small but centrally managed schools, you will end up with several small, failing schools! Small school size does create some of the benefits of community, but it does not guarantee that student loads can be reduced to eighty or ninety students in middle or high school. Neither does it automatically adjust primary school reading and math instruction so that children are taught these crucial skills in groups of five to seven students. To achieve those kinds of results, a school, whether large or small, needs the Four Freedoms.

Making good use of the Four Freedoms of school autonomy—control over budget, staffing, curriculum, and schedule—is a dauntingly complex exercise in a school of two thousand or four thousand students. Very few principals, even experienced principals, possess the skills that it takes to do that well. A school with four thousand students will have more than two hundred teachers and perhaps an additional two hundred non-teaching staff. School districts now have the ability to diagnose a huge variety of different kinds of learning, physical, emotional, and social needs, to the point that they can accurately describe exactly the kinds of services that each student must receive to succeed in school. However, those same districts typically lack the ability to organize the many specialists and the large number of teachers to get those services to the students who need them.

Very large school districts will likely always need to have a few very large schools that can deliver highly specialized services to the students who need those services, be they students with learning disabilities or high-achieving students. Those schools will always be very complicated and difficult to manage, and they will need principals and assistant principals who are highly skilled and deeply experienced.

No school district, not even the largest school district, has more than a small handful of principals who have the skill and experience to lead a very large school effectively. Therein lies the reason that large districts need small schools. Large districts can alleviate their bureaucratic disadvantages only through decentralization. There is no other antidote to the pathologies associated with large size. If a district delegates substantial autonomy to the principals who have been in charge of very large schools in a centralized district system, though, there will be trouble. The principals in a top-down district do not have much decision-making authority. If principals who have a bureaucratic mentality are suddenly set free, what do you think will happen? In the few cases in which districts have done it, the answer is that nothing happened. Principals who are of a traditional mind-set are aware that they lack experience, aware that they do not have the training that is necessary to make use of the Four Freedoms. Given sudden autonomy, they tend to keep things just as they have always been. A large district simply cannot, as a practical matter, hand over total control of a large school to a principal who is not prepared for that task. It is not likely that any school district can ever prepare enough of its principals to be able to run all of its existing large schools in a decentralized system.

On the other hand, a school of four hundred students will have perhaps twenty teachers and an additional three to six non-teaching staff. A school that small can be led effectively by a principal who lacks depth of experience, if that principal has already acquired strong teaching skills, has a thorough grasp of curriculum, testing, and the use of student performance data, and has had the benefit of a thorough training program for aspiring principals. Every school district has more than enough teachers who fill that bill and who can become successful principals with the proper training, coaching, and support.

In a small school, an energetic and sincere principal can develop personal relationships with every employee in the school. Once those employees trust that the principal cares about the right things, they will help out when things go wrong and will hesitate to criticize an inexperienced principal who is trying hard to do the right thing. As that new principal gains confidence and skill, she in turn becomes the teacher of her teachers. With about twenty teachers to lead, that principal has a total "student" load that she can handle successfully. Even in small schools, though, there is no guarantee that every principal will be successful. A fully developed accountability system operated by the school district is thus a necessity.

How small should a school be? Home schoolers can succeed with one or two students, so there's no theoretical minimum size for a school. There is, however, a financial minimum. If we consider the funding for the average student in a typical district, and if we factor in the typical salaries for school employees, the financial break-even point for schools tends to be between four hundred and five hundred students. That envisions a school that has a typical number of special education students, low-income students, and so on. Of course, that analysis rests on several assumptions, including assumptions about how much money the district will spend on central office staff. The four hundred to five hundred student range won't be correct in all instances. In most cases, though, that size range for small schools will produce schools small enough to be manageable by most principals and large enough to be financially reasonable for the district.

Big school districts have no choice but to decentralize the Four Freedoms to their principals. School districts will never have enough principals who have the capacity to effectively manage the number of big schools they now support. However, districts do have a large supply of current and future principals who can do an excellent job of managing small schools. Thus, big districts need small schools.

Lesson 2: Align Everything

In the real world, neither school districts nor any other kind of organization ever conforms perfectly to the conceptual models that books like this one advocate. Indeed, one of the basic rules for designing an organization is not to be compulsively neat. Organizations must always be designed with some flexibility if they are to be in step with the realities of their peculiar history and circumstances. On the other hand, it is important to understand that, by and large, the elements of the Five Pillars and the Four Freedoms must be substantially, if not perfectly, aligned with one another because the effectiveness of one element depends in part on its alignment with the others.

Consider, for example, what might happen if the Five Pillars—choice, empowerment, effective principals, accountability, and Weighted Student Formula budgeting—were not aligned. If any were absent, could the remaining four still be at least partially effective? The answer to that question must be no. As an example, let's imagine that one of our eight districts did not implement school choice, but did have the other four pillars in place. How would things work in that district?

Without school choice, every student would be assigned to attend the school nearest his family's home. A poorly performing school would not suffer a decline in enrollment, nor would a very good school be rewarded with increased enrollment. Thus, although principals in this hypothetical example might have all of the Four Freedoms that enable them to improve their school, they would not be strongly motivated to do so, and thus those freedoms would be wasted. The accountability system would also be vitiated, because principals who have full schools can come up with lots of excuses for their failures, blaming the parents for being indifferent, the students for being unprepared for school, or other factors beyond their control. When choice is in place, a poorly managed school will start to empty, and no principal can explain that away.

Without school choice, the effects of Weighted Student Formula are muted as well. An innovative principal who operates within a district that combines choice with WSF will be motivated to offer specialized programs that are attractive to students with higher "weights" and who thus bring with them more money. The reason for this is partly financial. If students are assigned to the nearest school, each school will have only a few students who have one or another type of special need, and typically the additional money that those few special students bring will be insufficient to enable the school to meet their needs fully. Even a partial servicing of those special needs will ordinarily cause the school to spend more money on those few than they bring in, thus causing the school to divert part of its budget from the needs of other students, as often happens in most school districts today. Knowing this, principals who operate within a district that combines choice and WSF budgeting take steps to implement specialized programs for high-need students in order to attract several such students, thus bringing in enough money to do the job right and to keep the school solvent. Without both choice and WSF, this result is unlikely to occur.

"Align everything" also goes for having in place not one, two, or three, but all of the Four Freedoms, because they too are intertwined. For example, if principals have control of their budgets, curriculum, and schedule, but do not control their staffing patterns, they are prevented from using their budget freedom to move money from hiring administrative personnel to hiring more classroom teachers. If they have control over their staffing pattern but not over their budget, they will be unable to replace one full-time employee with two part-time employees even if that would better meet the needs of their students.

In like manner, having control over schedule but not curriculum means that a school can replace the standard class periods of forty-five minutes with blocks of one hour and thirty minutes, but they cannot use those blocks to full advantage by combining English and social studies into a humanities course that is taught in a block two periods in length. There is little or no advantage to block scheduling without combined courses, at least in terms of reducing Total Student Load; both changes must take effect for TSL to be reduced by a meaningful amount.

Decentralization is simple in concept but difficult to implement. It is, however, the only solution for a large district. Although alignment of the elements is necessary, no district ever fully achieves complete alignment in all of its practices and organizational features. The closer a district can get to aligning everything, the more successful its students will be. As the great former UCLA basketball coach John Wooden often says, perfection might be impossible to achieve, but that's no excuse for not trying!

Lesson 3: Reorganize the Central Office

The central office must be aligned with the autonomy of the school if decentralization is to be sustained over the long haul. It is possible for a superintendent, through exhortation and force of personality, to coax or coerce a centralized district staff into acting as though they want to support autonomous schools for a while, but that won't last. Eventually, the superintendent will move on, and the next superintendent, who might not have the same level of personal commitment to decentralization, will allow the central staff to snap back into their habits like a stretched rubber band. We know from studies of large business organizations that the organization's structure and the leader's style are sometimes out of synch with each other, and that for a short while, style can overcome structure. But we also know that, over the long run, structure always wins. What this means is that a determined leader can for a while insist that a centralized organization be operated as though it were decentralized (or vice versa). As long as the leader is around, the staff will comply. Once that leader departs, however, the natural forces of organization will cause the staff to return to the behavior dictated by the structure.

Reorganizing a centralized staff is perhaps the single most daunting task in implementing permanent decentralization. In Edmonton, Mike Strembitsky achieved that end by organizing his central office staff into two parts. One part consisted of the functions that must always be in the role of monitoring and auditing the schools and maintaining the system of accountability. It also includes a few functions that are by their nature centralized, such as new school siting and construction, operating the choice system for families, performing legal and external communications work for the district, and selecting, training, and coaching principals and assistant principals. The second part of the central staff was designated as "consulting services." These consisted of activities like building maintenance, specialized psychological services for students, evaluating the needs of special education students, designing and operating professional development programs for teachers, and consulting with schools on curriculum design. Each of these service areas created an hourly billing rate to charge schools. The money for these services, which had previously been "free" to the schools, was sent to the principals, who could then choose to buy their services from the central staff or from an outside vendor of their choice. Several schools took advantage of this freedom to hire local farmers to plow the snow from their parking lots and saved money compared to what the central office or regional office would have charged. On the other hand, the building painting and maintenance staff at central turned 180 degrees from its former bureaucratic, uncaring attitude to one focused on customer satisfaction, and it managed to continue to win most of the building maintenance work from the schools. It took Edmonton several years to get to this point, though, and it will take our eight study districts time to get there, too.

Oakland, New York City, and San Francisco have made substantial organizational changes in their central offices, though none of them has yet reached a new stable equilibrium of the sort that Edmonton achieved. Boston, Chicago, St. Paul, and Seattle have also moved toward reorientation of their central staffs, though they've not yet gone so far as to reorganize. Oakland, for example, has reorganized along the lines of the Edmonton plan, establishing a central service organization that responds to school requests, with annual surveys of principals to rate the quality and responsiveness of that service. The next step would be for Oakland to establish billing rates, send the money to the principals, and let them decide where they would like to spend their money. New York City, as we've noted in an earlier chapter, has already moved certain of its central office functions into independent service organizations, including the Learning Support Organizations, Partnership Support Organizations, and the Empowerment Support Organization. The district has sent the money for those services to the principals, who are free to buy service from any of the alternative providers. The next step for New York City might be to realign the core central functions of budget, personnel, special education, and so on into school support teams and then to identify the central staffs that in reality are also service providers, as in Edmonton, and allow principals to buy services either from them or from outside vendors.

San Francisco has realigned its core central office functions, as we've already noted above, so that each central specialist in budget planning (and in all of the other central office functions) works both as part of her central department and as a member of one of the cross-departmental teams that support the schools. Seattle adopted its own version of that matrixed organization, though it did not include as many of the central office departments on each cross-departmental team as did San Francisco. This matrix concept, in which each central office specialist wears two hats, one as a personnel or budget specialist, for example, and the other as a member of a school support team, has long been used to good effect in business organizations. It seems to have worked quite well in these school districts, too.

The possibility of realignment or reorganization is typically viewed with suspicion and cynicism by central office staffers. In part, this is because the central office has long held the responsibility to protect the public purse from capricious or even unlawful behavior by principals. In part, it is also because realignment suggests a loss of power by the central staffs and a rise in relative power of the principals. Angus McBeath, who was one of Mike Strembitsky's successors in Edmonton, put the issue squarely on the table by saying to his central office staff, "Our job in central is to support the principals. If you want to be a star at EPS [Edmonton Public Schools], apply for a job as a principal."

All eight of our districts took steps to realign and/or to reorganize their central staffs so as to cause those staffs to support schools in their autonomy, rather than to resist that autonomy. The lesson is quite clear. In virtually every school district, large or small, the central office staff and its regional satellite staffs have traditionally been motivated and rewarded for keeping control in the central office, not for letting control flow to the schools. If a new leadership announces to principals that they now have autonomy, two things will happen. First, when principals attempt to make changes on their own, they will be stymied at every turn by the central staff; second, both the principals and the central staff will become frustrated and unhappy. The central staffs must be realigned right at the outset, and ultimately they must be reorganized if decentralization is to become a reality.

Lesson 4: The Leader Must Be a Serious Student of Change

There has been a fair amount of attention over the past several years to the topic of leadership. Much of the writing on leadership focuses on the attributes of "transformational leadership" or "charismatic leadership." We are sometimes left with the feeling that these great leaders somehow magically transform their organizations with the wave of a visionary wand or that they figuratively rewire their organizations through their personal electricity. This book has not adopted that point of view. Instead, it has attempted to describe the many changes in organization and in management process that accompany decentralization.

Although enduring change requires that the nuts and bolts of an organization be rearranged, there are without a doubt several ways in which personal leadership is also important. Getting the people in a large organization to abandon a decades-old centralized approach in favor of an unfamiliar decentralized one is more than changing the arrangement of the nuts and bolts, because unless the human beings who are being asked to make these changes are willing, they won't comply.

Among our eight districts, all had either a superintendent or, in the case of Boston, an outside nonprofit leader who provided the initial impetus that inspired others to take a chance on a new direction. Five were led by people who were nontraditional educators. Dan French in Boston had come from the state department of education rather than from a school district, and Arne Duncan in Chicago, Rod Paige in Houston, Joel Klein in New York City, and John Stanford in Seattle were all non-educators. In Oakland, St. Paul, and San Francisco, on the other hand, the leaders of change were drawn from the ranks of experienced educators. Both types of leaders succeeded, at least for a while.

The nontraditional leaders would be unusual in most industries, though not unknown. It is difficult to think of a major bank that has been headed by a non-banker or an accounting firm headed by a non-accountant, but in recent years, automobile companies, retailers, and other kinds of firms have been headed by presidents whose backgrounds were in other industries. From these examples, we might draw a variety of tentative conclusions. One is that when an organization is large, it requires a leader who understands how to manage large size. Managing large size, in a sense, is its own special area of knowledge and experience, and in at least certain industries, it appears to be transferable from one industry to another. Another conclusion is that when an organization is widely perceived to be in trouble and in need of fundamental redirection, people are more open to accepting a nontraditional leader than they otherwise would be.

Yet a third conclusion is that decentralization is also its own specialty, and these leaders all possessed both an understanding of and a belief in the efficacy of decentralization. In some cases, these leaders had not ever seen a large, decentralized school district in operation and thus had no firsthand knowledge that the idea would work in their district. However, they studied the few examples that did exist, and they believed, based on their other experiences, that decentralization would help their schools to improve.

Perhaps the most outstanding characteristic of these eight leaders, though, was their willingness to pioneer in the face of widespread doubt and skepticism. In particular, the leaders of the first generation (Boston, Houston, and Seattle) had only one point of reference from which to draw comfort, and that one example was from Canada, which many people thought was not relevant to the United States. Nonetheless, they were willing to launch full-scale decentralizations of their districts.

It is not surprising that the superintendents of the first and second generations did not publicly describe their reforms as decentralizations. Instead, they emphasized the improvements that they would bring about in teacher training, curriculum development, the creation of small schools, and increased parent involvement, all of which were themes that were familiar both in their local communities and across the nation. Had they said to parents and the press that they were about to launch a full-scale decentralization effort, it's likely that the public reaction would have been one of puzzlement and dismay.

By the third generation (Chicago, Oakland, and New York City), more people had heard of decentralization, though it was still only vaguely familiar to them. All three leaders in this generation emphasized their decentralization from the outset as a major objective. Once a big new idea has gained some acceptance, it's somewhat easier to implement. As the idea of school district decentralization becomes established, for example, the press understands something about it, teachers and families have heard of it, and consultants who have worked in other decentralized districts are more widely available.

But to return to the role of personal leadership in bringing about large-scale organizational change: in a sense, all eight of the leaders had to sell their vision of decentralization to a public that was largely unfamiliar with the concept, many of whom, not the least the teachers unions, were apprehensive about how such a change might affect them. I did not observe any systematic strategy or communications approach among these leaders in gaining acceptance of their new direction. There was consistency, though, in their approach to implementation. None of them plunged into district-wide decentralization all at once. All of them started with a portion of their schools, although a few announced at the outset their intention to go district-wide in the end. Some of these leaders attempted to broadcast their decentralization plans to their entire city, but the press didn't pay them much attention, perhaps because they didn't know what to make of this new idea.

If there was a crucial element of personal leadership in all eight districts, it was the personal style of the leader. Whether it was Arne Duncan in Chicago, Randolph Ward in Oakland, or Arlene Ackerman in San Francisco, these leaders walked their talk. They wanted their principals to be entrepreneurs, to exhibit creativity, and to willingly accept accountability, and so they behaved that way themselves. They were typically open to the ideas of others, they willingly experimented with a variety of approaches, and they accepted personal responsibility—and the occasional criticism that went with it—for their actions. Each of these leaders managed to build a team of dedicated professionals who put heart and soul into what they all believed was an exciting and revolutionary new direction that they firmly believed would benefit the students of their district.

Without this personal leadership, none of these districts would have been able to get its reforms off the ground. I am familiar with several other districts that have also attempted to launch decentralization but never managed to really get started. In some of these failed cases, the superintendent consistently exhibited authoritarian behavior that was at odds with the ideas of decentralization; in others, the superintendent failed to undertake a serious study of decentralization, causing people around him to lose confidence. There are other cases in which the leader was often spoken of as being charismatic or visionary, and in which decentralization was launched but then later faltered because the infrastructure had not been developed. Creating the infrastructure necessary for decentralization is like building the sidewalks and streets in the city. It's not glamorous work, but it's absolutely essential.

In the end, the eight leaders managed to exhibit enough "style" to give the people around them the confidence to come along. All of them, though, concentrated not on continuing to exhibit style but instead on building their management team, analyzing mounds of data, and poring over the details of the infrastructure that they needed to create. Yes, they did have some personal leadership style, and that style counted for something. Whether these leaders might qualify as charismatic or visionary is a question that I will leave to others. In the end, though, these leaders succeeded to the extent that they built the substance of realignment and reorganization. Style will get you going in the short run, but over the long haul, it the substance of organization and management that counts.

Lesson 5: The Infrastructure of Accountability Is Crucial

Accountability is surely among the most widely misunderstood and abused concepts in all of education. Many people think that accountability is a code word for getting rid of bad teachers. Others think that accountability means closing or reconstituting schools that fail to make adequate annual gains in standardized test scores. Our eight districts reveal that accountability is neither of these things.

A decentralized school district needs an accountability framework. Principals are the key managers in a decentralized district. They play a less crucial role in a traditional district. Traditional districts give principals little discretion. Traditional districts do not allow principals to change their staffing, design their professional development, or control their curriculum or schedule. As a result, traditional school districts cannot hold principals accountable for student performance, because principals do not control the instructional decisions that affect student performance. Instead, these districts measure principals by their inputs to the school, such as the number of days of district-mandated professional development that the teachers actually attend, the number of times that the principal met with the school site council, and the proportion of students who enroll in college-preparatory courses. In all of our eight districts, the change from centralized to decentralized operation was difficult for many principals because under the new accountability systems they were held accountable for outputs (actual student improvement) rather than inputs, and they were expected to make their own, creative decisions rather than follow central office rules.

Another important function of an accountability system is to give principals the feedback that enables them to make course corrections. To accomplish this, the accountability system must capture the subtleties of each school and provide feedback and guidance to principals on which new initiatives seem to be working and which do not.

Most large companies, as we've said earlier, are organized in a decentralized system of autonomously managed divisions or other subunits. In almost every company, the manager of each subunit is measured according to a set of financial items that correspond roughly to the standardized test scores of a school. Those measures are important and they ought to be taken seriously, but every company knows that if it were to rely exclusively on those financial measures, it would end up by encouraging the wrong behavior in its subunit mangers. Instead, the top corporate executives and the outside auditors personally visit the subunits and talk to managers and sometimes to employees at lower levels, with the objective of learning about the important subtleties and the human relationships within that subunit.

The most successful of our school districts are doing much the same. They rely on personal visits by the senior leadership of the district to the schools, and in some cases they supplement those visits with annual management "audits" by a team of experts from outside the district who interview school administrators, teachers, students, and parents. As a result, the senior executives of the district are in a position to look at the test scores with an understanding of the history and context of a school, and they are equipped to give useful guidance to the principals.

Some of the eight districts have also adopted Edmonton-style annual surveys of students, parents, teachers, and principals as another aspect of their accountability systems. In some cases these surveys occur once every few years rather than annually, and some districts publish the results for each school while others publish only the average scores for the district as a whole.

The benefit of surveys appears to be greatest when the results are publicly available for all to see, school by school. It is important for the school and the district staff to know if any of the stakeholder groups is systematically critical of a school or of its principal. It is conceivable, though perhaps unlikely, that an authoritarian principal could increase student test scores for a few years while coercing teachers and ignoring parents, only to have everything fall apart in one big bang at some later point. Public reporting of survey results is a strong protection against this possibility.

All of the leaders of these organizations would say that the choice program is among the most reliable elements of their accountability system. It might be that statistics and surveys can be manipulated, but when families vote with their feet and a school has lots of empty seats, the evidence of failing leadership is impossible to ignore.

Very few school districts across the nation employ the kinds of accountability systems that our eight districts are now using. None of these new techniques is overly complicated, and all of them can be put into use anywhere. If principals are to be empowered, there must be in place a robust system of accountability to guarantee that they get the feedback that will enable them to improve each year, and there must be a system that will detect any principal who is abusive or capricious in her treatment of any of her constituencies, or who fails to bring about improvement in student achievement.

Lesson 6: Site-Based Management Corrupts Accountability, but It Has Some Advantages

This is a strong statement, and perhaps even an overstatement, but it's meant to make an important point. As we've previously seen, site-based management (SBM) has not had a positive effect in very many districts, and most have dropped it. Versions of SBM were in existence in Chicago, St. Paul, San Francisco, and some of the other districts when they adopted decentralization, and the effect of decentralization in those cities was to grant even more power to the site councils than they had before. My own evaluation is that the existence of powerful site councils has hampered the implementation of decentralization, in much the same manner that the existence of school boards slowed things down in some, but not all, of the cases. On the other hand, site councils were deeply involved in the movement toward decentralization in both St. Paul and San Francisco, and they provided important impetus to change in some of the other cities. The existence of site councils is very much a double-edged sword.

On the negative side, many site council members have experience that is limited to knowledge of two or three schools, whereas principals have typically learned over the years from many colleagues in other schools. Teachers and parents typically have little familiarity with school budgeting, and council members in some cities have frequently failed to put in the time that it takes to be able to make constructive suggestions. In addition, some parents have proven to have a very short time horizon, limited to the number of years that their child will be enrolled in the school, while many of the changes that are most important will require sacrifices in the immediate future. Teachers on a site council may also have local agendas that are not in the best interests of the long-term development of a school. For example, the teachers who are elected to a site council will ordinarily be those who have served for many years in the school, and they may resist changes that they believe will favor younger or newer teachers.

On the positive side, teachers and parents can be the most ardent and effective proponents of change, and in some cases it is they who prod a reluctant principal into accepting the idea of school empowerment. In every school, it is essential that the principal consult with teachers and parents often and on many subjects, and the existence of a site council enhances the likelihood that consultation will take place. Site councils can also become a venue in which parents and teachers learn more about one another and develop trust in one another, another ingredient for a successful school. When WSF budgeting is implemented, school budgets become much easier to understand than before, and site council members often become very engaged in and knowledgeable about that process. Most important of all, site councils that are engaged and well informed are easily the most effective advocates at defending the autonomy of their school. They can become a bulwark against backsliding when the inevitable change of superintendents and school board members takes place.

Given the long list of advantages of site-based management councils, why am I opposed to them? The experience of our eight districts suggests that site councils that are purely advisory to the principal will bring with them virtually all of the potential advantages with none of the disadvantages of site councils that have the power to approve school plans and budgets or to hire and fire principals. An advisory council doesn't need formal authority to have influence, because unhappy members of an advisory can and likely will tell other parents and school board members if they are opposed to what a principal is doing. But when a site council has formal decision authority of some sort, it has authority without accountability, which is never a good thing.

The history of some of our eight districts shows that when site councils have formal decision authority, they sometimes fall into troubles of one sort or another that are difficult and time-consuming to correct. As we observed earlier, the site councils that Chicago had more than twenty years ago got into such trouble through their attempts to control school money that the state of Illinois convened hearings to air out their misadventures. When New York City introduced local elected boards, it ran into similar problems, which in some cases rose to the level of fraud and corruption. That's not to say that most such councils develop similar troubles, only that there is a tendency toward trouble whenever authority of any kind is granted without the protections of an accountability system. Because teachers cannot be held accountable for anything that is outside of their union contract, and because parents cannot be held legally liable for their governance role on a school site council, neither party can be accountable, and thus neither should have formal decision powers.

On several occasions when I have offered this argument, I have received angry replies from teachers and parents. They have not faulted my argument that site councils cannot be held accountable, but they raise their concern that if principals have final decision authority, some principals cannot be trusted and all principals should therefore be accountable to strong site councils. I agree that strong principals require strong accountability systems, but I would argue that school site councils, for the reasons already given, are not the proper method of establishing that accountability.

One final thought on this controversial subject—several of our districts have strong site councils that do have certain formal decision authority, and they have not gotten into serious trouble. The superintendents sometimes view these site councils as a bother, but one with which they can cope. Other times, superintendents view these site councils positively, both because they subject the annual school plan and budget to useful scrutiny and because they tend to strengthen community support for the school. As a result, it seems that our districts have been able to be successful with site councils that have formal decision rights, whatever my concerns might be. I would add, though, that where advisory site councils exist, which is the case in all of the other districts, they are universally regarded by teachers, parents, principals, and superintendents in a positive light. That's not to say that all of the advisory councils are equally engaged and well informed, but neither are all of the site councils that hold formal decision powers. Rarely have I heard the complaint that advisory site councils have created serious difficulties or have engaged in inappropriate or illegal conduct, as has sometimes occurred with the other type of site councils.

If and when site councils that hold decision authority get themselves into trouble, the consequences tend to be public and difficult to untangle. In more instances, powerful site councils have attempted to bully a principal and sometimes even to threaten a principal. If the parents or the teachers on a site council attempt to misappropriate school funds, to coerce the principal into giving a contract to a friend or hire a relative as a consultant, there isn't much that the district can do except to hope that person doesn't get re-elected to the council. If a principal were to engage in any of those inappropriate acts, the existing accountability system would call that principal to account in short order.

In short: accountability, yes; advisory site councils, yes; site councils with formal decision powers, no thank you.

Lesson 7: Continuity of Governance Is a Big Issue

If and when school district decentralization becomes as familiar as phonics-based instruction, Advanced Placement courses, or special education, continuity of governance won't be terribly important. By then, most candidates for superintendent will know something about decentralization, and most teachers, principals, and central office specialists will, too. But we're not there yet, not by a long shot. Today, education reporters from newspapers, magazines, and the electronic media have little or no idea what decentralization is all about, and virtually none has ever heard of acronyms like WSF or TSL. Today, a school board that continues to support decentralized decision making is an outlier, a pioneer, and even an isolate. A newly elected member of a school board is likely to be almost completely in the dark about district decentralization. If the district is under mayoral control, you can safely bet next month's pay that not one of the candidates for mayor will have any idea at all what this concept is all about.

For now, governance matters, and it matters a lot. As we have seen in the cases of Houston, Seattle, and St. Paul, even a well-established decentralization system can be vitiated through neglect from a new superintendent or school board. In the case of St. Paul, we have seen that a determined new leadership can undo six years of decentralization in just one year. As we've also seen, the DNA of decentralization still lives on in those districts, and it may well reassert itself again in the future, but the greatest threat today to decentralized districts is succession in the leadership.

Mayoral control has attracted quite a bit of controversy, and people tend to feel strongly about it one way or the other. Mayoral control has not produced a noticeable improvement in the schools in every case, but it has done so in Boston, Chicago, and New York City. These three make for a very informative comparison, because the mayor of New York City was at the time limited to two terms of four years each, which would have meant a succession every four or at most every eight years. If the next mayor of New York City does not support decentralization, then all that Joel Klein, Eric Nadelstern, and hundreds of others have worked so hard to achieve could be undone in a year or two. In Chicago, the mayor has no term limits, and thus the issue of succession might not be a problem there. It's possible that Mayor Daley will be in office for long enough for Chicago to establish decentralization as thoroughly as Mike Strembitsky did in Edmonton, though that's a tall order, and only time will tell.

The Edmonton school board is elected, and like any elected school board it experiences turnover. Despite that turnover, Edmonton Public Schools has consistently maintained its decentralized system for more than three decades, thus proving that decentralization can survive for quite a while under the governance of an elected school board.

So, what conclusions can we draw about the role of mayors and of school boards in providing continuity of governance? So far, the conclusions are precious few but of great importance. First, we can conclude that a mayor can play a crucial role in establishing decentralization, either by actively seeking to do so or by being supportive of a superintendent who wants to decentralize the district. Second, we can conclude that a school board can successfully take the initiative, find the right sort of superintendent, and initiate the process of decentralization. Third, we have ample evidence that no school board can afford to take for granted that, once established, decentralization will automatically continue into future years.

There does not appear to be any magic solution or basic strategy that can guarantee control over the risks that are part of the natural process of succession in the leadership of a school district. There is no issue of greater importance in the long-run sustainability of a decentralized school district. In time, the problem might take care of itself, if decentralization becomes the accepted norm rather than the bold new idea that it is today. So spread the word!

Some Final Observations

Decentralizing, as we observed at the beginning of this book, is more a continuous process than a one-time event. Decentralizing a school district is not like building a house—when you're done building, you're done for fifty years, except for occasional maintenance. As I pointed out earlier, decentralization is more like building a marriage: it's a living being that never stops changing and evolving, and you have to attend to it all of the time. More than anything, school districts are collections of people. As the people change and as the conditions around them change, the constantly decentralizing district must adapt. So the process of decentralizing never ends.

The many stories in this book about the people of our eight decentralizing districts are not simple stories. The districts are never completely, perfectly decentralized, nor will they ever again be perfectly centralized, either. Their stories are instead nuanced, subtle, and full of tensions, conflicts, and struggles. That these decentralizing districts are complex rather than simple, and diverse rather than uniform, is both an inevitable characteristic of human organizations and a necessity for their long-term survival. Internal diversity of opinions is not a bad thing. Any organization that lacks internal variation will have a limited repertoire of ideas and skills. If the environment around it changes, as it always will, a limited inventory of points of view will be a serious handicap in responding to change.

If large organizations need to include lots of variety, they will also be more difficult to manage. They'll be contentious, uncomfortable, and sometimes chaotic, but that's part of their sustainability. The people who work and live and are educated within these organizations ought to learn to cope with differences of opinion and with different kinds of people. It's a lesson that will make them more comfortable while they're part of the school district, and it's also a lesson that will help them to become more adaptable to the constantly changing world that they will inhabit.

I think that it's entirely proper to celebrate the internal dissension in districts like Boston, Houston, St. Paul, and Seattle, just as it's entirely proper to be greatly impressed by the apparently more unified nature of some of the other decentralizing districts. If we were to look even more closely than we have at the school districts in New York City or San Francisco, for example, we'd find there as elsewhere many divergent views about whether the district is truly decentralized or not, and about whether decentralization is a good idea or a bad one.

Herbert Simon was a great scholar who worked in the field of organization studies, among others. Simon won the Nobel Prize in Economics in part for his observation that a large, complex organization that is stable is always made up of parts that are largely autonomous, independent of one another and of any central office. He likened a complex organization to the inner workings of a complicated Swiss watch before the days of the digital chip. Imagine, he asked, that a Swiss watchmaker is building a timepiece out of several hundred parts. Imagine that he has to get all of the parts into their proper places before he takes his thumb off of his work, lest they all spring out all over the worktable. Now, imagine that the telephone rings every now and then, or that the watchmaker has to go to the bathroom. He'll never complete a single watch. As a result, watchmakers instead build many independent subassemblies, each consisting of a few parts. A watchmaker lays each completed subassembly on the worktable while he works on another one. In relatively good order, he will be able to build several watches.[1]

Perhaps Herbert Simon was right. It's the independent subassemblies, the schools of a large district, that must be built one by one. As long as each school can stand on its own, many schools can over time be assembled into one, large, complex school system without much fuss. If Simon's tale is a proper metaphor, the school boards and superintendents who are our educational watchmakers should focus on seeing to it that each school comes together in a sound manner. Then they should carefully and gently link these schools together into larger and larger assemblies, ultimately creating a smoothly operating, jewel-like school district.

APPENDIX 1: PERCENT OF SCHOOL
BUDGET UNDER PRINCIPAL'S CONTROL

District	Study One: 2000–2001	Study Two: 2005–2006
Boston	Not included	75.0% (Pilot Schools)
Chicago	19.3% (Sample of all schools)	13.9% (AMPS)
Edmonton	91.7% (Sample of all schools)	Not included
Houston	58.6% (Sample of all schools)	73.7% (Sample of all schools)
Los Angeles	6.7% (Sample of all schools)	Not included
New York City	6.1% (Sample of all schools)	85.0% (Autonomy Zone schools)
Oakland	Not included	60.5% (Sample of all schools)
San Francisco	Not included	22.8% (Sample of all schools)
Seattle	79.3% (Sample of all schools)	47.7% (Sample of all schools)
St. Paul	Not included	87.2% (Sample of all schools)

Note: Study One included the only three districts in North America that were decentralized at that time: Edmonton, Houston, and Seattle. They were compared to the three largest centralized districts: Chicago, Los Angeles, and New York City.

Study Two included the eight U.S. districts that were decentralizing in whole or in part at that time. Of these, three—Boston, Chicago, and New York City—had some decentralized and some centralized schools. The remaining five districts—Houston, Oakland, St. Paul, San Francisco, and Seattle—had decentralized all of their schools.

APPENDIX 2: EXAMPLES OF STUDENT WEIGHTS IN THREE DISTRICTS

Student Characteristic	Edmonton	Houston	Seattle
Limited English Proficient	126%	110%	127%
Special Education (lowest need)	199%	210%	195%
Special Education (highest need)	546%	700%	876%
Low Income	No weight	120%	110%
Gifted and Talented	126%	112%	No weight
High Mobility School	No weight	120%	No weight

Note: In each of these school districts, the "basic" student has a standard allocation of funds, perhaps $2,800. To this basic weight are added any additional weighting characteristics, such as those in the selected examples above. Each district also had other weights that are not shown. Each district also gives each school a "foundation" grant of perhaps $300,000 per year to cover the costs of a principal, office administrator, and basic utilities.

Sources for this table: Miles, Karen Hawley, and Marguerite Roza, "Understanding Student-Weighted Allocation as a Means to Greater Resource Equity," *Peabody Journal of Education* 81:3 (2006): 39–62. Also *Tackling Inequality and Antiquity in School Finance* (Washington, D.C.: Thomas B. Fordham Institute, June 2006). http://www.edexcellence.net/doc/FundtheChild062706.pdf

APPENDIX 3: TOTAL STUDENT LOAD IN EIGHT DECENTRALIZED SCHOOL DISTRICTS

School District	Average High School Total Student Load per Teacher
Boston	76.0 (Pilot Schools)
Chicago	141.9 (Sample of AMPS)
Houston	160.0 (Sample of all schools)
New York City	87.7 (Autonomy Zone schools)
Oakland	123.0 (Sample of all schools)
San Francisco	142.5 (Sample of all schools)
Seattle	125.7 (Sample of all schools)
St. Paul	129.0 (Sample of all schools)
Average for all eight districts	115 (442 schools in 8 districts)

APPENDIX 4: EFFECTS ON TOTAL STUDENT LOAD AND PERCENT PROFICIENT IN MATH OF A 10 PERCENTAGE POINT INCREASE IN PRINCIPAL'S BUDGET CONTROL

School District	Effect on TSL	Effect on Percent Proficient or Above
Boston	−4 students	No change
Chicago	−1 student	+0.1 percentage point
Houston	+1 student	+0.6 percentage point
New York City	−25 students	+11.0 percentage points
Oakland	+16 students	−3.2 percentage points
San Francisco	−7 students	+3.4 percentage points
Seattle	−4 students	+1.1 percentage points
St. Paul	+3 students	−2.9 percentage points
Average for all eight districts	−3 students	+ 1.2 percentage points

Note: This table shows the number of students by which the average TSL in high school either rises or declines if the principals' budget control is increased by 10 percentage points, for example, from .20 percent of budget to 30 percent. It also shows the number of percentage points by which student scores rise or fall on the state standardized test in percent who are proficient or advanced in math. The table does not show the total gains in student proficiency for each district. It only shows the amount of gain or loss in proficiency that results directly from changes in Total Student Load with other possible factors statistically accounted for. If a district had a larger gain in proficiency, it means that the district was more effective in getting its principals to use their autonomy to reduce TSL and through that means, to enhance student proficiency. For example, both Oakland and St. Paul made large gains in student proficiency over the years of this study, but in neither of the two districts did principals consistently use their autonomy to reduce TSL. As a result, average high school TSL rose in Oakland and St. Paul, and thus percent proficient or above as a result of TSL fell slightly. If Oakland and St. Paul had reduced their TSL, that would have resulted in additional gains in student performance. By comparison, New York City was the most consistent of our eight districts in getting principals to use their freedom to reduce TSL and through it, to increase student proficiency. Increases in principals' budget control greater than 10 percentage points were associated with proficiency gains greater than those shown in the table.

APPENDIX 5: THE FIVE PILLARS AND THE FOUR FREEDOMS

The Five Pillars of School Empowerment

1. Real choices for families
2. Empowering schools with the Four Freedoms
3. Effective principals
4. A system of accountability
5. Weighted Student Formula budgeting

The Four Freedoms of School Empowerment

Control of:

1. Budget
2. Staffing pattern
3. Curriculum
4. Schedule

Note: In addition to these essential elements, we have noted that equally important to our eight districts were two additional factors: a focus on reducing Total Student Load and a method for selecting, training, and coaching principals in how to use their autonomy effectively to improve student achievement.

APPENDIX 6: SOURCE NOTE FOR DATA DESCRIBED IN THIS BOOK

For those who are interested, there is available a full statistical analysis of the data drawn from the 442 schools described in this book. This analysis is described in full in a working paper that is available by e-mail from the author: www.william.ouchi@ander son.ucla.edu

The citation follows:

William G. Ouchi and Pete Goldschmidt, "A National Study of School District Decentralization and Student Performance," 2008 (under journal review)

About the authors of the paper:

William G. Ouchi is the Sanford and Betty Sigoloff Distin-guished Professor in Organizational Renewal at the UCLA An-derson School of Management, Los Angeles, California.

Pete Goldschmidt is Assistant Professor of Research Methods, California State University, Northridge—the Michael D. Eisner College of Education, and is Senior Researcher at the National Center for Research on Evaluation, Standards, and Student Test-ing at UCLA.

NOTES

Chapter One. Why Good Schools Are the Result of Good Management

1. B. A. Young, *Characteristics of the 100 Largest Public Elementary and Secondary School Districts in the United States: 2000–2001* (Washington, D.C.: National Center for Education Statistics, 2002, pp. 1–2.
2. William G. Ouchi, *Making Schools Work* (New York: Simon & Schuster, 2003).
3. William G. Ouchi, "Power to the Principals: Decentralization in Three Large School Districts," *Organization Science,* 17:2 (2006).
4. Karen H. Miles and Linda Darling-Hammond, "Rethinking the Allocation of Teaching Resources: Some Lessons from High Performing Schools," in *Developments in School Finance* (Washington, D.C.: National Center for Education Statistics, 1997), pp. 98–212.
5. F. C. Terrien and D. C. Mills, "The Effects of Changing Size Upon the Internal Structure of an Organization," *American Sociological Review* 20 (1955): 11–13.
6. Ouchi, 2006, and William G. Ouchi and Pete Goldschmidt, "A National Study of School District Decentralization and Student Performance," 2008, working paper under submission at a journal and accepted for presentation at the 2009 annual meeting of the American Education Research Association.
7. Ouchi and Goldschmidt, 2008.
8. Lydia G. Segal, *Battling Corruption in America's Public Schools* (Boston: Northeastern University Press, 2004).
9. Ouchi, 2003.

Chapter Two. The Five Pillars of School Empowerment

1. Ouchi, 2003, and Ouchi, 2006.
2. Theodore R. Sizer, *Horace's Compromise* (Boston: Houghton Mifflin, 1984); Theodore R. Sizer, *Horace's School* (Boston: Houghton Mifflin, 1992); Theodore R. Sizer, *Horace's Hope* (Boston: Houghton Mifflin, 1996).
3. K. H. Miles, M. Roza, and K. Ware, "Leveling the Playing Field: Creating Funding Equity through Student-Based Budgeting," *Phi Delta Kappan* 85:2 (2003): 114–19; M. Roza and P. Hill, "How Within-District Spending Inequities Help Some Schools to Fail," in D. Ravitch, ed., *Brookings Papers on Education Policy* (Washington, D.C.: Brookings Institution Press, 2004); working draft, 2003.
4. Sizer, 1984.
5. Deborah Meier, *The Power of Their Ideas: Lessons for America from a Small School in Harlem* (Boston: Beacon, 1995).
6. Arthur Powell, *Lessons from Privilege: The American Prep School Tradition* (Cambridge, Mass.: Harvard University Press, 1996).

Chapter Three. An Empowered School: Vanguard High School

1. Sizer, 1984.
2. Douglas McGregor, *The Human Side of Enterprise* (New York: McGraw-Hill, 1960).
3. Jay Greene, *High School Graduation Rates in the United States* (New York: Manhattan Institute for Policy Research, 2001).

Chapter Four. Scale-Up in New York City

1. We could go a bit deeper into these results, pointing out that New York City's fourth graders who are white were at or above the national averages for all white students in all tests save eighth grade math, where they were two percentile points below (58th percentile versus the national average of 60th percentile for white students), and that the city's fourth grade black students outperformed the national black averages in both reading and math in the 2007 tests. Hispanic fourth grade students in the city beat the national average for Hispanics in math and were one percentile point below the national average for Hispanic students in reading. In grade eight, New York City's black students were one percentile point below the national black average in math (26th percentile versus the national black average of 27th percentile) and were three percentile points below in reading. Hispanic students in the eighth grade were two percentile points below the national average for Hispanics in math (30th percentile versus the national Hispanic average of 32nd percentile) and were four percentile points below in reading. Overall, New York City is doing well among other urban school districts, but it, like its peers, has yet to find a way to close the gap between black and Hispanic students and the higher-performing white and Asian students.

2. Although New York City has made steady progress since 2002, its overall results are not yet exemplary. How, then, can I argue that the reforms in New York City are a success and that other districts should emulate it? To get at this issue, we need to look more closely at the recent nature of the decentralization and at the tests.

By the year 2007, New York City had granted autonomy to forty-two of its schools, most of them high schools. Only one of these autonomous schools was an elementary school, one was K–8, and one was a middle school. Some of these schools had been in operation since September of 2004, and others had begun in 2005. Those schools were not included in the NAEP tests of 2002, 2003, or 2005 (testing every other year began in 2003), and though they might have been included in the tests of 2007, there were only three autonomous schools that might have been tested—three new schools with a total of about 900 students between them (they were adding one grade each year and were not yet full). The NAEP sample included 4,500 students, or four-tenths of one percent of New York City's 1.1 million students. If 0.4 percent of the 900 students happened to fall into the sample, that would be 3 students out of the 4,500 who were tested. So, these NAEP tests do not shed any light on the performance of the autonomous schools.

The annual city and state tests of students in grades 3–8 and the Regents Examination results do shed light on the performance of the autonomous schools, as we have seen in the discussion of accountability at Vanguard. We analyzed these early test results, and we've already reported that they were extremely positive. To summarize that analysis: Our research included three years of student performance data on the forty-two autonomous district schools that were launched in 2004 and in 2005 (excluding the six charter schools in that group). What our analysis reveals is that these schools, as a group, along with the schools in Boston, reduced TSL dramatically more than did the autonomous schools in any of the six other study districts, and that they increased "percent proficient or above" more strongly than in any other district. If these schools had higher TSLs, at the level of Houston or San Francisco, their performance scores would have been 13 percentage points lower than they actually were. Whatever the other factors of poverty, prior student performance, or other considerations, a district that reduces TSL by these amounts can increase performance. We also found that some of these schools had very aggressively moved to reduce TSL, while others had not. In time, if all of the autonomous schools of New York City adopt the changes that reduce TSL, we can expect even greater gains in performance, above the 13 percentage point gain.

Districts that have smaller per-student budgets than Boston or New York City may not be able to achieve TSLs in the range of 80. They may, however, be able to reduce TSL substantially, perhaps from 170 to 120 or even 100, through the thoughtful implementation of decentralization. If these early results from our eight cities continue to be borne out in future studies, though, there will be a very strong argument for a substantial increase in school district budgets in most cities. At the same time, it is well to bear in mind that decentralization requires choice, accountability, and skilled principals to produce gains in student achievement. One can easily imagine a school district that has a large budget, a TSL of 80, but that has no meaningful accountability system, no school choice, and that is in a chronic state of failure.

3. Amy Rebecca Liszt, "Perceiving Empowered Leadership: A Qualitative Exploration of New York City Principals' Experience with Decision-Making Authority in Empowerment Schools," Ph.D. diss., Teachers College, Columbia University, draft of 2007, p. 54; not included in the final version of 2008.

4. Liszt, 2007, p. 54.

5. The planning cycle for the new Empowerment Schools consisted of three weeks during which teams met for three days each week. On day one, the fourteen network leaders met with Nadelstern and his staff; on day two, each network leader met with the other four members of their network team; and on day three, each of the fourteen network teams met with its network of twenty principals. The remaining two days of the week were for the principals to work with their school teams of teachers. The cycle was repeated three times over three successive weeks, so that as many issues as possible could be identified and resolved before school began in the fall.

Chapter Five. The First Generation: Boston, Houston, and Seattle

1. An evaluation of the results for ethnic groups reveals that Boston's white fourth graders were above the national average for white students in math (62nd percentile versus the national average of 60th percentile). Black students were also above the national average (31st percentile versus 26th for the national black average), as were Hispanic fourth graders (36th percentile in Boston versus 31st for the nation's Hispanic students). Boston schools made strong and steady progress under its long-serving former superintendent, Tom Payzant. In a reversal of the more familiar trend, Boston's eighth graders did as well as or better than fourth grade students, compared to their peers. In math, for example, Boston's black students scored in the 31st percentile, versus a national average at the 27th percentile, and Boston's Hispanic students were in the 38th percentile versus the national average 32nd percentile. Still, Boston's students of color scored below 65 to 75 percent of all students in grades four and eight, and Hispanic eighth graders fell below the national average for reading.

2. Atila Abdulkadiroglu, Josh Angrist, Sarah Cohodes, Susan Dynarski, Jon Fullerton, Thomas Kane, and Parag Pathak, "Informing the Debate: Comparing Boston's Charter, Pilot, and Traditional Schools." The Boston Foundation, January 2009, 54 pp. http://www.tbf.org/Home.aspx (accessed April 15, 2009).

3. Donald R. McAdams, *Fighting to Save Our Urban Schools . . . and Winning!: Lessons from Houston* (New York: Teachers College Press, 2000), pp. 132–33.

4. Over the past several years since Superintendent Abelardo Saavedra took office in 2004, Houston has pioneered in performance-based bonus systems for

teachers and other staff. In 2007, the district launched a bonus system based on student gains in performance. For the 2007–8 school year, 10,627 district teachers (about half of all teachers) received bonuses that ranged from $66 to $7,865, with an average bonus of $2,097. Among non-instructional staff, bonuses ranged from $62.50 to $500, earned by 4,187 staff (about half of the staff). In all, the district paid out about $23 million in bonuses. These performance bonuses are based on three components: (1) campus-wide improvement bonus of up to $1,000 per teacher if the school ranks in the top 75 percent of all district schools in average academic performance; (2) individual core teacher performance for teachers of English, math, science, and social studies of up to $5,000 per teacher whose students are in the top 25 percent of the district in academic performance gains; and (3) comparative campus improvement and achievement bonus of up to $1,300 per teacher if their campus is in the top 25 percent of all Texas schools that are demographically similar and is rated exemplary by the state. Teachers and non-teaching staff earn smaller bonuses if their students or their school is in the top half but not the top 25 percent and no bonus if they are in the bottom half in achievement gains. Houston intends to increase the performance bonuses as a percentage of base pay over time by allocating a portion of future pay increases to base pay and a smaller portion to the bonus pool.

Chapter Six. The Second Generation: St. Paul and San Francisco

1. A recent study by Jay Chambers and his colleagues at the American Institutes for Research (*A Tale of Two Districts: A Comparative Study of Student-Based Funding and Decentralized Decision Making in San Francisco and Oakland Unified School Districts*, September 2008) also reports that San Francisco Unified made these special allocations centrally (p. 21), while Oakland withheld smaller sums from its WSF for allocation by the central office to schools that disproportionately employed long serving and thus more highly paid teachers.
2. *Fund the Child: Tackling Inequity and Antiquity in School Finance* (Washington, D.C.: Thomas B. Fordham Institute, June 2006). 65 pp.
3. Mike Petko, *Weighted Student Formula (WSF): What Is It and How Does It Impact Educational Programs in Large Urban Districts* (Washington, D.C.: National Education Association, 2005). 24 pp.

Chapter Eight. Seven Lessons Learned Through Experience

1. Herbert A. Simon, "The Architecture of Complexity," *Proceedings of the American Philosophical Society* 106 (1962): 467–82.

ACKNOWLEDGMENTS

This book is the fruit of a long, intense research process. My research team and I spent two years visiting hundreds of schools in eight districts across the nation in order to find out what happens when principals are given nearly total freedom to run their schools. The lessons that we learned are many, and their implications for our schools are great. The data that we gathered were subjected to a sophisticated statistical analysis that Dr. Pete Goldschmidt and I performed together. The numbers from that analysis, which we have reported in an academic paper, are only briefly summarized in this book, but they provided the solid research foundation on which everything else reported here is based.

At first, no one wanted to fund the research that went into this book. Educational foundations and government agencies are not accustomed to the idea of a management school professor studying school districts. I wrote several proposals for funding and visited several education-related foundations, but all of them turned me down. I am therefore very grateful to the Conrad N. Hilton Foundation and the Riordan Foundation, which provided the money that was necessary to pay my research assistants, cover travel costs for them, and so on.

If the world of educators is skeptical of the idea that a management scholar might have anything useful to say about K–12 education, the same is not true of my colleagues at the UCLA Anderson School of Management. I want to thank them, along with Dean Judy Olian, for providing me with additional financial support and for never failing to encourage my efforts. I also received encouragement and advice from colleagues at the UCLA Graduate School of Education and Information Studies, and I thank them, too.

The hard work of living away from home, visiting schools—sometimes having to pry information out of people who were reluctant—was done by my research team. It included Sharon Harwood, my field manager; Radha Parikh, our excellent scheduler; and a capable interviewing team of Sylvia Gil, Jennifer Harris, Kennisha Malone, Greg Samarge, Kathryn Schreiner, and Joanna Smith. Dana Heatherton and Ellin Palmer transcribed the many pages of taped interviews and did so beautifully. Jonathan Fujioka and Jennifer Wahba provided valuable assistance in organizing the many interview transcripts. Jennifer Carvalo, John de la Torre, Kathryne Gadarian, Matthew Palmer, and Kristina Tipton were the administrative backbone that kept everything moving forward. Janet Breverman saw to it that all of the bills were paid, and Pete Goldschmidt provided expert consultation on thorny statistical issues and co-authored a research paper with me. Angelica Gutierrez and Erica Hamilton did a first-rate job of helping with parts of the analysis. These twenty-one people deserve my thanks.

The writing of this manuscript was, as it always is, both a joy and a tough job. That job was made much easier through the advice of my editor at Simon & Schuster, Bob Bender, who also edited my last book, *Making Schools Work*. Bob is a man of great intellect and skill, and I have learned to have complete confidence in his judgment. Amy Ryan, my copy editor, gave the book clarity. Victoria Meyer, who is responsible for publicizing this book, provided me with insights to understanding my audience. My agent, Michael Carlisle, was instrumental in helping me to conceive of this book, and I am grateful to him for his optimism and his experience.

Although I have spent many years as an advocate for school reform, as a board member of a charter school organization, and as a student of school district organization, my teaching experience of the past thirty-eight years has been limited to M.B.A. and Ph.D. students. I do not have the day-to-day experience of having taught in a public elementary or secondary school for three decades. As a result, I relied heavily on advice on each chapter from my sister, Carol Ouchi, who has had just that experience. When my sister told me that my first chapter was boring and confusing, I tore it up. When she said that my next try was only a slight improvement, I abandoned that, too. When she found that my third attempt was interesting and clear, I was overjoyed! Thanks to you, sister Carol.

I sent each section to the school district that it was about and asked its representatives to tell me about any errors that I had made. All of them replied, and I am grateful for the time that they gave me. A few friends took the time to read other sections of the book and give me their suggestions. Among them were Paul Grogan, Ben Haimowitz, and Jim Hamilton. I am grateful to them, as well. At several points, I needed an introduction to a key school district official somewhere, and Dan Katzir at the Broad Foundation never failed to make the connection for me.

No one readily invites an independent scholar to delve deeply into his organization, interview a variety of people, and then write whatever he feels he should. But all eight of the districts in this study did just that, and I am grateful to them for giving me that access. I hope that they will feel that the lessons that will now be available for others to follow make their inconvenience worthwhile.

This research project and the book that resulted are important to me. They are important because I believe deeply that our public schools are an essential part of the success of our democracy and because I believe that the study of management has much to offer to the success of those schools. I completely committed myself and my time to this effort for several years. That means that, in addition to my normal teaching and administrative tasks, I have spent long hours on the road, visiting schools and central office staffs, and months in my study at home, writing and revising this book. My wife, also named Carol Ouchi, cheerfully supported my intense attention to this project. Without her love and her willing support, I could not have done my work. Whenever we had dinner with friends, went on a vacation, or visited relatives, I could do nothing but talk about this project. Most of these people have tolerated my obsession, and I thank them for their patience. Lots of other people, I know, would just as soon not engage me in conversation. My friends haven't seen much of me for the past four years, nor have my children or grandchildren, and I look forward to making up for lost time with them now.

Before I began to work on this project, I was playing about fifty rounds of golf each year. In 2007 I played four rounds, and during 2008 I played three. It hasn't seemed like a sacrifice, but still, I look forward to working on my short game (and my long game and my putting) again!

William Ouchi
UCLA Anderson School of Management

INDEX